Political Theories and Social Reconstruction

Political Theories and Social Reconstruction

A Critical Survey of the Literature on India

THOMAS PANTHAM

SAGE PUBLICATIONS
New Delhi/Thousand Oaks/London

First published in 1995 by

Sage Publications India Pvt Ltd
M-32, Greater Kailash Market-I
New Delhi 110 048

Sage Publications Inc
2455 Teller Road
Thousand Oaks, California 91320

Sage Publications Ltd
6 Bonhill Street
London EC2A 4PU

Published by Tejeshwar Singh for Sage Publications India Pvt Ltd, phototypeset by Pagewell Photosetters, Pondicherry, and printed at Print Perfect, Delhi.

Library of Congress Cataloging-in-Publication Data

Pantham, Thomas.
    Political theories and social reconstruction: a critical survey of the literature on India / Thomas Pantham.
      p.   cm.
    Includes bibliographical references and index.
    1. Social science literature—India. 2. Social sciences—India—History 3. Political science literature—India. 4. Political science—India—History. I. Title.
    H62.5.I5P36   300'.954—dc20   1995   94–45237

ISBN: 0–8039–9216–5 (US-hb)   81–7036–447–7 (India-hb)
          0–8039–9217–3 (US-pb)   81–7036–448–5 (India-pb)

To the memory of *chachan* and for *amma*:
Chacko and Annamma Panthamakal

Contents

Preface and Acknowledgements

This book is the outcome of a survey of the literature undertaken for the Indian Council of Social Science Research as part of its Second Survey of Research in Political Science. The theme assigned to me was entitled 'Models and Strategies of Change: Problems of Value, Order and Change.' In the course of the study, I felt it appropriate to choose the present title.

I also felt it advisable to survey not only the contributions of Indian political theorists but also the political theorizations of the other Indian social sciences. I have also taken into account what seemed to me to be major India-focussed political theorizations made by some Western social and political theorists.

Roughly speaking, the present survey covers the publications of the period from 1971 to 1992. In this way, the present study is a continuation of two previous trend-reports in political theory, written by Rajni Kothari and Sudipta Kaviraj, as parts of the First ICSSR Survey of Research in Political Science. In chapters 1 and 7, I have tried to relate the present study to those previous trend-reports. I should however clarify that the present book can also be read and used independently.

My primary addressees are the advanced-level fellow-students of Indian politics, who I hope will find my interpretive summaries and commentaries helpful for undertaking further inquiries into, or contributions to, the political-theoretical visions and constructions of the basic organizing principles, ideals and values of the Indian society.

During the last few years, in addition to my regular teaching and administrative responsibilities, I have been devoting my research time to this study and to another project on contemporary political thought. During these years, I have received help and encouragement from many institutions and individuals. First of all, I thank the Indian Council of Social Science Research for inviting me to undertake this study. From the Council, Iqbal Narain, V.R. Mehta, D.N. Dhanagare and the late Sukhamoy Chakravarty have been sources of encouragement.

I thank the Maharaja Sayajirao University of Baroda for giving me a sabbatical leave and for providing a generally supportive environment for research and writing. I am also grateful to St. John's College, Cambridge, for electing me to an academic visitorship for the 1989 Easter Term and to the South Asia Institute of Heidelberg University and the Maison Des Sciences De L'Homme, Paris, for giving me research facilities during my visits to their excellent libraries. In India, I received help, largely in the form of photocopies of articles, from the Social Science Documentation Centre of the ICSSR, the Nehru Memorial Museum and Library, New Delhi, the library of the Indian Council of Historical Research, New Delhi, and the Centre for Social Studies, Surat.

I acknowledge the helpful conversations I have had with John Rawls, Hans Georg-Gadamer, Jacques Derrida and Charles Taylor. Although those conversations pertained to another on-going study, they have also helped to clarify some of the theoretical issues discussed in the present study.

For their sustained help and encouragement, I remain indebted to Quentin Skinner, Bhikhu Parekh, Fred Dallmayr, John Dunn, D.L. Sheth, Rajni Kothari, Claus Offe, K.L. Deutsch, Ashis Nandy, Sudipta Kaviraj, Manoranjan Mohanty, V.N. Kothari, Partha Chatterjee, Ghanshyam Shah, A.P. Rana, Dietmar Rothermund, Ronald Terchek, Dennis Thompson, William Connolly, Jan Nederveen Pieterse, Maurice Aymard, D.H. Mohite and H.C. Shukul. Some of them gave me the benefit of their reactions to specific aspects of the present survey. I am also thankful to Yogendra Yadav, Sunil Khilnani, Sivananda Patnaik, Kanti Bajpai, Rajendra Vora, Jyotirmaya Sharma, Amit Dholakia and Prakash Chandra Upadhyaya for helpful comments or discussions on parts of the study. My thanks go also to Brijbala Tewari for her valuable assistance in research and to P.R. Chalke, V.M. Karandikar, Jaganath Dalvi and my niece, Mercy Alappattu, for their help with the typing and word-processing of some of the chapters.

At home, the numerous ways in which Annie, Prakash and Preeti have contributed to the completion of this book formed only a small reflection of their sustaining love.

Obviously, the greatest indebtedness I have incurred in writing this book is to the political and social theorists, whose writings have been critically surveyed here. I must admit that it has not been easy for me to make interpretive comments on their theoretical positions. But the attempt to understand them has been an enormously enriching experience to me. If some of my readers would come to have a similar experience, I shall feel amply gratified.

Thomas Pantham

1

Political Theories and Social Reconstruction: An Introduction

On the Politics of Social Reconstruction

At the dawn of Indian independence, Mahatma Gandhi stated: 'The Congress has won political freedom, but it has yet to win economic freedom, social and moral freedom. These freedoms are harder than the political if only because they are constructive, less exciting and not spectacular' (cf. Ostergaard and Currell, 1971: 3). In saying this, Gandhi was only reiterating a view which he and the other leaders of the Indian national/freedom movement had long held, namely, that political independence or parliamentary *swaraj* was to be a means to social transformation.

Thus, in its 1931 session held at Karachi, the Indian National Congress had declared that India's freedom struggle was aimed at securing not only political independence from British rule but also an 'end to the exploitation of the masses . . . and real economic freedom for the starving millions'. A few years later, Jawaharlal Nehru (1938: 11) wrote that political freedom would be only 'a means to an end, that end being the raising of the people . . . to higher levels and hence the general advancement of humanity.' In the Constituent Assembly, Sarvepalli Radhakrishnan spoke of political independence and democracy as the beginning of a process of 'socio-economic revolution', or, in other words, 'a fundamental change in the structure of Indian society.'

In this *swaraj–sarvodaya* discourse of our freedom movement, the national democratic state was thought of as a necessary, quasi-autonomous instrument of social reconstruction. The political system, to use Rajni Kothari's words, was seen to be taking on 'an importance that is central to the whole enterprise of building a new society' (1976: 2). As noted by Ravinder Kumar (1983: 1), the Indian national movement and its culmination in the 1947 transfer of power from British to Indian hands constituted 'one of the most important historical processes of the twentieth century'; they set afoot processes of momentous socio-economic change both in the domestic sphere and in the international arena. The autonomous role of the political sphere in social change in India has also been emphasized by Atul Kohli (1991: 19–20 *et passim*).

While the centrality of politics in social transformation has thus been universally recognized, political leaders and social theorists in post-independence India have differed among themselves on the question of whether it is political *stability* or political *change* that is required for, or entailed in, changing the overall structure of the society. Some have maintained that political stability, political order, or, in other words, the stability of the governing/moderniz-ing elites is necessary to generate and manage the processes of economic growth with social justice. Others have argued that given their origins in, or affiliations with, the dominant, entrenched classes, the governing elites 'can only operate on the margins of the status quo' and that therefore political change, and not political stability, is required to 'restructure and regenerate the economy towards a path of true national independence and prosperity' (Partha Chatterjee 1977: 35). The overall structure or principle of organization of the society, we are reminded, cannot be changed except through political change (Kothari, 1976: 2).

There has been a controversy not only over the question of whether *political* stability or political change is required for *social* reconstruction but also over the question of which model of the polity or which mode of political organization and action is best suited to bringing about the good society. No doubt that within the modern western-educated middle class there has been a majority view in favour of the liberal-democratic model of modernization. But, as we shall see later, different versions or models of the liberal-democratic path of modernization have been advanced by social and political theorists. Other political models and strategies of social change have also been advanced, viz., the Marxist, Gandhian and Hindu nationalist models.

These models or theories of the politics of social transformation or reconstruction differ in their assumptions about, as well as conceptions of, human needs and potentialities, which are to be maximized or fulfilled through political institutions. These theories also differ in their conceptions of the interrelationship, first, between political institutions on the one hand and the individuals, groups and classes on the other hand, and, second, between the transformation of India's domestic socio-economic and political structures and that of the larger capitalist world system. These theories or models, to use Manoranjan Mohanty's words, generate 'an exciting battle of ideas' about the basic principles of organization of our social life (1979: 45; and 1989).

How have Indian and India-oriented political theorists faced the challenge of social change? Is the necessity or desirability of social transformation recognized in their writings? If so what political models and strategies of change have they preferred? What are the values which they seek to maximize by their preferred models of political modernization, development or revolution? Who are to be the agents, beneficiaries and losers (if any) of the type of social and political change they advocate or favour?

These are the types of questions that are addressed in this critical survey of the literature on the political theories of social reconstruction in India, which I have categorized as belonging to four varieties, viz.: the liberal-democratic, Marxist-Leninist, Gandhian and Hindu-nationalist varieties.

Preparatory to such a survey of the literature, I shall, in the next section, give a brief introduction to the nature, functions and varieties of political theories. In a subsequent section, I shall indicate how the present survey of the literature relates to the corresponding trend-reports of the previous ICSSR survey.

On the Nature and Varieties of Political Theories

'In the absence of a paradigm or some candidate for paradigm,' writes Thomas Kuhn (1962: 15), 'all of the facts that could possibly pertain to the development of a given science are likely to seem equally relevant.' It is for this reason that the development of both the physical and social sciences has depended on 'paradigms,' or theoretical models. To quote Karl Deutsch (1963: 12):

. . . we all use models in our thinking all the time, even though we may not stop to notice it. When we say that we 'understand' a situation, political or otherwise, we say, in effect, that we have in our mind an abstract model, vague or specific, that permits us to parallel or predict such changes in that situation of interest to us.

Deutsch goes on to suggest that good theoretical models contribute to 'the development of human powers of insight and action' by performing such functions as the heuristic function of leading to discoveries of new facts and methods, and the organizing, predictive, explanatory and measuring functions with respect to the phenomena under study. Similarly, Isaiah Berlin (1962) writes:

The first step to understanding of men is the bringing to consciousness of the model or models that dominate and penetrate their thought and action. Like all attempts to make men aware of the categories in which they think, it is a difficult and sometimes painful activity, likely to produce deeply disquieting results. The second task is to analyze the model itself, and this commits the analyst to accepting or modifying or rejecting it, and in the last case, to providing a more adequate one in its stead.

Models of social life, unlike those of physical or natural objects, deal with phenomena which are variable by human will. They highlight the sources and goals of political and social change. Models or theories of the polity, in particular, seek either to justify a given political ordering of social life or to advocate an alternative to it. They do so on the basis of their specific assumptions as to what human nature is and what it is capable of becoming in a given historical situation or technological context. 'Men,' writes Marx, 'make their own history, but they do not make it just as they please; they do not make it under circumstances chosen by themselves, but under circumstances directly encountered, given and transmitted from the past'.

Generally speaking, what a political theorist or model-builder does is to advance a specific conception of human needs and potentialities in a given socio-historical and technological context and then to argue which type of polity is best conducive to the fulfilment or realization of those human needs and potentialities. In other words, it is with reference to their conceptions of human needs and potentialities and of the order of priority among them that political theorists argue that a certain way of structuring political-power relationships are deserving of political obligation, while some other ways of structuring the same would have to be resisted and changed through civil disobedience or revolution.

Political theories or models are thus not only an aid to understanding a given political tradition or practice but also a means of the political reconstruction of society.[1] In fact, major socio-historical transformations have been associated with major revisions in political philosophies. To quote William Connolly (1974: 203):

> Conceptual revision is not, . . . a sufficient condition of political change, but it is indispensable to significant political change. It is part of that process by which events once considered mere facts come to be seen as the outcome of a political process . . . . Conceptual revision is involved in any political strategy that aims at reconstituting social life in modest or in radical ways.

That the history of political theories is a history of a succession of political paradigms of social life and social organization has been suggested by Sheldon Wolin, whose argument is summarized in what follows.

Wolin follows Thomas Kuhn's theory of the structure of scientific revolutions. According to Kuhn, in the history of the natural sciences, periods of *normal* scientific activity alternate with periods of *revolutionary* scientific activity. A *normal* scientific activity is one that is governed by a paradigm or 'disciplinary matrix.' Kuhn defines paradigms as 'universally recognized scientific achievements that for a time provide model problems and solutions to a community of practitioners' (Kuhn 1962: viii). The achievements which serve as paradigms may be 'law, theory, application, and instrumentation together.' Normal scientific activity is the activity of solving the puzzles thrown up by the given, reigning scientific paradigm.

Sometimes, scientists encounter problems, which are more

---

[1] In this survey, I use 'theory,' 'model,' 'approach' and 'paradigm' interchangeably. On the distinctions and inter-relationships among them, see Keohane (1976), Dunn (1985), Held (1989), Bernstein (1976), Miller and Siedentop (1983), Miller (1987) and Horton (1990).

complicated than puzzles, and which therefore come to be viewed as *anomalies* that cannot be resolved in terms of the norms, expectations, procedures and assumptions of the reigning paradigm. Anomalies, in other words, signify a crisis in the scientific community and lead to *revolutionary* scientific activity. Those trying to resolve the anomalies of a scientific discipline, in other words, are led to abandon the governing paradigm and to search for a new paradigm that can explain or resolve what cannot be explained or resolved by the existing paradigm. Such a search entails 'recourse to philosophy and to debate over fundamentals.' When the scientific community finally assents to a new paradigm, a scientific revolution has occurred.

Applying Kuhn's notion of scientific paradigms to the history of political theories, Wolin suggests that 'we conceive of political society itself as a paradigm of an operative kind.' He writes (1968: 149):

> From this viewpoint society would be envisaged as a coherent whole in the sense of its customary political practices, institutions, laws, structure of authority and citizenship, and operative beliefs being organized and interrelated. A politically organized society contains definite institutional arrangements, certain widely shared understandings regarding the location and use of political power, certain expectations about how authority ought to treat the members of society and about the claims that organized society can rightfully make upon its members . . . . This ensemble of practices and beliefs may be said to form a paradigm in the sense that the society tries to carry on its political life in accordance with them.

It must be noted here that Wolin stresses the fact that political paradigms/political theories are *moral* in the sense that they entail notions of what is correct, right or appropriate behaviour. They are, in other words, value-laden. Hence, as noted by Alan Ryan (1972), they 'define the range of *possible* moral arguments, and define what *sort* of puzzle a particular moral puzzle is.' A model or paradigm of politics is also ideological in the sense that it is a 'more or less systematic set of ideas about man's place in nature, in society, and in history (i.e., in relation to particular societies), which can elicit the commitment of significant numbers of people to (or against) political change.' Such a model, in other words, contains 'elements of explanation (of fact and history), justification (of demands), and faith or belief in the ultimate truth (of rightness of their law)' (Macpherson, 1973: 157–58).

To continue with Wolin: after characterizing the 'political society' as a moral or ideological paradigm, he goes on to argue that 'political theories can best be understood as paradigms and that the scientific study of politics is a special form of paradigm-inspired research.' He invites us 'to consider Plato, Aristotle, Machiavelli, Hobbes, Locke and Marx as the counterparts in political theory to Galileo, Harvey, Newton, Laplace, Faraday, and Einstein.' The former group of writers, Wolin (1968: 140) goes on to say,

> inspired a new way of looking at the political world; in each case their theories proposed a new definition of what was significant for understanding that world; each specified distinctive methods for inquiry; and each of their theories contained an explicit or implicit statement of what should count as an answer to certain basic questions.

The masters of political thought, says Wolin, are those who sought to change or restructure the existing political system or the operative political paradigm, which they perceived to be crisis-ridden or deranged. They argued that through redefinitions of human needs and potentialities, of socio-political roles and expectations, and through the restructuring of socio-political relationships and institutions, what they saw as deranged polities can and must be re-railed on to the path of a normal, creative, just or good society.

Political theories are systematic meshes of interconnected concepts which describe, explain and evaluate the political structuring or ordering of a community or society at the local, national or transnational levels. The central question which all political theories address is this: what political arrangements are best for protecting and promoting the common good or well-being of the society and, simultaneously, the fulfilment of the human needs and potentialities of each member of the society. Marx and Engels expressed it well when they wrote that the aim of their political theory was to bring about a form of society in which 'the free development of each is the condition for the free development of all.'

Given this central concern, political theories in modern times invariably focus on the structuring of state power in relation to such ideals, values or principles as freedom, equality, justice, rights, obligation, *swaraj, sarvodaya*, etc.

Different traditions or varieties of political theories differ from one another either in terms of the ultimate value which each of them upholds (e.g., liberty or equality or community or justice) or, if they happen to uphold the same general ultimate value, in terms of the different interpretations they give of it. According to Ronald Dworkin (1977) all plausible political theories of modern times, ranging from libertarianism to communism, uphold the same ultimate value, namely, an abstract notion of equality which stipulates that all persons are to be treated 'as equals.' However, while sharing the same 'egalitarian plateau,' the different political theories define and imagine the meaning of equality and its social, economic and political requirements differently.

Liberal political theories uphold the values of freedom, reason and toleration, which are said to be necessary to liberate people from the hold of custom, tradition, status, absolutism, etc., of the pre-liberal order.[2] In their opposition to the latter order, the liberal theorists advanced the idea of the 'free and equal' individuals with natural rights, which cannot be taken away even by the rulers. Liberalism thus defines and defends a 'private' sphere of the life of the individuals and their 'civil society' (family, schools, business, etc.), which are to be free from state interference.

A central problem of liberal political theory has been that of the conflict between the freedom of the individuals and the authority of the state. This conflict, along with the political organization of the workers, led eventually to the invention of the institution of representative democracy, which seeks to justify the sovereign power of the state and at the same time to limit its power through constitution, law, separation of powers, independent judiciary and democratic franchise.

Marxism departs from liberal-democratic theory by pointing out that the individual cannot be the starting point of political analysis.[3]

[2] On the nature of liberal political theory, see Skinner (1978), Gray (1986), Held (1987), Macpherson (1977), Kymlicka (1990) and Dunn (1992).

[3] On the nature of Marxist political theory, see Jessop (1982), Bottomore (1983), Callinicos (1989), Held (1989) and the following works which are included in the bibliography of chapter 3: Kaviraj et al. (1978), Bharadwaj and Kaviraj (1989) and Parekh (1982).

Marx wrote that 'man is not an abstract being squatting outside the world' but a species-being whose nature and needs are determined by the relations of production through which he gets or does not get his means of life and labour. These, according to Marx, are essentially class relations, which he places at the centre of his political theory. While liberal-democratic theorists conceptualize the state as an impersonal, class-neutral institution, Marxism interprets it as a class institution, which tries to coordinate the society in the interests of the dominant class. Hence, Marxist political theory emphasizes the differences among 'the bourgeois state,' 'the proletarian state' and the stateless, communist society in which there would be no class divisions. In bringing about this ideal society, Marxism recognizes the necessary role of revolutionary violence.

Gandhian political theory pursues a line of thought and action which seeks to overcome the individualism, utilitarianism and imperialism of the liberal and liberal-democratic tradition without resorting to the class war approach of Marxism-Leninism.[4] Through the 'experiments' of a novel way of political struggle, namely, *satyagraha*, Gandhi 'imagines' or 'theorizes' that the conflictual relationship between the 'self' and 'other' can be played out through political action informed by the twin moral principles of *satya* (truth) and *ahimsa* (non-violence *and* love). In a *satyagraha* movement or struggle, the contested truth of a social system or norm is sought to be validated through the use of 'truth force' or 'love force,' which does not seek to eliminate or annihilate the opponents but to bring about a restructuring of the conflictual or oppressive situation so that both parties to the initial conflict can realize a heightened mutuality or moral interrelationship. 'The claim for *satyagraha*,' writes Joan Bondurant, 'is that through the operation of non-violent action the truth as judged by the fulfilment of human needs will emerge in the form of a mutually satisfactory and agreed-upon solution' (1959: 195). Besides *satyagraha*, the central concepts of Gandhian moral-political theory are *satya*, *ahimsa*, *tapas* (self-suffering), *swaraj* (self-rule and self-restraint) and *sarvodaya* (the welfare of all).

---

[4] The nature of Gandhian political theory is discussed in the following works, which are included in the bibliography of chapter 4: Iyer (1973), Bondurant (1959), Pantham (1983 and 1986a), Roy (1985) and Parekh (1989a & b).

The varieties of political theories, which have been briefly introduced, are not to be taken merely as rival representations or mirror-images of a realm of politics which exists *independently* of those theories. Such a mirror-conception of the nature of political theories is not quite correct; political theories do not merely mirror an independently existing world of politics but serve to constitute or construct that world. In other words, political theories help to politically construct and reconstruct societies.

A politically ordered society, unlike a chaotic situation, is one whose members live and interact with one another in accordance with a political theory that is at least implicitly accepted by them. To quote MacIntyre (1983: 19–20):

> Every society is constituted by members whose behaviour embodies a set of beliefs about the workings of that particular society: how individuals are to be classified and ranked, who owes what to whom under what circumstances, what the consequences are likely to be of breaking rather than keeping different types of rule.

Formally articulated political theories are sometimes the explicit, systematic and extended presentations of the implicitly held political theories of the ordinary people. But this is not the case always. Very often, political theorists challenge and criticize the prevailing political self-understanding of a given community or society and thereby contribute to new self-understandings and reconstructions of social and political structures.[5] Charles Taylor (1983: 64) brings out this task of political theory in the following words:

> In fact the framing of theory rarely consists simply of making some ongoing practice explicit. The stronger motive for making and adopting theories is the sense that our implicit understanding is in some way crucially inadequate or even wrong. Theories do not just make explicit our constitutive self-understandings, but extend, or criticize, or even challenge them. It is in this

---

[5] Some of the best defences and explorations of the critical tasks of social and political theories can be found in the writings of Jurgen Habermas and Charles Taylor. Cf. Habermas (1990) and Taylor (1985). Cf. also Bernstein (1976 & 1991), Dallmayr (1991), McCarthy (1991) and Benhabib (1986).

sense that theory makes a claim to tell us what is really going on, to show us the real, hitherto unidentified course of events.

The foregoing considerations on the nature and varieties of political theory are admittedly brief and simplified. Yet, I hope they are sufficient to serve as an introduction to the survey of the literature reported in the following chapters.

Theorizations of Indian Politics: Two Previous Trend Reports

Since the present study has been undertaken as part of the *second* ICSSR Survey of Research in Political Science, it is pertinent to relate it to the previous survey. In it there were two trend-reports, which may be regarded as benchmarks for the present study, viz.: (*a*) 'Contributions to Theory,' by Rajni Kothari (1986); and (*b*) 'Marxian Theory and Analysis of Indian Politics,' by Sudipta Kaviraj (1986). These reports were completed in 1971, but were published only in 1986.

In his report, Kothari pointed out that even though 'a mammoth virgin laboratory for original research' was provided by India's post-independence project of nation-building, polity-making and an array of momentous public policy-making in an open, democratic framework, the response of Indian political scientists has been dismal. 'The response,' he writes, 'has been the weakest in respect of theoretical contributions and on that basis a systematic study of goals, strategies, and instrumentalities.'

Kothari reported that original Indian thought on these matters has come much more from 'non-professional thinkers, political activists, and philosophers of a general kind' than from professional social and political scientists. He observed: 'As compared with the rather original contributions to Indian political thought by such men as Rammohun Roy, Dadabhai Naoroji, M.K. Gandhi, M.N. Roy, and Jayaprakash Narayan, the contributions of the social scientists to fundamental thought adds up to rather little.'

Kothari made two suggestions. First, he said that Indian social and political theorists would have to turn to the issues raised by Gandhi and Jayaprakash Narayan, which, he added, are of continuing relevance to the development of a theory of Indian politics in particular and of global politics in general. Second, he wrote that serious and urgent attention had to be given 'to enriching the Marxist heritage in the light of the liberal-democratic commitment of India, employing the vast conceptual and philosophical bag of tools left behind by Marx, integrating the powerful insights into the Indian mind left by Gandhi, and thus producing a more acceptable version of socialist reconstruction' (p. 14).

In his trend-report, Sudipta Kaviraj critically reviewed Marxist writings on Indian politics with special emphasis on the works of M.N. Roy and R. Palme Dutt. There is also a brief section devoted to Nehru's Fabianized Marxian views, which, according to Kaviraj, constituted a trend of radical *thought* rather than a trend of *action or praxis* within the Congress.

Kaviraj noted that in contrast to Indian nationalist scholarship which adopted a healthy *critical* approach to Western theories, the social and political sciences in the immediate post-independence years came under the conservatism of the empiricist or behavioural *science* of politics. 'Our social sciences,' wrote Kaviraj, 'were recolonized' (p. 166). In his view, a central shortcoming of the behavioural–functional model of politics, with its claim of value-neutrality, was that it did not recognize the relevance of the central Marxist idea of class conflict.

After giving due recognition to the important contributions of M.N. Roy and R. Palme Dutt, Kaviraj observed that Marxist political theorizing in India never attained the level it did in Russia, central Europe or China. In his view, the only two men who developed integrated theoretical structures in India were Gandhi and Nehru, who were not Marxists, though the latter, during a certain stage of his life, did espouse a Fabian version of Marxism.

According to Kaviraj, macro-structural theorizing on contemporary Indian politics is 'one of the greatest absences in the Indian Marxist tradition.' What is available from it, he says, are only *ad hoc* commentaries or negative criticisms. He wrote: '. . . Marxists have, in the end, specialized in negation, criticizing the analyses done by others in frequent reviews. But negatively criticizing an academically hegemonic paradigm is not a substitute for replacing it' (p. 180).

For remedying this situation, Kaviraj made the following suggestions: (*a*) Marxist scholars should abandon their 'dogmatic incubus' by distancing themselves from party lines. They should 'proceed from the fact to theory and not the other way round.' (*b*) They should turn from micro-fragmented investigations to studies in 'high theory' and methodology. (*c*) They should reject any 'empiricization of the dialectic' and the positivistic conception of science and adopt the more complex and richer paradigm of the Marx–Lenin–Lukacs–Gramsci tradition. Being sensitive to the specifics of *historical* contradictions and to the influence of *superstructural* factors, this tradition of Marxism is, according to Kaviraj, of particular relevance to the analysis of Indian politics and society.

Like Kothari and Kaviraj, I too shall be concerned in the present survey, not with abstract political philosophy, but with political theorizations of the Indian society as a whole. While they surveyed the period up to 1970–71, I shall focus on the years since then, though for reasons of continuity of presentation or argument, I shall also include some major earlier studies. While my main focus will be on the theorizations of political scientists, I shall, in a selective way, also deal with the works of scholars belonging to such other social and human disciplines as history, economics, literary criticism, social psychology and philosophy.

2

Models of Liberal Democracy
and Modernization

Introductory Remarks

The overriding concern of theoretical writings on the direction of
Indian politics has been to provide justifications or critiques of, or
alternatives to, one or another *liberal* model of democracy and
modernization. These models differ from one another in their
assumptions about the nature, needs and potentialities of human
beings, the structure and character of the good society and the
nature and role of the state. These models also differ from one
another in their conceptions of the nature and tasks of modernization, development, social transformation and world order.

The various alternatives to the liberal models of democracy and
development will be taken up in the following chapters. In the
present chapter I take up the literature on the liberal models.

Taken as a whole, the various liberal models of democracy and
modernization are presented by their advocates as superior,
liberating alternatives to the old, traditional, pre-liberal or non-
liberal organization of social life. This can be seen best in the
liberal-democratic optimism of the Indian constitution, in the
Nehruvian model of modernization and in the writings of those
who provide structural-functional explanations of the same process. In these writings, the liberal-democratic order, based on the
ideas of individual choice and social contract/consent, liberty and
equality, is presented to be a liberating alternative to the traditional social order based on custom, ascriptive status, hierarchy
and inequality.

A second category of 'liberal' writings (e.g., the theory of the modernity of tradition) stresses the need for a certain accommod-ation or adaptation of the institutions and processes of liberal-democratic change to the institutions and processes of Indian tradition as they have come down to the present. Third, there is a division within the broad liberal school between those who favour an elitist, techno-bureaucratic, state-oriented, 'political economy' model of liberal democracy and development and those who advance one or another form of radical, social-democratic, people-oriented transformation of liberal democracy and development.

Preparatory to surveying the literature on these different liberal models of democracy and development, it is useful to note that as a combination of liberalism and democracy, 'liberal democracy' has an internal or in-built tension between the logic of liberalism and the logic democracy.

Liberal democracy is found only in those countries whose eco-nomy is wholly or predominantly capitalist. In these societies, democratic franchise came as a late 'top dressing' on the firmly established liberal/capitalist market-society and the liberal-repre-sentative state. What this democratization of liberalism and liberal-ization of democracy did was to bring about a particular combination of the possessive individualism and inequalities of the liberal-capitalist market-society with the 'common good' and equalities of democratic politics (Macpherson, 1972, 1973 and 1977a; Pantham, 1976–77 and 1985; Parekh, 1992).

In India this tension between the inequalities of the capitalist economy and the equalities of democratic politics has been com-pounded by the colonial nature of the introduction of the capitalist relations of production on to the indigenous society. How this problem is addressed by the subaltern Marxists and Gandhians will be examined in the next two chapters. Our concern in the present chapter is with how the various liberal writers have seen the interaction, first, between modern liberal democracy and the tradi-tional order and, second, between the possessive individualist/ inegalitarian logic of liberalism/capitalism and the egalitarian logic of democracy.

The Liberal-Democratic Optimism of the Indian Constitution

An excellent examination of the liberal-democratic road to 'social revolution' taken by the Indian Constitution is contained in Austin

(1966: chapter 2). Among the liberal-democratic features of the Constitution which he singles out are universal adult franchise, constitutionally guaranteed fundamental rights, a directly elected Lok Sabha and an independent judiciary. In his view, these features make the Constitution different from the Gandhian model of a decentralized, village-based system of governance.

After reviewing the brief consideration given by the Constituent Assembly to a proposal for a Gandhian constitution, Austin notes the following reasons for the choice of the Westminster model of liberal democracy: (a) The modern western-educated Indian leaders were favourably disposed towards liberal democracy; (b) India had a long period of experience with modern parliamentary institutions under the colonial government; (c) The victory of the Allied Powers over the Axis Powers in the Second World War created a favourable atmosphere for liberal democracy; (d) The problems created by the Pakistani invasion of Kashmir, the Telengana rebellion, Hindu–Muslim riots, the imperative of planned economic change and industrialization all called for a centralized, parliamentary democracy rather than the Gandhian, decentralized, village-based system of government.

As noted by Austin, several members of the Constituent Assembly affirmed optimistically that the values and institutions of liberal democracy would transform India's tradition-bound social structure. Sarvepalli Radhakrishnan said that modern parliamentary democracy would bring about a 'socio-economic revolution' or, in other words, 'a fundamental change in the structure of Indian society.' Another member of the Constituent Assembly, K. Santhanam, wrote that the new Constitution was meant to help India to get out of 'the medievalism based on birth, religion, custom, and community and reconstruct her social structure on modern foundations of law, individual merit, and secular education.' He went on to state that the liberal-democratic Constitution would help India to make a 'transition from primitive rural economy to scientific and planned agriculture and industry (Austin, 1966: 63–64). Similarly, K.M. Panikkar, who too was a member of the Constituent Assembly, wrote in his book, *Hindu Society at Cross-Roads* (1955: 83), that parliamentary democracy based on universal adult franchise presented the masses 'with dynamite for the destruction of social institutions based on privileges or on hereditary inequality.'

In the recent literature of political science there is a general recognition that the Indian Constitution provides a liberal-democratic framework of governance and development. A.H. Somjee (1982: 41) writes:

> On an essentially traditional and hierarchical society the founding fathers superimposed a democratic political system which had its own norms, goals and assumptions concerning social equality and political participation. Through these, they hoped, Indians would be able to transform their society into one that would be just and free.

Ernest Barker (1951: vi) finds the Preamble of the Indian Constitution to be stating in a 'brief and pithy form' the argument of his book on the principles of liberal democracy. Similarly, A.R. Desai (1984: 26–27) finds the Indian Constitution to be upholding the bourgeois norms of social life, while for V.R. Mehta (1983: 20) the Constitution is 'almost an essay in liberal ideology,' which he, as we shall see in chapter 6, thinks is unsuitable to India.

The Nehruvian Model

Nehru has himself given some explanations of the distinctiveness and relevance of his approach to modernization through the political framework of parliamentary democracy and the economic model of mixed economy. These together constituted his democratic-socialist model of modernization, which he believed to be 'a third way which takes the best from all existing systems—the Russian, the American and others—and seeks to create something suited to one's own history and philosophy.' Nehru saw modern imperialism to be 'an outgrowth of capitalism,' whose remedy, he said, lies in 'the socialist structures of society'. However, given the class composition of the Indian national movement, in which the nationalist-capitalist class was a dominant force, Nehru felt compelled to make a strategic postponement of the pursuit of socialist policies until the more pressing tasks of national independence and unity were attended to on a priority basis. Unless political independence was attended to as 'our immediate objective,' he said, 'we will have neither socialism nor independence'. He however entertained the hope that 'the logic of events' in the setting up of an independent and democratic state in India 'will lead it to socialism, for that seems to me the only remedy for India's ills.' As noted by Bipan Chandra and his associates, Nehru believed that 'to break away from the National Congress and Gandhi's leadership would be counter-productive for socialist and radical goals' and that 'the left had gradually to transform the Congress in a socialist direction.'

Several scholars concur with Nehru's claim that his model of modernization was an alternative to the standard models of capitalist and communist modernization. Thus, H.K. Manmohan Singh notes that Nehru's mixed economy framework was a 'middle path' between a free enterprise economy and a fully-controlled economy (Singh, 1975: 1325). Regarding the relevance of that framework for India's development, Singh raises the following questions about some of its assumptions:

> How do we turn over control of production from the capitalist class to the whole people? Can a socialist sector develop from a public sector which has not cut off its moorings in a capitalist economy? Can the socialist man emerge in a system in which the means of production are in large part in private hands? Those who seek the regeneration on Indian economy and society in terms of Nehru's *weltanschauung* must face these questions (Singh 1975: 1337).

The distinctiveness and basic soundness of Nehru's mixed economy model has been endorsed by V.K.R.V. Rao and P.C. Joshi in their article, 'Some Fundamental Aspects of Socialist Transformation in India' (1982). They differentiate the Nehruvian model from the classical/Soviet strategy of socialist transformation and credit the former with considerable success in giving a measure of autonomy and growth to the Indian economy and society. They however maintain that in its actual operation, the mixed economy has moved in the direction of capitalism rather than that of socialism. This they attribute to the failure of Nehru and his successors in creating 'the *socio-cultural* and *political* conditions' which could have led the mixed economy in a socialist direction. According to them, the framework of mixed economy and parliamentary democracy is a necessary but not sufficient condition for socialist transformation; what was additionally required but not actually provided was a pattern of political mobilization in which the modernizing leadership brought about an alliance between the intermediate and lower classes. In their view, such an alliance could have used the levers of power to bring about a socialist transformation. They conclude that what has actually occurred is a pattern of 'political alliance of the intermediate classes with the upper classes resorting to socialist ideology only to win mass support but using all levers of power to facilitate a type of capitalist development in the interest of a narrow section of the Indian society' (p. 22). Rao and Joshi call for increasing the 'weight of the non-capitalist classes in general and the working masses in particular in the country's state structure' (p. 12).

Baldev Raj Nayar (1989) has argued that Nehru's conception of the mixed economy was not an instrumental–capitalist one but an instrumental–socialist one in that it was aimed at bringing about 'a steady advance to a socialist pattern of economy' through the relatively greater expansion of the public sector (p. 207; cf. also Chakravarty, 1987: 90). In its operation, however, Nehru's 'middle way' between capitalism and communism, says Nayar, 'harboured the danger of combining the ills of both systems, that is, inequality and bureaucratic domination' (pp. 204–05). Nehru, according to Nayar, underestimated the vested interests of the intermediate strata which controlled the state; for them the public sector was 'a source of autonomous economic power to be added to their already existing political power' (p. 209).

In a path-breaking study of Indian nationalist thought, Partha Chatterjee (1986) interprets Nehru's political ideology as that of an *etatisme* that is wedded to capitalism. Nehru, in Chatterjee's view, simply crowned the passive, capitalist revolution of India with a sovereign national state, which he legitimised 'by a specifically nationalist marriage between the ideas of progress and social justice.'

Following Gramsci's ideas, Chatterjee points out that the Indian bourgeoisie, blocked by imperialism and the colonial state, was unable to carry out any full-scale bourgeois revolution against the old, pre-capitalist dominant classes. Thus failing to establish hegemony over the 'civil society', it tried to bring about a passive revolution by spearheading an all-class nationalist struggle against the colonial state so that a politically independent national state could be set up and used for establishing capitalism as the dominant mode of production. In this 'passive revolution,' the bourgeoisie made a political appropriation of the masses or the peasantry and brought about 'a "molecular transformation" of the old dominant classes into partners in a new historical bloc'.

What is particularly noteworthy, according to Chatterjee, is that the political independence that is thus brought about 'does not attempt to break up or transform in any radical way the institutional structures of 'rational' authority set up in the period of colonial rule, whether in the domain of administration and law or in the realm of economic institutions or in the structure of education, scientific research and cultural organization.' Those 'institutional structures of 'rational authority', we are reminded, are subservient to capitalist imperialism.

Gandhi, according to Chatterjee, was the supreme leader of the penultimate phase or 'moment of manoeuvre' of India's passive capitalist revolution in the sense that he 'succeeded in opening up the historical possibility by which the largest popular element of the nation—the peasantry—could be appropriated within the evolving forms of the new Indian state.' In other words, Gandhi is said to have made the peasantry 'willing participants in a struggle wholly conceived and directed by others,' namely, the bourgeoisie. According to Chatterjee, the Indian passive revolution of capital owes its 'moment of arrival' or 'the final, fully mature' phase to Nehru; he appropriated the Gandhian political legacy of the partially mobilized peasantry and crowned it with a sovereign national state, assigning to it a 'central, autonomous and directing role in the further development of capitalism,' which he legitimised 'by a specifically nationalist marriage between the ideas of progress and social justice.' Chatterjee sums up the Nehruvian, *etatist* phase of the Indian passive revolution of capital, in the following manner:

> It is now a discourse of order, of the rational organization of power. Here the discourse is not only conducted in a single, consistent, unambiguous voice, it also succeeds in glossing over all earlier contradictions, divergences and difference and incorporating within the body of a unified discourse every aspect and stage in the history of its formation. This ideological unity of nationalist thought it seeks to actualize in the unified life of the state. Nationalist discourse at its moment of arrival is passive revolution uttering its own life-history. (1986: 51)

Chatterjee goes on to argue that after independence Nehru abandoned socialism and that instead of pursuing equality 'by means of politics, through the violent struggle between classes,' he resorted to the rational, realistic management of the government by the technicians of power.

Chatterjee notes that since the Age of Enlightenment, there has been an historical partnership between the universal march of Reason and the universalist urge of capital. Anti-imperialist nationalism, of which the paradigmatic case is the Indian one, did, according to him, administer 'a check on a specific political form of metropolitan capitalist dominance' and gave a 'death-blow . . . to such blatantly ethnic slogans as the civilizing mission of the West, the white man's burden, etc.' But all this, Chatterjee maintains, has been achieved in the name of capitalistic rationality. 'Nowhere in the world,' he writes, 'has nationalism qua nationalism challenged the legitimacy of the marriage between Reason and capital.' Nationalist thought, according to him, has lacked the ideological means to make such a challenge.

In an insightful attempt to uncover the 'apparent paradoxes' of Jawaharlal Nehru, Sudipta Kaviraj (1980) gives him credit for his innovativeness in setting up a politically independent bourgeois state and pursuing a relatively independent path of reformist welfarist capitalist development. Nehru, however, according to Kaviraj, resorted to an 'irresponsible' technique of legitimation, namely, 'a manipulation of the evident appeal of the socialist idea in a poor and illiterate country'. Nehru's socialism, Kaviraj notes, brought him political success in the electoral arena but historical failure against such impersonal or 'structural problems' of capitalism as poverty, inequality, exploitation, etc. 'Nehru,' writes Kaviraj, 'was a political success and at the same time a historical failure.'

In a paper, entitled 'Understanding Nehru's Political Ideology' (Pantham, 1991), I have argued that while Chatterjee and Kaviraj are indeed right in pointing out that the Nehruvian state and ideology have not transcended capitalist rationality or established socialism, they fail to appreciate the positive aspects of the relative autonomy of the Nehruvian state vis-à-vis the imperialist reason of capital. As both Chatterjee and Kaviraj admit, the independent, national, non-aligned, liberal-democratic state, in the setting up of which both Gandhi and Nehru played a world-historic role, braving strong opposition from within and outside the country, has a *greater* relative autonomy from imperialist capital than would have been the case if a non-democratic, non-socialistic, aligned, satellite-type state had been set up. In bringing about that greater relative

autonomy or, in other words, a form of 'decolonization' or dissoci-
ation of the reason of the states system from the imperialist reason
of capital, the Nehruvian 'mixture' of liberalism, Marxism and
Gandhism seems to me to have played a positive historic role.

This ideological mixture was correctly seen by Nehru to be
constituting a necessary, though far from sufficient, condition for
the politics of transition to a post-capitalist or 'socialistic' social
order. In my view, he and Gandhi correctly perceived that the
minimal requirement for the politics of exit or transition from the
capitalist–imperialist system of states was the setting up of independent, non-aligned, democratic nation-states which were to constitute counter-hegemonic spaces against that system and which
were to become instrumental in bringing about social and economic
change at both national and international levels. Even though
Nehru did not pursue socialism 'through the violent struggle between
classes,' the non-aligned, democratic-socialist state which he strove
to institutionalize seems to me to constitute a crucial step in a
larger political movement of exit or transition from the two versions
of imperialism which the two superpowers were trying to impose
on the rest of the world since the Second World War. Nehru's anti-
imperialist democratic socialism did serve to prevent or check 'the
selling out of national economic and political interests' and to a
certain—though far from sufficient—degree of sharing of the fruits
of economic growth with the disadvantaged sections of the society
(cf. Mukherjee and Mukherjee, 1988: 541).

Modernization: The Structural-Functional View

During the 1950s and 1960s, several Anglo-American political
scientists advanced a neo-evolutionary, unilinear, liberal-democratic, Westcentric path of modernization for India. These scholars
operated from a sense of complacency with, and optimism about,
the Anglo-American model of liberal-democratic industrial
modernity. The contributing factors to this Westcentric liberal-
democratic optimism were the defeat of the Fascist Powers in the
War, the disrepute of the Stalinist model of Marxism, and a feeling of
satisfaction with the prosperous and expanding nature of the
America-led world capitalist economy. To many scholars North
America seemed to be 'the good society.'

To them, further philosophical or ideological exercises in search of any better conception of society seemed irrelevant. Declaring ideology to have come to an end and political philosophy to have died, they busied themselves with making empirical (or behavioural) generalizations of the operative features and supporting values of the American model of the modern. Those features and values of the American polity were held out to be the ideal-typical variables of the modernization of the less developed countries.

In the immediate post-World War II period, it was widely recognized that the economic development of the less developed countries (LDCs) and their participation in international free trade would facilitate the rebuilding of the war-shattered economic system of the world. It was further realized that such economic development of the LDCs, depended on their social, cultural and political modernization. The LDCs, in other words, were required to follow in the footsteps of the advanced industrial nations. In their social evolution, the LDCs were believed to be stuck at the traditional stage. Their development was said to depend on their reaching and crossing the stage of economic take-off, which the advanced industrial countries had crossed long ago. Accordingly, the modernization/development of the LDCs was taken to mean their transition, in a unilinear and teleological sense, from the 'ideal-typical pattern variables' of tradition to those of Western-style modernity. 'What America is . . . the modernizing Middle East seeks to become' (Lerner, 1965: 79)! Or: 'The Anglo-American politics most closely approximate the model of a modern political system' (Coleman in Almond and Coleman, 1960: 533). 'Now that colonialism is ended,' wrote Lucian Pye of MIT in 1966, 'we see the United States and others through various forms of foreign aid and technological assistance continuing the effort to shape numerous loosely structured societies into reasonable facsimiles of the modern nation state' (p. 8).

The theory of liberal-democratic modernization is rooted in Talcott Parsons' neo-evolutionary model of the development of social organization. In his typology of the structural and cultural characteristics of societies at different stages of general societal evolution, Parsons found greater structural differentiation and integration or, simply, greater generalized adaptive capacities in the developed or modern societies than in the primitive or traditional societies. This superior adaptive capacity of the social system was seen to be best exhibited in the modern liberal-democratic industrial society of the United States of America. Its key structural features were identified as a complex money and market system, a universalistic legal system, bureaucratic administration and a liberal-democratic political framework.

Corresponding to this politico-economic structure of modernity, there are, according to Parsons, certain 'pattern variables' or value orientations (at the level of role-actors). These were called the ideal-typical pattern variables of modernity. They were said to constitute the telos or terminal stage of the natural evolution of backward societies. Accordingly, their modernization was interpreted as a process of transition, from the 'pattern variables' of tradition to those of modernity, viz., from particularism to universalism, from ascriptive considerations to achievement orientations, from functional diffuseness to specificity, from affective motivations to affectively neutral motivation and from collectivity orientations to individualist orientations.

Parsons' neo-evolutionary paradigm of general societal evolution has been applied by several Anglo-American social scientists to the analysis of the politics of the developing or modernizing areas of the world. For instance, in advancing the ideal of American-type liberal-democratic modernity as the terminal stage of the political pilgrimage of the less developed countries, Gabriel Almond admits that he has been influenced by Parsons' theory. 'Our theory building and modelling,' he writes, 'first took on simple dichotomous form. Working from the classic formulations of Max Weber, Ferdinand Tonnies and Talcott Parsons . . . several innovative social scientists . . . constructed models of traditional and modern forms of society and polity' (Almond et al., eds., 1973: 1). Almond, following Parsons, maintains that the modernization of the developing areas is a process of transition toward the structural differentiation, sub-system autonomy and secular or 'civic' culture of the western liberal-democratic paradigm of capitalist industrialism. In typical neo-evolutionary, ideal-typical pattern variables language, he writes:

The political scientist who wishes to study political modernization in the non-Western areas will have to master the model of the modern, which in turn can only be derived from the most empirical and formal analysis of the functions of modern Western politics. (Almond, 1960: 64)

Almond favours cultural diffusion from the Western metropolis, aimed at aiding the modernizing elite of the developing areas in transforming their 'rigid, diffuse, and ascriptive patterns of tradition.' He is optimistic that 'in the new and modernizing nations of Asia, Africa and Latin America the process of enlightenment and democratization will have their inevitable way' (Almond, 1970: 232). He and his co-author, Sydney Verba (Almond and Verba, 1963: 9), state that '(t)he civic culture and the open polity . . . represent the great and problematic gifts of the West.'

Lipset, like Almond and Verba, equates political development with stable political democracy. He identifies a 'syndrome of conditions' of the stable democratic order, which he believes can help 'men to develop it where it does not now exist.' That syndrome, he notes, is made up of a rich capitalist economy, industrialization, education, urbanization, an open class system, an egalitarian value system and extensive cross-cutting participation in voluntary organizations. He is particularly wary of the fact that 'political extremism based on the lower classes, communism in particular, is to be found not only in low-income countries but also in newly industrializing nations' (Lipset, 1960: 54). Such extremism, he maintains, must be and can be prevented through policies aimed at preserving the syndrome-character of the socio-economic prerequisites of stable democracy. 'To clarify the operation of Western democracy in the mid-twentieth century,' he writes, 'may contribute to the political battle in Asia and Africa' (p. 417).

According to Edward Shils, the model of the future of the developing societies is contained in the present-day advanced Western liberal representative democracy. The modernizing elites of the new states are those, in whom is 'reflected' the light of the Western model of the modern and who are 'drawing what inspiration and self-esteem they can from their efforts to conform with the model and to come thereby closer to the centre' (Shils, 1972: 361). Recognizing the crucial importance of the acculturation of the elite of the new states to the diffused culture of the 'centre' of the international system, Shils writes: '(I)f he denies that culture, he negates himself and negates his own aspiration to transform his society into a modern society' (p. 368). The ethnocentrism, unilinearity and conservatism of Shils' modernization theory come out clearly in the following passage:

> The orderly understanding of the new states requires that they be seen *sub specie aeternitatis*, or at least within the categories of known human experience. To escape from *ad hoc* explanations, in which the causes of explanations are historically accidental, we must promulgate categories that are equally applicable to all states and societies, to all territories and epochs—variations must be subsumable within these categories (Shils, 1963: 16–17).

These writings, especially of Shils, Pye and Almond, have had a tremendous influence on Indian political scientists. Some of the former scholars have been visiting faculty members at all-India summer institutes in political science, and some of their books have been widely used in Indian universities.

During the 1960s, as O'Brien writes, 'the political value preferences which accompanied the theoretical statement [of liberal modernization] appear to have been too well incorporated into a prevalent scholarly mood even to have given rise to a comment . . .' (O'Brien, 1972: 354). In the heyday of the behavioural revolution in political science, models which actually were value-laden were offered—and generally accepted—as value-free. This has prompted Arora to remark that 'of all the difficulties and lacunae in the current literature on political development, the most crucial is this tendency to project a value-preference without ever dealing directly with questions of value' (Arora, 1968: 112). As noted by Thapar, the policy scientists of the poor countries have been 'reluctant to espouse concepts which would be considered primitive' and, therefore, they 'seldom moved beyond the mechanical application of Western experience' (Thapar, 1968: 5).

In concluding this section on the structural-functional account of political modernization in India, I would like to note that a *modified* version of the same framework can be seen in the early works of Rajni Kothari (i.e., till about the mid-1970s), which also has some affinities with the model of 'modernization revisionism,' discussed later. I shall review Kothari's writings under the rubric of 'The "Congress System" of Political Modernization' in chapter 6, where I shall also take up Kothari's recent works, which advance a conception of 'alternative democracy and humane development.'

Modernization Revisionism

Modernization revisionism rejects the liberal-diffusionist neo-evolutionary assumption that the relationship between tradition and modernity is of a zero-sum character. Instead of regarding the process of change in the developing countries as a unilinear, West-centric transition *from* tradition *to* modernity, the theorists of modernization revisionism term it 'the modernity of tradition'. This revisionist theory of political development sees the traditional social structures as adapting to, and supporting, the modern institutions just as the latter are seen to modernize and democratize the former.

Fred Riggs maintains that the process of change in the ex-colonial societies cannot be interpreted as the simple replication of the process through which the pioneer societies evolved from tradition into modernity. He refers to the 'new states' as 'prismatic' societies in the sense that they are in a permanent transition or incomplete refraction of their 'fused' or undifferentiated traditional set-up into a diffracted or differentiated, modern set-up.

In their book, *The Modernity of Tradition: Political Development in India* (1967), Lloyd Rudolph and Susanne Rudolph provide an empirically grounded corrective to the 'overly simple and Occident-centred view of the relation between tradition and modernity.' They challenge the equation of modernization with Westernization and reject the 'prerequisites' theory of modernization, according to which democratic modernity had to be preceded by industrialization, urbanization, literacy and mass communications. They claim that in India the traditional culture and structure of caste have adapted to democratic modernity. This is seen in the operation of caste associations and caste federations. Following M.N. Srinivas, they maintain that changes in the traditional culture and structure of caste were due to the spread of communications, Western education, market economy and state intervention in the social and economic spheres. They see the modernity of tradition or the democratic re-incarnation of caste as occurring in four sub-processes of national integration, viz. (*a*) the expansion of ascriptive boundaries; (*b*) the downward spread of the culture and status of the twice-born *varnas* to the Sudra castes; (*c*) Westernization; and (*d*) secularization. Finding that 'political man in democratic India has been wrought out of traditional materials,' the Rudolphs choose to 'accord tradition a higher priority in the study of modernization than has often been the case in previous analyses of it' (pp. 10 and 62).

Purporting to show that the pattern or sequence of socio-historical changes which led to the stable liberal-democratic modernity of the West need not be replicated in the non-Western countries, they pose the rhetorical question: 'Will the muse of history, having prescribed a particular historical sequence for the Atlantic nations, suffer a failure of imagination and repeat herself endlessly into future historical time?' (p. 13).

This question seems to me to be obfuscating the fact that the 'particular historical sequence' followed by the imperialist Atlantic nations has already altered the history of their colonies in such a way that the question of their repeating the history of the former does not arise any more. I am suggesting, in other words, that a self-contained view of the Atlantic nations or of the decolonizing or post-colonial nations is not appropriate for understanding the tradition–modernity problem. It must, however, be acknowledged that the contributions of the Rudolphs did serve to correct the Occident-centredness of the theories of modernization/Westernization.

The modernity of tradition thesis, moreover, under-emphasizes the types of changes which the ex-colonial countries may need to bring about in order to overcome their underdeveloped or distorted pattern of growth.

The Authoritarian Model of Liberal Democracy

During the mid-1960s, Western development planners and social scientists came to realize that there were serious 'limits to growth' and that the widening economic inequalities both within and between the nations of the world posed serious threats to the capitalist world system. In such a situation, the 'diffused' values of liberal-democratic modernity, which roused the people into increased political activity and greater demands for economic equality, were seen as a new source of political instability and developmental crisis. The containment of this crisis and instability became the concern of the advocates of the order-and-stability model of liberal democracy. They effected a normative reversal in development thinking in the sense that 'the interest in order of those at the top is given logical precedence over the interest in social justice of those below' (Sandbrook, 1976: 80–81).

In place of the values of liberty, equality, participation, structural differentiation, sub-system autonomy and cultural secularization (which were advocated by the liberal-democratic diffusionists), the proponents of the order-and-stability model of liberal democracy favoured the political passivity of the ordinary people, the security and capability of the governing elites, political institutionalization and political order. Pool (1967: 26) articulated this line of thinking in the following words:

> In the Congo, in Vietnam, in the Dominican Republic, it is clear that order depends on somehow compelling newly mobilized strata to return to a measure of passivity and defeatism from which they have recently been aroused by the process of modernization. At least temporarily, the maintenance of order requires a lowering of newly acquired aspirations and levels of political activity. The so-called 'revolution of rising expectations' creates turmoil as new citizens demand things which the society is unable to supply. Movements which express demands that cannot be satisfied do threaten the cohesion of those commonwealths.

While the liberal diffusionists believed in the desirability and possibility of making the underdeveloped countries follow the model of Western liberal-democratic industrial modernity, the theorists of order and stability deny both the desirability and feasibility of Western-style liberal-democratic modernization of these countries. According to these theorists, the underdeveloped countries have either to be content with just 'reasonable facsimiles' of liberal-democratic modernity or opt for an authoritarian form of government. They propound a doctrine of double standards, according to which the peoples of the developed and developing countries should be governed by different norms and values of the good life. Apter (1965) articulates this new doctrine in the following words:

> Difficulties arise for comparative study because we have enshrined moral principles in models that have served well in a Western political context. The models we derive from concepts of justice, equity and good society may be quite inappropriate for modernizing societies.

Similarly, Robert Ward (1963: 596) remarks that 'perhaps only modern societies with modern political cultures . . . are practical candidates for democratization.' Going a step further, Samuel Huntington argues that for the developing countries a strong, authoritarian regime is a prerequisite for economic development. According to him, the recent 'sharp increase in political consciousness, political participation and commitment to egalitarian and democratic values' has led to an expansion of governmental activity and a decline of governmental authority (Huntington, 1975: 106). The 'democratic surge' of the masses and, especially of the unions of industrial workers and governmental employees, has led the government to expand its regulative and welfare functions. This, without a corresponding increase in taxation (which would hamper capital accumulation), has necessitated budgetary deficits and inflation, which in a situation of low or negative rates of economic growth, have had an alarming impact on the society.

In this situation, according to Huntington, the advocacy of democratic and egalitarian values could be dangerous. He says that there has already been an 'excess of democracy' and that therefore, what is 'needed . . . is a greater degree of moderation in democracy'. In his view, the claims of expertise must take precedence over the claims of democracy! In his 'post-industrial' society, he sees greater tensions and conflicts, which require a technocratic pattern of governance. In that way, he says, any demand-overload on the government can be avoided and 'more self-restraint on the part of all groups' enforced. He writes that for the less developed countries, 'the primary need is the accumulation and concentration of power, not its dispersion, and it is in Moscow and Peking, and not in Washington that this lesson is learned' (Huntington, 1968: 138).

The order-and-stability model of democracy is defended for India by B.K. Nehru (1980). 'Liberal democracy and the removal of poverty,' he writes, 'do not go together in a poor society.' For its economic development, such a society needs to generate and increase capital accumulation internally. While this requires the reduction of consumption, democracy forces governments to pursue policies which deplete, rather than increase, capitalist accumulation. Hence, argues B.K. Nehru, liberal democracy is not suitable for the removal of poverty through economic development, even though he believes that 'liberal democracy is, for advanced societies, perhaps the best system of political organization man has been able to devise' (p. 13). After noting that the 'closed totalitarian communist society' of China has made more impressive achievements than India in economic growth and nuclear weaponry, he warns the developing countries to 'think twice before adopting an open democratic society' (p. 14). He reminds them that their own tradition of government has been authoritarian and that they would be inviting 'institutional instability' and 'disaster' if they were 'to discard their own ancient gods . . . and begin suddenly to worship this Venus [i.e., liberal democracy] who has arisen fully formed from the western seas . . .' (p. 13).

According to him, a full-fledged totalitarianism may be inevitable in those few countries which have an 'unmanageable' ratio of population to resources. The other countries, including India, which are not so badly off, he feels, can still manage to scrape through with a modified version of democratic government. The modification he justifies is 'the concentration of great power in the hands of the executive, together with stability and continuity of policy' (p. 15). The presidential executive is preferred to the parliamentary executive as the former entails greater executive autonomy. Under it, 'the supremacy of reason and inductive logic' will check the growth-inhibiting, consumption-oriented egalitarian 'passions' of the demos (pp. 9–10). It is only when such a 'modified system of democracy' has brought about a considerable improvement in the material well-being of the society can it sustain a social order through a non-authoritarian state (p. 20).

Some Criticisms of the Authoritarian Model of Liberal Democracy

Several Indian and India-oriented social scientists have criticized the authoritarian model of liberal democracy and offered alternatives to it. Some of their writings are surveyed here (cf. also chapter 6).

According to Partha Chatterjee (1974), the authoritarian models which are prescribed for the underdeveloped nations 'flow from the material and ideological interests of world monopoly capitalism.' Sudipta Kaviraj (1984) writes that the legitimacy-deficit of bourgeois-democratic institutions in India is prompting the state elite to pursue strategies of 'frenetic centralization' and the disaggregation of the institutional structures with a view to defending the 'core sector' at the cost of the periphery. Arun Shourie (1978) suggests that India's internal emergency had symptoms of fascism and that it marked the beginning of the take-over of power from the representatives of the intermediate class by 'the representatives of the means of production.'

W.H. Morris-Jones rejects the authoritarian thesis that democracy prevents the eradication of poverty and the reduction of inequalities. He notes that even in Western Europe, 'the most substantial erosion of mass poverty took place only after liberal democracy had been extended far enough to create strong pressures from the ranks of the disadvantaged.' Regarding the authoritarian argument that a strong government, undeterred by any democratic overload, is needed to reduce consumption and thereby increase the capital investments needed for economic growth, Morris-Jones points out that the major impediment to economic growth is not consumption (except the conspicuous consumption of the rich) but rather the stagnation of the demand side, which, he says, can be improved by raising the poor above their miserable levels of living. For such a task, democracy, according to him, is an aid, and not a hindrance (Morris-Jones, 1980 and 1984).

In his view, democracy can be used by the disadvantaged as a weapon against the established privileges and power of the few. It can also be used to bring about structural reforms, e.g., land reforms, which can accelerate economic development. Finally, the 'cultural argument' that the tradition of the Third World countries is authoritarian and not democratic is, in Morris-Jones' view, a pernicious argument against any social-democratic change.

In two articles (Pantham, 1976–77 and 1985a), I have argued that the political-theoretical justification of the authoritarian model of liberal democracy is derived from the neo-elitist/neo-pluralist theory of liberal democracy provided by the Schumpeter–Dahl line of democratic thought, which, in its turn, is a revisionist re-formulation of the 'protective democracy' of the Locke-to-Bentham line of thought. Both the neo-elitist and protective models of democracy, I have argued, are morally flawed and must therefore be abandoned in favour of a participatory–egalitarian model of democracy.

The arguments *against* the protective and neo-elitist/neo-pluralist models of liberal democracy and *for* the participatory–egalitarian model may be briefly summarized as follows:

1. The protective model of democracy is based on a descriptivist/positivist concept of man, whereby the *whole* of a man's powers is taken to be his *present* powers to extract benefits from others. The purpose of people's participation in politics and the task of the good (i.e., representative) government is taken to be the protection of the people's established private interests from arbitrary rule. This model of democracy is not concerned with the frustrated human *potentialities* of, say, the members of the non-possessing class of people. This model, to use Macpherson's words, 'left people free to do each other down in their economic relations, provided they did so by free contact and free market operations. It lacked altogether any idea of social equality or fraternity, leaving unequal classes as they were' (Macpherson, 1978: 20–21; 1977a, chapter 2).

2. Schumpeter reduced democracy to a *political method* or market model, in which the voters are mere consumers, with the competitive political elites performing entrepreneurial roles. Similarly, Dahl regards public contestation involving at least two parties to be the central feature of democracy, which he prefers to call 'polyarchy'. As noted by Macpherson (1977a: 77) the Schumpeter–Dahl model of liberal democracy is:

   > pluralist in that it starts from the assumption that the society which a modern democratic political system must fit is a plural society, that is, a society consisting of individuals each of whom is pulled in many directions by his many interests, now in company with one group of his fellows, now with another. It is elitist in that it assigns the main role in the political process to self-chosen groups of leaders. It is an equilibrium model in that it presents the democratic process as a system which maintains an equilibrium between the demand and supply of political goods.

3. The limitations of this model of liberal democracy are that it produces an equilibrium of inequality, an illusion of consumer sovereignty, and a negation of 'the central democratic tenet of equality of individual entitlement to the use and enjoyment of one's capacities' (Macpherson, 1977a: 77). This model of liberal democracy, in other words, does not pay attention to

the *moral or developmental* power of the members of the non-owning class, who, because they do not have free or equal access to the means of life and to the means of labour, are subjected to a continuous process of class-determined transfer (or alienation) of their labour/human power to the owning class.

4. The participatory–egalitarian model of democracy regards the human being not as a mere consumer of utilities but as an agent or doer who can develop and realize his/her human potentialities through participation in politics. This model of democracy also assigns a market-correcting role to democratic politics. According to this model, democracy is not merely a method of government but also a kind of society which seeks to maximize the human potentialities or developmental powers of all its members.

The 'Economic Efficiency' and 'Basic Needs' Approaches to Development

These two interrelated approaches to development have come into prominence since the mid-1970s. In the literature, they are interpreted, as two versions of international or global Keynesianism, which are seen by several commentators as responses of the development planners and social scientists to the following developments:

1. the argument of dependency theory that the underdevelopment of the Third World countries was related to the development of the First World countries;
2. the successful defiance of the West by the OPEC countries in raising the export price of petrol;
3. the 1974 U.N. General Assembly *Declaration on the Establishment of a New International Economic Order (NIEO)*;
4. the adoption by the U.N. General Assembly of the *Charter of Economic Rights and Duties of States (1974)*;
5. the first Club of Rome report on the 'limits to growth'; and
6. the global economic crisis of the early 1970s (cf. Kegley and Wittkopf, 1981; Hoogvelt 1982; Cox, 1979).

These developments brought home to the development planners and social scientists of the First World that the development of the

Third World countries had to be approached in terms of some form of international or global Keynesianism, which stipulated that a *new international deal or redistribution* was necessary for ensuring the viability and efficiency of the world economy. From now on, the developmental problems of any country, be it of the first, second or third world, had to be approached from a *global* and *futurological* perspective (cf. Hoogvelt, 1982; chapter 4).

The Brandt Report (1980: 21) stated the need for international Keynesianism in the following words:

> Just as employers at the turn of this century had to be made aware that higher wages for workers increased purchasing power sufficiently to move the economy as a whole . . . the industrialized countries now need to be interested in the expansion of markets in the developed world.

The global Keynesian approach to development recognizes the 'interdependence' between the rich and technologically advanced First World countries and the Third World countries, some of which have important natural resources and raw materials. The second Club of Rome report refers to 'the worldwide dependence on 'common' stocks of raw materials; the worldwide problems in providing energy and food supply; the sharing of common physical environment of land, sea and air' (Mesarovic and Pestel, 1976: 18).

There are two versions of, or approaches to, international Keynesianism, namely, (*a*) the 'economic efficiency' approach and (*b*) the 'basic needs' approach. They, as pointed out by Robert Cox (1979), represent the two faces of global capitalist hegemony. He writes:

> They share the same fundamental assumptions about the progressive nature of world capitalism bringing about a new international division of labour, and both recognize the need in addition for an international welfare programme to be carried out as far as possible by the poor themselves (p. 279).

As pointed out by Cox as well as by Amin (1977), global Keynesianism, in either of its two aforementioned versions, fails to deal adequately with the structural, political-economic causation of the inequalities and marginalizations of the underdeveloped countries. While the 'political economy' or 'economic efficiency' version of global Keynesianism emphasizes the *minimal* international and intra-national economic redistributions required for ensuring the functional stability of the capitalist world system, the 'basic needs' approach represents a '*broader and somewhat more generous* view of the adjustments that can be made without fundamentally disturbing the existing hegemony' (Cox, 1979: 261. Emphasis mine).

Thus, the third Club of Rome report advocates economic redistribution among and within the nations with a view to ensuring for every citizen of the world his rights to life, employment, education, leisure and cultural autonomy. The same report makes out a case for imposing welfare-oriented controls and regulations over the operations of the MNCs. It states:

> In the long term, transnational enterprises will still form part of the world structure, in either their present form of private enterprises or in a renovated form comprising genuine international ventures . . . . The statutes of transnational enterprises should be under the supervision, and their profits taxed by, an inter- or supra-national authority. Transnational enterprises should form part of an international framework of concrete economic activities and their labour conditions should be negotiated with representative national and international trade unions.

In their well-researched and comprehensive book, *In Pursuit of Lakshmi: The Political Economy of the Indian State* (1987), Lloyd I. Rudolph and Susanne Hoeber Rudolph claim that their analysis of the 'political economy' of the Indian state gives a better account of 'the dynamics and direction of change' than does either the dependency theory or the theory of methodological individualism/ rational choice. They do not find the dependency theory applicable to India because foreign investment has been marginal and controlled, commercial debt low and trade diverse. Methodological individualism and rational choice are seen by them as exaggerating atomistic rationality and ignoring the social and historical determinants of private and public choices.

In their 'political economy' approach, therefore, the Rudolphs 'adapt' and 'mutually adjust' the concepts of class and state and use them to explain the dynamics and direction of change in India. In one of these adaptations, they depart from Marxist class analysis and, following Weber, 'posit interest rather than class as the basic motivating and organizing principle of political economy' (pp. 248 and 399). Another of the Rudolphs' adaptations of the concept of class pertains to their notion of the class of 'bullock capitalists' (independent, self-employed agricultural producers), who neither exploit nor are exploited by the other classes. According to the Rudolphs, this class is the 'fulcrum' of India's 'centrist politics' in the rural sector in the sense that it 'constrains' class polarization.

Central to the Rudolphs' analysis of the political economy of the Indian state are the notions of 'demand polity' (voter sovereignty and societal control over the state) and 'command polity' (state sovereignty and state hegemony over politics and society). Both can, according to them, operate either through democratic or authoritarian regimes. Accordingly, they periodize Indian politics into the following combinations:

1. democratic regime and command politics (1952–64);
2. democratic regime and demand politics (1964–75; 1977–86);
3. authoritarian regime and command politics (the emergency of 1975–77).

The Rudolphs observe that in post-independence India, demand politics has been compatible with, and contributive to, economic growth and the legitimacy of the state or, in other words, to development and social justice. They write: 'The notion that authoritarian rule in India has been positively associated with economic growth and that democracy has not is more contradicted than supported by the available evidence' (p. 223). They go on to point out that authoritarianism in India has not only a legitimacy-constraint but also productivity- and efficiency-constraints. Development, they add, must address 'basic human needs' (p. 215).

The Rudolphs also argue that Indian politics is characterized by '[t]he marginality of class politics and the predominance of centrist politics,' in which 'the state as third actor' plays the principal role vis-à-vis the two other actors of the organized economy, viz., private capital and organized labour. 'The Indian state,' they write, 'will remain the economy's guide, tutor and patron, particularly with respect to investment. Nor is it likely to surrender the industrial, financial, and infrastructural resources it controls, that is, abandon the economy's commanding height' (p. 399). According to them, the Indian state is not only relatively autonomous but also self-interested and self-determined (i.e., able to resist determination by societal forces). They write:

> Even while retaining conventional state attributes and powers, the state as third actor has become a major component of the economy and of society. It may or may not be subject to direction by command or demand politics or become the agent of dominant class, elite, or interest group coalitions. The self-determining state is in a position to serve itself and, like other self-interested actors, to be a source of exploitation or injustice. (p. 400)

The Rudolphs' 'political economy' of development has been subjected to critical review, among others, by Rajni Kothari (1988) and T.J. Byres (1988). Both of them point out that the politics of economic development, which the authors analyze, is different from political economy in the Marxian sense, in which modes of production and class conflicts are of basic importance. Byres writes that the Rudolphs' 'demand groups' approach distorts the bitter class conflicts that are taking place in India. He also rejects the portrayal of the Indian urban bourgeoisie as a dependent class. Concerning the authors' view about the marginality of class politics, Byres points out that the rich peasants are organized very effectively as a class.

Rajni Kothari acknowledges that the Rudolphs' book has considerable merits such that it can definitely be recommended as an advanced text for university-level courses on the politics of economic development in India. He however criticizes it for analyzing the phenomena of state-building and economic development from the vantagepoint of the 'sources of stability and order' as seen 'from the viewpoint of elites and managers of the system at the apex' rather than 'from the viewpoint of the people, of the vast social peripheries and ethnic upsurges, and of the victims of state policies and elite endeavours.' Since the latter viewpoint was not adopted, the Rudolphs, says Kothari, fail to deal with the mass upsurges based on class, ethnicity, ecology and gender. In his view, this politics of transformation and struggle would modify the thesis of the Rudolphs about the predominance of centrist politics in India.

A basic needs or social-democratic model of development is advocated for India in F. Frankel's *India's Political Economy, 1947–1977: The Gradual Revolution* (1978). Frankel maintains that an evolutionary growth model, in so far as it neglects the issue of 'prior institutional change,' e.g., radical agrarian reform, cannot solve India's poverty. Given India's grossly inegalitarian social and economic structure, she argues, an 'undiluted capitalist approach' to economic development would only widen the inequalities. She also rules out the feasibility and desirability of any violent, revolutionary transformation of society. There are, according to her, 'insurmountable barriers' in organising a revolutionary class-based movement of the poor and landless who are hopelessly fragmented along caste, religious, linguistic and regional lines. More importantly, she fears that the revolutionary model would result in 'incalculable levels of destructive violence' and 'fearful costs in human life.' She maintains that India still has the option of a 'third way' of a 'gradual revolution' for democratic socialism. According to her, what is required for its success is the abandonment of the vertical, class-accommodative strategy of party-building or political mobilization and its replacement by a horizontal, class-based strategy of mobilizing the peasantry. Given such a class-based political mobilization, political democracy, she believes, can 'bring to bear the strength of numbers of the poor in such powerful pressures on the ruling classes that they would be compelled to move in the direction of economic democracy' (p. xiii). Such a leftist-liberal model of democracy is her preferred alternative to revolutionary class struggle for bringing about the social-structural transformation that can put India on the path of growth with justice for 'the minimum needs of India's diverse social groups.' Frankel ends her book with the following advice:

> The middle class intelligentsia professing a commitment to democratic socialism may yet have much to gain in attempting to organize the poor peasantry while it is still possible to bring them into politics in a way that will strengthen political stability, that is by augmenting the capacity of elected governments to complete the second part of the gradual revolution for structural changes. (p. 582)

In a paper, entitled 'Elites, Classes and the Distortions of Economic Transition in India' (Pantham, 1980), I have developed an argument analogous to that of Frankel. I have suggested that it is possible for India's politico-intellectual groups to engage in a type of democratic-political mobilization of the masses which can bring about a shifting of the social basis of state power in their favour and which can thereby bring about a people-oriented pattern of economic change and development.

In a review of Frankel's book, A.K. Bagchi (1980) has noted that its language reflects the attitude of the typical western aid-negotiating official, whose concern is not so much with meeting the human needs of the poor as with ensuring the functional stability of the world capitalist system.

Atul Kohli criticizes Frankel's social-democratic model of change for its failure to recognize that 'inequalities of power are not merely a consequence of the degree of organization.' Such inequalities, Kohli says, are 'prior' to the 'political' in the sense that they are a function of the division of labour according to which some people manage, control and/or own the means of economic production, while others serve, obey and/or sell their labour power according to the 'rules' of selling and buying (Kohli, 1980). Kohli maintains that a stable democratic framework cannot eliminate those inequalities of power, though it may mitigate them to some extent. He points out that a strategy of horizontal, class-based political organization of the poor and landless aimed at establishing a social-democratic regime for the redistribution of property and income would face formidable 'layers of obstacles at the ideological organizational, electoral, governmental, and bureaucratic levels.'

In his book, *The State and Poverty in India* (1987), Kohli uses a state-oriented approach to explain some of the reformist changes taking place in India's democratic-capitalist path of development. According to him, in India, as in many other Third World countries, 'development' is less of a demand from the society and 'more of a political goal which state authorities wish to impose upon their societies'. He endorses the idea of Rajni Kothari that politics has been the 'driving force' of social change in India.

The 'political logic' of this process of change, says Kohli, is not adequately captured by the 'core theoretical logic' of either the modernization/structural-functional or the Marxist approaches; they seem to him to be reducing politics to society. Concerning the former, Kohli maintains that its 'liberal' assumption that growth will 'trickle down' to the poor is empirically and normatively inadequate. Concerning the latter, he points out that even though it does recognize the significant role of the state in development, it sees that role as reflecting the interests and goals, not of the political elite, but of economic actors. Calling for an abandonment of 'the logic of social determinism in political analysis' and the adoption of a 'political logic,' he writes:

> Many issues of state intervention for development are simply better analysed by abandoning the analytical commitment to a social logic of politics and admitting that political structures and process result from a partially autonomous logic—a political logic that is not reducible to or derivable from social variables. (p. 20)

The autonomous role of the state, however, says Kohli, is not an invariable phenomenon; it does vary from situation to situation. The degree of autonomy and its role in development and social change vary from regime to regime, say, from communist regimes to the national-democratic, dependent-authoritarian or social-democratic variant of capitalist regimes.

After distinguishing the 'popular'/'organize the poor' model of social democracy from the 'disciplined, left-of-centre' model, Kohli argues that the latter is the appropriate model for bringing about a poverty-reducing pattern of democratic-capitalist development. The former model, i.e., popular social democracy, which is advanced by Raj Krishna, Francine Frankel and Marcus Franda, seeks to alter the political and policy balance in favour of the poor by expanding the social base of state power through the political mobilization and organization of the poor. Kohli criticizes this model by arguing that inequalities of power are not simply a consequence of organization but are rather rooted in the class structure. In his view, class inequalities get reproduced in the dominant political institutions. Hence in a democratic-capitalist framework, political attempts at reform would remain constrained by the class structure at the ideological, organizational, electoral, governmental and bureaucratic levels. He writes: 'Class inequalities, therefore, can never be reversed within the framework of a stable, developmental-capitalist state. They can at best be mitigated' (p. 42).

Kohli's thesis is that the exercise of effective power by the lower classes over the direction of state policy requires disciplined left-of-centre parties as ruling parties. These he says can 'institutional-ize—ideologically and organizationally—the power of the lower classes' and use state autonomy to implement redistributive reforms, e.g., land reforms. He writes:

> Mobilizing hitherto excluded groups into the political arena is by itself an invitation to political instability and reaction . . . . Disciplined left-of-centre parties are . . . crucial for the controlled mobilization of the lower classes and for institutionalizing reformist goals within the state. Such parties also create a partial insulation of the state from society, making reformist intervention possible.

Kohli concludes that from a perspective that holds the short-term alleviation of mass poverty in the poorest of the Indian states to be an important goal, the installation of disciplined, left-of-centre parties in power would be 'a desirable direction for political change.'

In a recent book, Kohli (1991) has examined the crisis of the liberal-democratic state in India. 'No problem in contemporary India,' he writes, 'is likely to prove more serious than the disinte-gration of its major problem-solving institution: the democratic state' (p. 387). Such a disintegration or, in other words, 'crisis of governability,' he writes, is manifest, first, in the decline in the legitimacy of the state which is increasingly relying on force to maintain order in the society and, second, in a slow, inefficient and deficitary pattern of economic development, especially industrial growth. He argues that this crisis has been brought about primarily by politics, i.e., by a 'wrong' kind of democracy, which, he main-tains, needs to be, and can be, remedied by a 'right' kind of democracy.

In his view, a 'wrong' kind of democracy is discernible in such political processes as the undermining, weakening or de-institu-tionalization of the organizations of democratic politics and govern-ment, the political mobilizations of various social groups and communities merely for electoral victories or for securing access to the state's resources, and the increasing conflicts between the rich and the poor. In the literature, deinstitutionalization is shown to include the following phenomena: the erosion of intra-party democracy, the concentration of power in the Prime Minister's Office, the declining role of legislatures, growing centralisation in Union-State relations, decreasing neutrality of the civil servants, electoral malpractices, the rise of persons to top political positions by non-institutional pathways, the rise of 'coteries' of power and the increase of political violence. (cf. Sridharan, 1993, Kothari, 1983 and 1988, Mitra, 1991, Dasgupta, 1989 and Kohli, 1991). According to Sridharan and Kohli, it is this deinstitutionalization of democratic politics and government which is responsible for the state's fiscal deficits, public sector inefficiency and the underdevelopment and imbalances of the industrial sector.

To remedy this situation, what they recommend is not the replacement of democracy with authoritarian rule but the reconstruction of democratic political institutions in the 'right' way. What this entails is the *reversing* of each of the aforementioned political phenomena or processes of deinstitutionalization. Both Sridharan and Kohli emphasize the significance of democratically organized political parties and properly institutionalized consultations among them, consultations between the centre and the states, the strict implementation of the Anti-Defection Law, etc. The case of West Bengal, writes Kohli, demonstrates the significance of a 'well-organized reformist party for generating political order' in a highly mobilized political environment (1991: 15 & 295).

Kohli and Sridharan also maintain that the recent policy of liberalization of the Indian economy should not be interpreted as justifying a libertarian market-system and that the reinstitutionalization or reconstruction of democratic political institutions, which they advocate, is of primary importance for revitalizing India's political economy.

According to Sridharan, a policy or programme of fiscal discipline, public sector efficiency and international economic competitiveness does not necessarily constitute 'a liberalizing, privatizing, rightist agenda,' because the exigencies of external and internal debt will force such policies on to the agenda of even a leftist or centrist government. In the politics of India's economic liberalization, he sees 'a redefined rather than reduced role for the state.' He describes this redefined role of the state as that of 'skimming some of the gain from industry's growth and putting it into long-neglected, productivity-raising (and equalizing and empowering) investment in education, health, rural infrastructure, and minimum needs' (1991: 1204). It is for the performance of these and other tasks that Sridharan and Kohli call for the reinstitutionalization of democratic political organizations, procedures and norms (cf. also Kothari, 1988 in chapter 6 *infra* and Nayar, 1992).

Before leaving the present chapter, it may be noted in anticipation that brief references will be made in chapters 6 and 7 to how the liberal theory of democracy and modernization is criticized by the theorists of postmodernization. Before coming to it, I shall, in the next chapters, take up for review the works on the Marxist, Gandhian and Hindu nationalist alternatives to liberalism.

3

Marxist and Neo-Marxist Theories of Social Transformation

Introductory Remarks

Marxist theories of social change and development/underdevelopment in India and other Third World countries fall into two broad groups. First, there are the 'classical-Marxist' theories (of Marx himself, Lenin, Hilferding and Bukharin), which regard capitalism as playing a regenerative, though brutal, role in the colonies. In these theories, capitalism is seen essentially as a mode of *production*, which, through the employment of free but propertyless wage labour by competing capitals or firms, develops the material forces of production and creates the class forces which will bring about decolonization and/or socialist revolutions.

The second group of theories are those of the neo-Marxists such as Frank, Wallerstein and Amin, who conceptualize capitalism as a *world system*, in which the development of the countries at the core or centre is seen to have brought about the underdevelopment of the countries at the periphery.[1] These theories justify such

---

[1] According to Gorman (1985: 6–22), 'neo-Marxism' includes all the 'non-materialist' versions of Marxism such as idealist/Hegelian Marxism (Lukacs, Gramsci, Marcuse, Kolakowski, etc.), empirical Marxism (Eduard Bernstein, Lucio Colletti, E.P. Thompson, Frank, Wallerstein, Amin, etc.), the Critical Social Theory of the Frankfurt School (Horkheimer, Adorno, Marcuse, Habermas, Offe, etc.) and experiential Marxism (Sartre, Merleau-Ponty, etc.). Gorman notes that although these 'children' of Marxism have gone their separate ways, they are all based on one or another of the Marxist texts and that they share the following Marxist blood-traits: the conception of reality as a dialectical totality, the view of capitalism as an

courses of action as the delinking of the Third World countries from the capitalist world system and revolutions against capitalism's 'development of underdevelopment' in the peripheral capitalist countries.

In this chapter, I shall indicate the nature of these Marxist and neo-Marxist theories and survey some of the Indian contributions to them. I shall also review the *Subaltern Studies*, which, as we shall see below, claim to mark a departure from the 'nationalist' and 'orthodox' versions of Marxism.

Historical Materialism

Marx, it may be recalled, encapsulated his historical-materialist theory of social change in his preface to *A Contribution to the Critique of Political Economy* in the following words:

> In the social production which men carry on they enter into definite relations that are indispensable and independent of their will; these relations of production correspond to a definite stage of development of their material power of production. The sum total of these relations of production constitutes the economic structure of society—the real foundation on which rise the legal and political superstructures and to which correspond definite forms of social consciousness. The mode of production in material life conditions the general character of the social, political and spiritual process of life. It is not the consciousness of the men that determines their being, but on the contrary, their social being determines their consciousness. At a certain stage of their development, the material forces of production in society come into conflict with the existing relations of production, or—what is but a legal expression for the same thing—with the property relations within the framework of which they have operated hitherto. From forms of development of the forces of production these relations turn into their fetters.

alienating, exploitative system, and the view of socialism as the desired, disalienating form of human organization. It may be noted, incidentally, that while Gorman's book on 'neo-Marxism' does not deal with any Indian Marxist, his companion volume on 'Marxism' (Gorman, 1986) includes biographical sketches on several Indian Marxists (see the contributions by Arun Bose, A.N. Das, Thomas Pantham, K. Seshadri and G. Shah in Gorman, 1986).

Then comes the period of social revolution. With the change in the economic foundation the entire immense superstructure is more or less rapidly transformed. (Marx, 1970: 20–21)

In this theory, the central category is that of the mode of production so much so that changes in it are said to be what social change or social transformation is all about. As noted by Asok Sen (1985: 16), the 'three couples' of Marx's theory of social transformation are production forces/production relations, base/superstructure and civil society/state. These together form a dialectical totality, whose contradictions over-determine its historical development.

The relationship between the economic 'base'/'structure' and the 'superstructure' of politics, law, government, ideology, etc., has been explained by Marxists according to three models, viz., the deterministic, organic and dialectical-totality models. The deterministic model, which regards the superstructure as mere epiphenomena of the base, does not do justice to the Marxist notion of political praxis or conscious revolutionary activity. The model of organic unity does violence to the Marxist idea of contradictions, through which revolutionary social transformations come about. The model of historical dialectical-totality recognizes the economic-structural determination of socio-historical change in the first instance without denying the relative autonomy of the instances of the superstructure. The superiority of this model over the two previous models is being increasingly recognized in the literature (cf., among others, Kaviraj, 1989 and Tripathy, 1990).

In her widely read book, *The Third World in Global Development* (1982), Ankie Hoogvelt points out that while bourgeois liberal writers only outline a *taxonomy* of human social organization along some logically perceived stepladder of evolution, Marx's historical materialism gives us a *theory* of socio-historical changes in terms of 'the struggle between emerging and obsolete relations of production, consequent upon the quantitative growth and qualitative change of the forces of production.' Hoogvelt goes on to add that while the bourgeois tradition of social analysis tries to establish 'logical fits' or 'structural compatibilities', the Marxist analysis 'does exactly the opposite: it seeks to trace the contradictions engendered by any mode of production, to clarify and deepen them' (pp. 157 & 158).

According to Partha Chatterjee (1978; 63), compared to bourgeois liberal political theory, the historical materialism of Marx is 'far better adapted to analyze society in terms of the historical development of social structures and their interrelationships, and particularly to tackle the problems of instability and change.' To Chaube, Marxism is 'fundamentally oriented to changing the given social system' (1978b: 98). Similarly, B. Sen Gupta (1973: 1) writes that Marxism is 'the first system of social science conceived primarily, indeed almost exclusively, in terms of models of development,' which, he goes on to suggest, are 'viable alternatives to the gradualist, incremental models of growth based on private enterprise.' In D. Banerjee's view (1987: 171), the *historical* problematic of development/underdevelopment in our Third World societies can be best addressed within the broad theoretical universe of Marxian discourse. According to Bhambhri, the strengths of Marxist political economy are that it separates the 'real social facts' from their appearances and shows the superstructure of politics to be 'solidly rooted in the material forces of society' (1989: 335 & 336, cf. also 1981).

In his book, *The Political Economy of Underdevelopment* (1982), A.K. Bagchi maintains that although Marx's formulation of the method of political economy is still highly relevant, it needs to be combined, first, with the ideas of Luxemburg, Kalecki and Keynes, who, in his view, have made 'a more extended analysis of problems of effective demand and capitalist crises' and, second, with the ideas of Lenin and Mao, who, he notes, have provided a 'finer typology of social classes' (pp. 2–3).

Marx on India and the Asiatic Mode of Production

According to Marx, Europe has progressed through 'social revolutions,' whereby the *ancient* mode of production (characterized by the conflict between slaves and masters) was replaced by the *feudal* mode of production (characterized by the extra-economic coercion of the serfs by the lords), which, in its turn, has been replaced by the *capitalist* mode of production, in which the class of free but propertyless workers are employed by competitive capitalists. Turning to the pre-colonial history of the Asiatic societies, Marx, according to several interpreters, noted that their mode of production, unlike that of Europe, had certain change-resisting features and that their major disruption came about under the impact of outside forces (e.g., by colonial rule).

Marx noted that the Asiatic mode of production, unlike the other pre-capitalist modes of production (e.g., slavery and feudalism) was characterized by a 'subsistence economy' of self-sufficient village communities in which there was a unity of agriculture and crafts and in which there was no private property in land, with the king, as the representative of the community, owning all the land. The *despotic and extra-economic* coercion by the state and its agents, who extracted absolute rent without themselves contributing in any way to the management or improvement of the productive process, is said to have prevented the emergence of any forces of change from within the society. Hence, while in Europe capitalism could emerge through the break-up of feudalism which came about through the expulsion of the peasants from the land in the process of the conversion of feudal property into bourgeois property in land, in India and the other *Asiatic* societies, such a transformation (from within) was precluded by the absence of private property in land and/or by the self-sustaining unity of agriculture and manufacture.

In his famous pair of articles on the impact of British rule on Indian society, Marx referred to that rule as having brought about 'the only social revolution ever heard of in Asia.' 'England,' he wrote, 'has to fulfil a double mission in India: one destructive, the other regenerating—the annihilation of old Asiatic Society; and the laying of the material foundations of the western society in Asia' (Marx in Marx and Engels, 1977, vol. I: 495).

On the *destructive* side of British colonial rule in India, Marx placed the neglect of public works and the destruction of handicrafts and textile production, both of which caused unprecedented misery for the masses. He also referred to the naked barbarism and profound hypocrisy of the bourgeois civilization that was introduced into India.

Turning to the *regenerative* role of British rule in India, Marx singled out the developmental impact of the political unity brought about by the British sword, the railways and the electric telegraph, the organization and training of the army by the British drill-sergeant, the free press ('a new and powerful agent of reconstruction') and, in particular, the introduction of the system of private property in land, which, he noted, had been 'the great desideratum of Asiatic society.' Marx also noted the emergence of a new middle class in colonial India, one which was 'endowed with the

requirements for government, and imbued with European science.'
This class, he believed, would be able to operate a modern nation-
state and promote industrial capitalism.

With admirable prevision, he wrote that although British rule
was creating the *material premises* for the development of the
productive forces, which could be appropriated by the mass of the
people, the latter potentiality would be actualized only when the
rule of the English bourgeoisie would be replaced by proletarian
rule (in England) or by the decolonization of India. Marx wrote:

> All the English bourgeoisie may be forced to do will neither
> emancipate nor materially mend the social condition of the
> mass of the people, depending not only on the development of
> the productive powers, but on their appropriation by the people.
> But what they will not fail to do is to lay down the material
> premises for both. Has the bourgeoisie ever done more? Has it
> ever effected a progress without dragging individuals and peoples
> through blood and dirt, through misery and degradation?
>
> The Indians will not reap the fruits of the new elements of
> society scattered among them by the British bourgeoisie till in
> Great Britain itself the now ruling classes shall have been sup-
> planted by the industrial proletariat, or till the Hindoos them-
> selves shall have grown strong enough to throw off the English
> yoke altogether. (1969: 137)

While most Indian political scientists have ignored Marx's views
on the Asiatic mode of production and on the impact of British
rule in India, Sudipta Kaviraj (1983) has argued that Marx's references to the Asiatic mode of production were not meant to be a
theory of pre-capitalist Asian forms but were only intended to
support the theory of the capitalist mode by contrasting it with its
negations.[2]

The noted Marxist historian, Irfan Habib, writes that in essentials
Marx's analysis of the impact of British rule 'remains of lasting
value and has ever since formed the bedrock not only of Marxist,

---

[2] Similarly, Carver (1985) maintains that Marx's views on non-European development only constituted 'notes towards a theory' and that they were meant to play
only a supportive role politically and intellectually in his overall theory of the
distinctive and transitory nature of the capitalist system.

but of all progressive evaluations of the history of British imperialism in India' (1975: 20). In particular, Habib (1983a) acknowledges Marx's insight and prevision in thinking of India's national liberation and in linking the emancipation of the Indian people with a socialist transformation of England.

Habib, however, finds that Marx's views on the Asiatic mode of production in pre-British India were incorrect as they failed to take note of its features of slavery, feudalism, private property, etc. Habib goes on to argue that in their later works, Marx and Engels themselves came to realize the limitations of the information on which their earlier views were based and that they therefore abandoned them. Habib also attacks Hobsbawm's view that Marx did not abandon the Asiatic mode thesis. In Habib's view, the thesis of the Asiatic mode would amount to denying class contradictions and class struggles in Asian societies and to emphasizing 'the existence of the authoritarian and anti-individualistic traditions in Asia, so as to establish that the entire past history of social progress belongs to Europe alone, and thereby to belittle the revolutionary lessons to be drawn from the recent history of Asia' (1975: 24).

Unlike Irfan Habib, Amalendu Guha, Harbans Mukhia and S. Naqvi maintain that Marx did not abandon the idea of the Asiatic mode.[3] Guha, however, shows that the later Marx 'revised his earlier stand that the stagnation of Indian village communities could be forcibly broken up only by bourgeois intervention from outside' (1985: 51).

According to D. Banerjee, Marx did not discard any of his pre-capitalist modes of production (including the Asiatic mode) either as analytical or as historical constructs, even though he did not define any of them in *sufficient* terms. More importantly, Banerjee argues that 'the much-maligned Marxian concept of the Asiatic mode of production . . . can be of some help' to us in understanding such problems of India's underdevelopment as the emergence of 'eunuch capitalists,' the overdevelopment of the state and the underdevelopment of a production-oriented civil society.

Under the Asiatic mode, he notes, the mainstream productive process was 'out of bounds' for the ruling groups, represented by

---

[3] Similarly, Jaksic (1985) argues that Marx's theory of the Asiatic Mode cannot be separated from his general theory.

the state and its officials and agents. They were not involved in the management or improvement of the productive process. Their interest was in extracting *absolute* surplus labour/product through extra-economic and despotic means. According to Banerjee, under the impact of capitalist imperialism, such a society entered a path of distorted development marked by such features as the persistence of labour-intensive, low-wage ventures, the rise of a class of eunuch capitalists from among the usurers and merchants, the continued overdevelopment of the state and the underdevelopment of the civil society. He notes that in the West, civil society was 'beholden to the production principle of a rising bourgeoisie,' whereas in societies dominated by the Asiatic mode of production, 'the historical-structural bases of a civil society had always been exceedingly frail during pre-colonial times, in the midst of non-individualistic, community-oriented way of life . . .' (1987: 22). He goes on to suggest that we need to take seriously Gramsci's view that without a transformation of the 'primordial and gelatinous' civil society there can be no transition to socialism.

Underdevelopment and Social Crisis: Some Neo-Marxist Theories

Marx, as we have seen, has been interpreted by his 'orthodox' followers as having maintained that British capitalist imperialism played a 'developmental,' though brutal, role in India by disrupting/transforming its 'Asiatic' mode of production and thereby setting in motion a process of change that had the long-term potential of leading to the decolonization of India and/or a world-wide socialist revolution. The neo-Marxist theorists make some important departures from this orthodox explanation of the sources of change and development/underdevelopment in India and other Third World, ex-colonial countries. These departures will be indicated with reference to the contributions of Frank, Wallerstein, Emmanuel, Laclau, Amin and Alavi.

According to Frank, capitalism is a world system of monopolistic trade and exchange, in which the development of the metropolises and the underdevelopment of the export-oriented, satellite countries are the two sides of the same coin. Accepting Paul Baran's identification of monopoly capitalism as a cause of the stagnation of the less developed countries, Frank maintains that by their incorporation into the capitalist world system, the presently underdeveloped countries have been expropriated of their economic surplus, which have been appropriated by the presently developed metropolitan countries through the mechanism of the world market. Thus, the poverty and underdevelopment of Asia, Africa and Latin America, we are told, has not been caused simply by their original, internal 'causes of backwardness' but by their incorporation, on exploitative terms, into the chain of metropolis–satellite relationships. Frank writes:

> The satellites remain underdeveloped for lack of access to their own surplus and as a consequence of the same polarization and exploitative contradictions, which the metropolis introduces and maintains in the satellite's domestic economic structure. (1967: 7–9)

Thus, departing from Marx's thesis of England's 'double mission' in India, Frank maintains that the 'historic mission' of the capitalist-imperialist system has been to *underdevelop* the satellized regions of that system. Moreover, according to Frank, the underdevelopment of these satellized regions occurs not so much in the relations of production as in the sphere of trade and exchange.

According to Frank, the underdeveloped countries must attempt to overcome their structural dependency and underdevelopment by breaking with the world-wide monopoly network of capitalism; without such a break, the 'lumpenbourgeoisie' of the satellized countries would continue to follow a policy of underdevelopment or 'lumpendevelopment' (Frank, 1972). In the case of India, without such a break, Frank notes, there would be a 'permanent emergency' for the institutionalization of economic, political and military repression . . . designed to favour Indian and foreign monopoly capital still further without solving any of the structural problems of the Indian economy (Frank, 1977: 463).

Like Frank, Wallerstein too maintains that in studying the sources and direction of change in any particular country in the modern era, the capitalist world-system must be taken as the unit of analysis. He points out that since the emergence of 'the modern world system' in the sixteenth century, the transformational problematic of each country or region of the world must be seen as fitting into the cyclical rhythms and secular trends of the world economy, which is 'a single division of labour comprising multiple cultural systems, multiple political entities and even different modes of surplus appropriation' (1980: 5). To him, the key to capitalism is 'hierarchically-integrated production processes within the framework of an interstate system, in which the penalties for acting other than to maximize accumulation are severe in the middle-run' (1986: PE34).

The Indian subcontinent, he argues, was incorporated into this world system during the period from 1750 to 1850. That incorporation is shown to have involved a restructuring of production processes and the creation of India into a subordinated political entity that had to operate within the rules of the interstate system (Wallerstein, 1986: PE34).

Wallerstein concludes his analysis of the incorporation of India into the capitalist world economy by indicating that his world system perspective marks a departure from orthodox Marxism. He writes:

I should perhaps end by suggesting against what alternative explanation I am placing mine. There is one standard explanation which sees British colonization as part of a world-wide process of modernization, wherein the shock of outside influences and pressures unlocked India . . . from the relatively non-dynamic and non-progressive system or culture within which it was living. This argument . . . usually implies a system of historic stages through which peoples or nations . . . pass. This has long been the dominant view in the world; it is not mine (1986: PE 34).

According to Wallerstein, the capitalist world system is composed of not only the core and the periphery but also a semi-periphery, which serves as a balancing or buffer zone between the core and the periphery. In his view, the former Soviet bloc countries have also been part of the capitalist world market.

In the transfer of surplus from the peripheral countries of the world system to its core countries, Wallerstein recognizes the interplay of economic and political mechanisms. The market mechanism of unequal exchange, he notes, is underpinned by the differential strength of the different states which make up the world system. Core economies have states which are strong in relation to others, while peripheral economies have states which are weak in the international sphere. The latter are unable to alter the terms of international trade which is structurally unfavourable to their economies.

He maintains that in the long run the contradictions of the capitalist world system may lead to a transition to socialism (1980: 83). But in the short run, the peripheral and semi-peripheral nation-states should, according to him, try to improve their positions within the world system by strategies of seizing whatever chances are available to them in the course of the cyclical rhythms of that system.

The mechanisms of transfer of the surplus from the periphery to the centre of the world system is the focus of attention in the 'unequal exchange' theories of Emmanuel and Amin.

In their view, in the formation of the capitalist world system, there has come about an international division of labour in the sense that the production tasks requiring skilled labour, superior technology and greater capitalization are located in the core areas, with the peripheral countries specializing in the production of primary products requiring 'raw' labour power and 'raw' materials. Moreover, capital and goods, as pointed out by Emmanuel (1972), are mobile across international boundaries, while labour remains immobile in their respective countries or regions. The rate of profit from *internationally mobile capital and goods* is much higher than the value of the *geographically and occupationally fragmented labour*. Given the differential wage levels in the core and the periphery of the world market system, the products of the core get overpriced, while the products of the peripheral regions get underpriced. This mechanism makes for *unequal exchange* within the capitalist world system.

According to Emmanuel, the exploited countries should take effective steps to 'shake off the international exploitation to which they are subject' (1972: 330). In his view, instead of waiting for the capitalist relations of production ('exploitation of man by man') to be transformed into socialist relations in the core countries, the peripheral countries should pursue such strategies of national development as the raising of wages, the diversification of production and the taxation of exports.

I shall turn next to Samir Amin's contribution. But before doing so, I shall pause to take note of Laclau's 'productionist'/'articul-ationist' critique of Frank's 'circulationist' thesis.[4] As I shall indicate, Amin combines that critique with aspects of the circulationist thesis.

In his critique of Frank's position, Laclau (1971/1977) maintained that capitalism is not so much a mode of exchange as a mode of production involving the separation of the producer/worker from the means of production and the surplus-expropriation from the worker through economic or market means. He noted, moreover, that while capitalist relations of production have supplanted the pre-capitalist relations of production in the core countries of the capitalist world system, capitalism in the colonies has come to be *articulated with* pre-capitalist relations of production. Such an articulation of different relations of production is, according to him, the essence of capitalist imperialism. He pointed out that in Latin America, for instance, feudal relationships entailing exploit-ation of the producer through extra-economic (i.e., political or ideological) coercion were *intensified* in the wake of the increased production of commodities for the capitalist world market. In this way, as noted by Hoogvelt (1982: 175),

> capitalism overseas came to have the best of both worlds: it introduced commodity exchange all over the globe arranging for an international division of labour most suited for its own needs, and at the same time it could get the overseas products at prices which were obtained through extra-economic means.

The combination of the extra-economic with the economic

---

[4] It is pertinent to note here that a similar critique has been made of Frank and Wallerstein by Banerjee. According to him, Frank and Wallerstein fail to consider the impact of the pre-colonial history of the peripheral capitalist societies on their incorporation into the capitalist world-system. Banerjee brings out the limitations of their theory in the following words:

> The antecedent historical societies of the periphery founded upon these PCMPs [pre-capitalist modes of production] are for them a *tabula rasa*—or nearly. They are the wombless whores of the market-place and greedily receive the capitalist world-economy in their passive bosom. The assumption is unambiguous: the antecedent PCMPs of the periphery can scarcely affect the process of their interaction with the quaquaversal world-capitalism. (1987: 8)

modes of surplus extraction in the peripheral social formations of the capitalist world system keeps their wage levels much lower than those in the core countries. This is underpinned by the alliance between imperial capital and the exploiting social forces of the peripheral social formations. This 'articulation' permits 'the super-exploitation of human and physical resources in the Third World' (Hoogvelt, 1982: 178).

Moreover, as pointed out insightfully by Claude Meillassoux (1972), the pre-capitalist subsistence sector of the domestic economies of peripheral social formations *subsidizes* the reproduction of the lowly paid labour power required by the capitalist sector. What this means is that the capitalist sector of the economy which requires the *reproduction* of wage labour does not fully bear the costs of that reproduction. The children of those workers in the urban/capitalist sector who are paid very low wages have to be brought up by their rural families who survive on the pre-capitalist subsistence economy.

The net result is that the Third World commodities which contain doubly extracted labour value are exchanged for the commodities of core countries which do not contain such super-exploited labour value. There is thus the interlocking of exploitation in the sphere of exchange with exploitation in the sphere of production.

The nature of the class alliance between the exploiting social forces of peripheral regions and imperial capital varies according to the particular interests which metropolitan capitalism has in those regions. As noted by Hoogvelt (1982: 183–84), if the MNCs are interested in the extraction of raw materials, the alliance will be with feudal structures. MNCs interested in exploiting cheap labour will tend to strengthen authoritarian regimes, while democratic alliance with the local bourgeoisie would be preferred by those MNCs which benefit from the fast-growing markets in those locales.

Because of the sub-imperialist structural articulation of the capitalist relations of production with the pre-capitalist relations of production in the peripheral regions, any bourgeois revolution of the classical type is ruled out in those regions. By the same token, also lacking are the conditions ripe for a proletarian socialist revolution. Is there then any relevant strategy of transformative action by the Third World?

To this question, Samir Amin provides an answer that is different from that of Emmanuel. According to Amin, Emmanuel's policy prescription to raise the wage levels in Third World countries to offset the mechanism of unequal exchange is not based on a correct understanding of the economic mechanisms *and* political structures (i.e., class alliances) through which the peripheral capitalist mode of production reproduces itself through time. Amin does accept Emmanuel's idea that high wages at the centre and low wages in the periphery lead to unequal exchange. The former however goes beyond Emmanuel in recognizing that unequal exchange, resulting from inequality in wages, leads to, and, in turn, is reinforced by, a process of *unequal international specialization*. Some aspects of this unequal international specialization are:

1. the resource-based export-oriented activities of the periphery, as contrasted with the technologically advanced and high productivity activities of the centre; and
2. the autocentric accumulation at the centre, contrasted with the dependent or blocked development of the periphery, where segments of the population depend for their survival on elements of the pre-capitalist relations of production.

In Amin's view, the native bourgeoisie of the peripheral capitalist countries is structurally implicated in the process of mutual reinforcement between unequal international specialization and unequal international exchange. He writes: (1977: 234):

The bourgeoisie as a whole stops being national: it cannot fulfil the historical function of primitive accumulation, i.e., radically destroy the pre-capitalist modes, 'save' the surplus value, and so on. It has to be reactionary ('protect' the pre-capitalist modes in order to dominate them), wasteful (consume the surplus value), and dependent. We can therefore understand that 'dependency' is not 'imposed' but necessary to generate the surplus.

Even after their political independence, the ex-colonies, says Amin, continue to be the periphery of the capitalist world system. There is no halt to the disarticulation of their economies, to unequal exchange and to the resultant pauperization of their peoples. He recognizes that within the periphery, i.e., the Third World, considerable differentiation has occurred and is still occurring as a result of some of those countries having become the favoured sites for the relocation of certain declining sectors of industry from the capitalist metropolises. There is also an international dispersal of the production process (excluding R & D) of certain manufacturing industries by the MNCs. In this context of the dispersal of the autocentricity of metropolitan capitalism, Amin sees hopeful signs for effective resistance by regional formations of the marginalized peoples of the world system.

For autocentric and self-sustained growth, the countries of the peripheral regions should form *regional economic formations* and break with the world system. Such a break is, according to him, both necessary and possible at the present time. (In this he differs from Wallerstein.) The national independence of the former colonies, in his view, constitutes a 'break towards socialism.' He even maintains that the transformation of the global system can *start* only at its periphery. He writes: '[W]hen a system is outgrown and superseded, this process takes place, not in the first place, starting from the centre, but from its periphery.' He believes that it is only when the periphery of the capitalist world system revolts successfully that imperialist capital is forced to 'transfer the contradictions to the metropoles' (1980: 194–95).

Influenced by Amin, Frank, Laclau, Baran, Banaji, Chattopadhyay, etc., Hamza Alavi has put forward a thesis, which is best captured in the title of his article, 'India and the Colonial Mode of Production' (1975). How this thesis came to be advanced and what it means are indicated hereafter.

In an article on the mode of production in Indian agriculture, Utsa Patnaik (1972) noted that the 'specificity of the colonial system' marked it off from the capitalist mode of production of the 'core' countries. This was soon followed by an article by Paresh Chattopadhyay (1972), who pointed out that British imperialism 'preserved as well as destroyed the conditions of India's pre-capitalist economy, accelerated as well as retarded the development of capitalism in India.' Then, in an article, entitled 'For a Theory of Colonial Modes of Production' (1972), Jairus Banaji argued that the mode of production in colonial India was 'neither feudal nor capitalist, though resembling both at different levels.' In his view, the colonial mode of production served as a circuit through which capital was drained out of India and which contributed to 'the accumulation process in the metropolis without unleashing any corresponding expansion in the forces of production' in India.

Taking off from Banaji and bringing in, among other ideas, some of the productionist/articulationist ideas of Laclau, Hamza Alavi (1975) argued that imperial capital brought about an internal disarticulation of India's pre-colonial/pre-capitalist economy and external articulation of it into the world-wide structure of imperialism. In his view, this structural specificity of India's colonial mode of production makes it distinct from both feudalism and capitalism in the metropolis.

Although Alavi spoke, in 1975, of a 'postcolonial' mode of production in post-independence India, he, in 1980, chose to speak rather of the *subordinate, peripheral capitalism* of post-independence India. Even in 1975, he had maintained that in what he then called the 'postcolonial' societies, the native bourgeoisie was a subordinate partner of the metropolitan bourgeoisie in an 'unequal and hierarchical' system of world capitalism. By 1980, he became more emphatic in maintaining that a proper understanding of the structural features of India's *peripheral* (rather than 'postcolonial') capitalism is necessary for evolving a suitable strategy of transforming it.

There are, he says, crucial differences between the structure of metropolitan capitalism and that of peripheral capitalism. In the metropolitan economy, the development of capitalism has been characterized by a *complementary, integrated* development of the various sectors of the economy, viz., agriculture, industry and the various branches of industry, especially the consumer goods and capital goods industries. By contrast, internal *disarticulation* of the various sectors of the economy and *external integration* into the imperialist network are among the important structural features of colonial/peripheral capitalism. In the colonial/peripheral social formations of the world capitalist system, Alavi writes, 'the circuit of generalized commodity production was not completed within an integrated and internally balanced economy but only by way of the linkage with the metropolitan economy, through dependence on exports and imports' (Alavi, 1980: 393). In this way, according to Alavi, India's colonial/peripheral social formation is subordinate to the metropolis of the capitalist world system and as such it cannot be properly understood in isolation from its 'imperialist integument.' The structure of the colonized/peripheral social formation, in other words, 'transcends the geographical and societal boundaries of the colonized country' (Alavi, 1980: 395). What this means, in other words, is that in India, seen as a peripheral region of the capitalist world system, there is *no* structural conflict between the rural 'capitalist' class and the 'feudal' landlords.

Since the structure of peripheral capitalism is a part of the hierarchically structured world capitalist system, the former cannot be transformed without its structural de-linking from the latter. Advancing this position, Alavi writes:

> The structure of the colonial mode of production will not be transcended within the framework of peripheral capitalism and world imperialism for it is itself an aspect of the global capitalism of our times. But it is neither a universalized world of undifferentiated capitalism, as some tend to suggest, but a hierarchically ordered, colonial capitalism which can be superseded not by national independence within the framework of world capitalism (with a 'dependent' relationship) but by a decisive structural break with it (1980: 398).

Alavi seems to believe that for bringing about this 'structural break' with imperialism/neo-imperialism, the relative autonomy of India's peripheral capitalist state is a positive factor (1982: 302). For such a disengagement from the imperialist network he recognizes the role of struggles by the subordinate classes, viz., the workers and the rural poor, against the class-coalition of feudal landowners and the bourgeoisie.

How the 'dialectical unity' of a triangular alliance among the native bourgeoisie, the feudal landlords and the foreign imperialist bourgeoisie sustains an unequal exchange between India and the metropolises of the neo-imperialist system is examined by R. Sau in *Unequal Exchange: Imperialism and Underdevelopment* (1978). These classes, he says, are the 'joint exploiters' of the people of the Third World. There are, however, he notes, conflicts of class interests *within* this coalition. As a result, he says, the state does enjoy a measure of autonomy from each one of those classes. But in trying to accommodate the conflicting demands of the partners of the dominant class coalition, the state 'performs a balancing act all the time' and as such is unable to promote national economic development or socialism (ibid., 156).

According to Pranab Bardhan (1984), India's fiscal crisis and retarded industrial development has to do with the conflict of interests within the dominant class-coalition consisting of the industrial capitalists, the rich farmers and the professional-bureaucratic class. The industrial capitalists are interested in cheap inputs from the public sector, export subsidies, etc., while the rich farmers seek subsidized fertilizers and seeds, higher procurement prices, etc. The politico-bureaucratic class has an interest in ruler's rents and other benefits through public controls and regulations. For nearly two decades following independence, the framework of liberal democracy served to umpire the bargaining game among the partners of the dominant coalition. Such a politics has brought about a 'fiscal crisis' of the state, which, along with the impact of the political mobilization of the subordinate classes, has slowed down industrial growth very considerably. In this situation, some of the partners of the ruling class-coalition have been trying to set up a centralized, secure or repressive form of state. India, writes Bardhan, has 'a centralized powerful state, combining its monopoly of the means of repression with a substantial ownership of the means of production, propelling as well as regulating the economy' (1984: 36). The politico-bureaucratic class, he notes, is able to exercise its regulatory role on a selective basis in order to prevent any class-based challenges from the industrialists and the traders. In this way, according to him, 'the autonomy of the Indian state is reflected more often in its regulatory (and hence patronage-dispensing) than developmental role' (p. 39). In his view, it is this regulatory role of the state that is being altered by the policy of economic liberalization (Bardhan, 1993).

Bardhan's analysis has been praised by Sridharan (1993: 21 & 28) for providing 'the most robust theory of India's political economy.' He finds in it an admirable fusion of Marxian political economy with neo-classical rational choice political economy, which is also referred to as New Political Economy (cf. Toye, 1987 and Roemer, 1985). In Bardhan's rational choice Marxism, the Indian state appears as being characterized neither by the class-neutrality of liberal-pluralism nor by the mere relative autonomy of neo-Marxist theory but by an autonomous interest in ruler's rents, which (interest), however, is in conflict with the interests of the other partners of the dominant class coalition as well as of the subordinate classes. Bardhan's theory, however, has a major flaw in that it fails to recognize the political autonomy which the *top* political leadership has vis-à-vis not only the agrarian and industrial bourgeois classes but also the state-bureaucratic professionals. It also underplays the role of such other *political variables* as regime organization and the institutional-procedural matrix of politics (cf. Sridharan, 1993, Nayar, 1992 and Kohli, 1989).

In an article, entitled 'On the Crisis of Political Institutions in India' (1984), Sudipta Kaviraj has provided a subtle Marxist argument to the effect that the state-bureaucratic approach (as opposed to a revolutionary class approach) to social transformation, which was pursued by the Indian modernist elite (led by Nehru) in the first two decades after independence, was a wrong approach and that given the 'circumstantial weakness' of Nehru's successors, it was bound to lead to a deep social crisis. This argument is briefly summarized in what follows.

Like Asok Sen and Partha Chatterjee, Kaviraj maintains that India's transition to capitalism has features of what Marx called the 'second way' to capitalism (like in Germany or Italy) or what Gramsci referred to as a 'passive' bourgeois revolution. In such a transition, unlike in the 'first way' of bourgeois revolution (in England and France), the bourgeoisie, because of its relative weakness, is unable to establish its 'hegemony' or moral-political leadership in the civil society. Instead of hegemony, it seeks to gain 'domination' over the society through the instrumentality of the state bureaucracy.

A society under the 'second' or 'passive' way of bourgeois revolution suffers from an incoherence or asymmetry between the logics of its economic, political and cultural levels. This is in contrast to societies of first-way capitalism, in which there is a congruence or class-based 'social design' between the civil society and the political institutions.

According to Kaviraj, the Indian National Congress, as a multi-class organization, did not have a revolutionary social design. Under Nehru's modernizing leadership, the Congress assumed that there would come about an evolutionary modernization of the Indian society, which had only to be 'managed' through the instrumentality of the state bureaucracy. This, according to Kaviraj, was a wrong approach to social transformation. To quote:

Evolutionism is . . . the direct opposite of a mobilizational pic-
ture of a social revolution. These evolutionist beliefs provided
the fundamental ideology of the passive revolution. Transformation of the society, it was believed, was not to be achieved
through a mass movement, it could be safely left to a large
bureaucracy to supervise. The logical obverse of this bureau-
cratisation of the problem of development was the demobilization
of the Congress from its earlier militant political form into ordinary
ministerialism. The mixed character of the Congress, an invalu-
able asset in the struggle against imperialism and a considerable
instrument for winning elections, made it an inappropriate agency
for directed, decisive social change. (Kaviraj, 1984: 231)

Kaviraj goes on to point out that while Nehru sought to change
the pre-capitalist logic of the society (e.g., of caste and religion)
through the political imposition of the logic of democracy, his
successors, for a variety of reasons, tended to make political
institutions accept rather than change the old or traditional logics
of the society.

From this story of Indian politics, which he has reconstructed
through the categories of Marxian political theory, Kaviraj draws
an important historical proposition: 'In transitional societies, the
question of social design is not a dispensable consideration, to be
taken up only if politicians feel philosophically disposed. It per-
meates all other questions' (p. 242).

Paths to Socialism: Some Marxist Writings

Commenting on Marxist writings on the Indian state, Baldev Raj
Nayar writes: 'A striking feature of Marxist analyses of the Indian
state is that the field is dominated by formulations by practitioners
of politics in the Communist parties than by scholars' (Nayar,
1989: 71; cf. also Kaviraj, 1986: 167). Such party-theorizing, he
notes, has had both merits and demerits. He considers the integration of theory and practice as its merit and the hold of dogma and
ideology as its demerit. He notes that for a long time the Indian
communists supported whatever line the Comintern advocated,
often out of concern for the foreign policy interests of the Soviet
Union rather than out of any concern for 'the specific Indian
situation.' This, he notes, has had such outcomes as the unjustified

labelling of Mahatma Gandhi as 'a police agent of British imperialism in India' (Nayar, 1989: 73–74).

Besides Nayar and Kaviraj, Bhabani Sen Gupta, Manoranjan Mohanty, T.R. Sharma, etc., have made notable scholarly analyses of the revolutionary models of social change being pursued by the different Indian communist parties. In their studies, the three major communist parties are shown to differ from one another in their understanding of the overall balance of class forces, the nature of the state, the degree of national autonomy from, or dependence on, the foreign bourgeoisie, and the strategies and tactics of mobilizing the non-capitalist and/or anti-capitalist forces.

Turning to the contributions of Marxist academicians, we can see three paths of transition to socialism being advanced, namely, (*a*) a national democratic path of 'non-capitalist transition' to socialism; (*b*) the path of the 'intermediate regime'; and (*c*) various forms of revolutionary class struggles, including a 'subaltern' form. Relegating the 'subaltern' model for treatment in the next section, I shall take up here the other models of socialist transformation.

The idea of the non-capitalist path to socialism was initially put forward by Lenin to suggest that countries which were at a pre-capitalist or semi-capitalist stage could move directly or almost directly to socialism, i.e., without their having to wait for the full maturation of capitalism (cf. Sharma, 1990: 162–73). In an article entitled 'Marxism and the Pettybourgeois Default' (1969), Asok Sen has argued that 'the next step forward in our history' lies along the national-democratic path of non-capitalist transformation. In his view, that path calls for a carefully planned development of certain sectors of the economy, especially the public sector, aided by credits from the socialist countries. Such a path of development was claimed to be able to bypass the capitalist transformation of the entire economy and lead directly to socialism. Accordingly, Sen called for a programme of national economic emancipation through collaboration between the working classes and all other national-democratic forces, including the anti-imperialist, anti-monopoly and anti-feudal sections of the bourgeois class.

In his recent writings, Sen has come to emphasize that since the Indian transition to capitalism is clearly a 'passive revolution' in the Gramscian sense, the national bourgeoisie is incapable of pursuing an anti-imperialist, anti-monopoly and anti-feudal path of development. He therefore thinks that the non-capitalist transition of the Indian society to socialism requires a fusion of anti-imperialist struggles with struggles directed against the national/internal forces of capitalism. This recent viewpoint of Sen will be surveyed along with the views of his colleagues on the subaltern studies project in the next section.

Before turning to that section, I need to consider the models or paths of 'intermediate regimes' and revolutionary class struggles.

Adopting the ideas of the Polish economist, Michael Kalecki, K.N. Raj suggests that India is governed by an 'intermediate regime,' in which the lower middle class and the rich peasantry perform the role of the ruling class. According to Kalecki and Raj, in several countries of the Third World, certain conditions have made the petty bourgeoisie or the intermediate classes somewhat autonomous from the big bourgeoisie and the feudal landlords. Those conditions are: (*a*) the numerical dominance of the lower middle class; (*b*) the increasing involvement of the state in the economic sphere, and (*c*) economic aid from the socialist countries. The white- and blue-collar workers, according to Kalecki and Raj, are the allies of the intermediate regime. These authors suggest that by striving to assert a measure of autonomy from the foreign bourgeoisie, carrying out land reforms and using state capitalism for continuous economic growth, the intermediate regime can establish its efficient viability (Raj, 1973; Jha, 1980. Cf. also Bardhan, 1993).

Pursuing the analyses provided by Asok Sen and K.N. Raj, I have, in a paper entitled 'Elites, Classes, and the Distortions of Economic Transition' (1980), argued that because of its lack of hegemony over the society, the rule of the dominant bourgeois–landlord class coalition is *crucially* dependent on the support of the elite groups of intermediate classes, which perform the functions of coercion, bureaucratic control, political manipulation and electoral legitimation. I suggested that given the democratic framework and the poverty and illiteracy of the masses, the political-intellectual segment of the intermediate classes can use their quasi-autonomy *either* to support the non-hegemonic rule of the dominant bourgeois–landlord class coalition *or* to shift the social bases of state power in favour of the masses. Even though the actual course of change since independence has been in the former direction, I suggested that through mass literacy and mass mobilization we can still try to usher in a mass-based polity.

An appropriate entry into the models of revolutionary class struggles is provided by Arvind Das's critique of the 'intermediate regime' theory of Kalecki and Raj.

Das's standard of critique is Lenin's view that the state can only be 'an organ of class *rule*, an organ for the *oppression* of one class by another' and that the idea of class reconciliation or class accommodation by the state is a petty-bourgeois distortion of the Marxian idea of the socialist/proletarian revolution (Das, 1974: 27–28). According to Das, the idea of a class-accommodating state 'leads to fascism at the worst and confusion at the best.' Particularly objectionable to Das is Kalecki's and Raj's idea that the 'intermediate regime' of any non-socialist country can be 'benevolent and looks after the interests of many classes.' In Das's view, the theory of the intermediate regime should be rejected in favour of the theory of the dictatorship of the proletariat. He quotes and endorses the following passage from Lenin:

> The main thing that socialists fail to understand and that consti-
> tutes their shortsightedness in matters of theory, their subservi-
> ence to bourgeois prejudices and their political betrayal of the
> proletariat is that in capitalist society, whenever there is any
> serious aggravation of class struggle intrinsic to that society,
> there can be no alternative but the dictatorship of the bourgeoisie
> or the dictatorship of the proletariat. *Dreams of some third way
> are reactionary, pettybourgeois lamentations* (Lenin as cited,
> with added emphasis, in Das, 1974: 36).

The case for a proletarian revolution against the bourgeois state is made out by Patankar and Omvedt in their article, 'The Bour-geois State in Postcolonial Social Formations' (1977). In it, they reject the thesis of the relative autonomy of the capitalist state. They maintain that in the Indian social formation, the capitalist mode of production is dominant and that therefore the bourgeoisie holds state power. In a capitalist society, they note that the state '*cannot have relative autonomy* from the requirements of the bour-geoisie as a whole, and the bourgeoisie does not have to exercise its interests through direct links' (1977: 2170). Hence they argue that in the politically independent bourgeois states of the Third World, it is no more appropriate to pursue any revolutionary strategy of alliance with the so-called 'national' sections of the bourgeoisie. In the post-World War II phase of imperialism, they note, the (native) bourgeoisie as such 'will not be part of the revolutionary movement . . . but is its immediate enemy' (p. 2165). This new phase of imperialism, is characterized by the 'internalization' of imperialism in the dominated social formations and the 'disarticulation' of their peripheral-capitalist development both from any radical-capitalist transformation of agriculture and from any proper development of the home market. As a result, they write,

we have a situation in most dominated social formations of the third world where there are bourgeois states, where the capitalist mode of production is dominant, where the local (formerly 'national') bourgeoisie is the ruling class but where this bourgeoisie cannot complete the democratic revolution, cannot carry through an agrarian revolution, cannot escape from dependence on imperialism, and cannot wipe out feudal or other pre-capitalist relations in the social formation. (Ibid., 2174)

The politically independent bourgeois state, Patankar and Omvedt maintain, serves the reproduction of peripheral capitalism and as such cannot be an agency for overcoming the 'internalization' of imperialism and the disarticulated development of capitalism. In their view therefore the bourgeoisie of a dominated social formation 'is in basic antagonism to the masses, and it is its state, the bourgeois state, that will be the object of any mass revolutionary upsurge' (p. 2174).

According to Weisskopf, India's class structure as it has been shaped by the colonial experience has been conducive to the pursuit of neither a purely capitalist nor a completely socialist strategy of economic development. As a result, the minor socialist modifications of India's essentially capitalist strategy of development has, in his view, retarded economic growth without contributing to any greater equality. Weisskopf believes that a clear socialist strategy is best suited to achieving rapid economic growth with distributive justice. He writes:

In order to achieve rapid economic growth in the context of a substantially more equal distribution of income, there is really no alternative to a socialist strategy in which private property ownership is sharply curtailed and the state assumes most of the responsibility for resource mobilization and capital accumulation. Such a strategy is politically feasible only when and where a coalition of anti-capitalist classes has succeeded in wresting power from property-owning elites. (1978: 61)

Weisskopf however notes that a powerful coalition of anti-imperialist classes which can promote such a socialist strategy of change does not exist in India. Rather, he writes, 'it seems most likely that the governing members of the educated elite will choose to ally themselves with indigenous and foreign capitalist elites in whose benefits both can share' (1978: 64).

That India's neo-imperialist dependency has remained undiminished since its political independence is an argument put forward by Gough (1980). She notes that the capital intensity of industries and the drain of capital to Indian and foreign monopolies have both been instrumental in the increasing unemployment and poverty of the Indian masses. In this situation, according to her, peasant struggles for wage increases or for the prevention of eviction of tenants are insufficient to 'solve the structural contradictions of the capitalist mode of production.'

According to Prabhat Patnaik, in the immediate post-independence years, Indian economic nationalism was characterized by 'the fight against foreign capital and the growth of state capitalism' (1975: 147). State capitalism, he argues, was necessitated by the peculiar class basis of the Indian state. 'The colonial structure having left no single strong class, state power continues to be based on a coalition between the bourgeoisie and large landowners' (1975: 148). This class-coalition, he writes, has three elements: (a) the monopoly bourgeoisie; (b) the small urban bourgeoisie and the professional groups; and (c) landlords and rich peasants. Given this alliance of classes, state capitalism was preferred to private capitalism. The former, as noted by Patnaik, received support from the Soviet bloc (1975: 150).

In Patnaik's view, since the 1962 Chinese aggression, India's subordination to imperialism has been increasing. He however argues that India can secure total freedom from imperialism by removing the internal obstacles to growth, or in other words, through a transformation of the social structure, in which he sees a growth-inhibiting compromise between the forces of feudalism and capitalism. 'Today in India or other "Third World" countries, the bourgeoisie, arriving too late on the scene, is forced to ally itself with the remnants of feudalism; and having no colonies and being threatened by the increasing political consciousness of the people, it is reintegrated into the imperialist structure. Compromising with feudalism, it is forced to compromise with imperialism' (1975: 162).

According to Patnaik, the subsequent 'liberalization' of the economy is part of the centralization of capital at the international level. It can *at best* make a segment of the Indian economy a lateral extension of the metropolitan economy, but will not solve the problems of mass unemployment and poverty. On the contrary, as noted by Bagchi (1982: 236), the policy of export-oriented liberalization may lead to the use of authoritarian measures against labour and popular unrest. For the solution of those problems, Patnaik notes, India needs to replace the set of institutions associated with the capitalist mode of production (in either its 'independent-national' or 'liberalized' form) with the institutions of 'a different mode altogether' (1973: 209).

An orthodox Marxist conception of class struggle is defended by Randhir Singh (1991). He finds that disenchantment with the conventional class politics of the established communist parties is leading some radical intellectuals of the left of the Indian political spectrum to advocate 'identity struggles' (i.e., struggles for an identity of dignity and honour) by such long-oppressed groups (= 'identities') as religious and ethnic minorities, tribals, *dalits* and women. He admits that these groups or identities are in fact victims of 'double oppression,' i.e., class oppression and oppression specific to each of the concerned groups or identities. He also grants that their struggles constitute a most justifiable part of the peoples' struggle for a just and humane social order. He however finds identity-consciousness and identity-politics to be falling short of the revolutionary class consciousness and class struggle, which, he believes are required for resolving the basic economic-structural contradictions of the Indian society (1991: 116–17).

'Subaltern Studies' and Problems of Social Transformation

Subaltern Studies constitute a new school in the historiography of colonial/post-colonial India (Guha, ed., *Subaltern Studies* [hereafter S.S.], I to VI). It has a distinctive political theory of social transformation in colonial/post-colonial India. According to a knowledgeable commentator, the subaltern historiography 'will pave the way for research that will illuminate important aspects of the politics central to an understanding of social, cultural and political change in colonial India and in the post-colonial era' (Sathyamurthy, 1990: 139).

Among the authors of these studies, the disciplinary perspective of political science is represented by Partha Chatterjee, most of the other authors being historians.

Since the *Subaltern Studies* project has yet to have its due impact on Indian political science, I have felt it advisable to give, in the present section, a detailed and interpretive summary of some of its leading theoretical formulations. Some important critical commentaries on the Subaltern Studies project will be surveyed in the following section.

Departing from the *colonialist, liberal-nationalist* and *Marxist-nationalist* forms of *elitist* historiography, which interpret Indian nationalism as the achievement, exclusively or predominantly, of elite groups and which fail to acknowledge the role of the politics of the 'people' or the 'subaltern classes,' the authors of *Subaltern Studies* recognize the autonomous or independent role of the politics (especially the uprisings) of the subaltern peasantry in Indian history. They view the insurgent subaltern or peasant as 'a subject of history in his own right even for a project that was all his own.' 'The central aim of the *Subaltern Studies* project,' writes Dipesh Chakrabarty, 'is to understand the consciousness that informed and still informs political actions taken by the subaltern classes on their own, independently of any elite initiatives' (S.S. IV: 374).

According to the authors of *Subaltern Studies*, the nationalist historiography, like the imperialist/colonialist historiography, fails to recognize the historical limits of capital. They maintain that the former shares in the latter's meta-narrative of the modern state and portrays all anti-imperialist struggles of the people as struggles for setting up a sovereign national state. In nationalist historiography, in other words, the life of the people gets subsumed into the biography of the nation-state. 'All politics,' writes Partha Chatterjee, 'is now sought to be subsumed under the overwhelming requirements of the state-representing-the-nation' (1986: 168).

This is exactly what subaltern historiography seeks to correct; its central assumption is that the subaltern classes or groups had 'other notions of community than that of the nation.' For the subaltern historians, what the nationalist historiography presents is simply the history of the 'appropriation by elite (and elitist) Indians, on behalf of their project of building an Indian state, of diverse historical struggles of the subaltern classes.' Departing from that perspective, the subaltern historiography seeks to show that the subaltern classes have acted (i.e., rebelled) time and again against the 'statist project and politics of the nationalist elites' (Chakrabarty, 1991: 2163). What the *Subaltern Studies* pursue, in other words, are the *different* political and cultural ideas which the subaltern classes and groups had *against* the bourgeois-liberal nationalist ideas of the elite classes and groups which led the Indian freedom struggle.

Subaltern Studies also depart from 'nationalist Marxism,' including Nehruvian socialism, which regards colonialism as the overarching source of all problems of popular politics in India, including the problems of casteism, communalism and regionalism. For the nationalist Marxists and the Nehruvian socialists, the solution to all these problems lies, at least initially, in 'liberal-bourgeois nationalism.' The Subaltern theorists thus see a complicity between nationalist Marxism and liberal-bourgeois nationalism in so far as they both uphold the *ideology* of the nation and the national state. A questioning of this ideology is one of the central tasks of the Subaltern Studies project.

It questions the category of the 'nation' and 'poses the failure of the "nation" to come to its own as a fundamental problem of modern Indian history' (Chakrabarty in S.S. IV: 373). As we shall see, this 'failure' of the Indian nation-state is interpreted by the *Subaltern* contributors as an expression of the *historical limits of capital*, which it is never going to be able to overcome.

Differentiating Subaltern historiography from 'orthodox Marxism,' Partha Chatterjee points out that while the latter explains historical transitions in terms of a linear determination by the economic level (the forces of production), the former takes into account the interrelationship among the different instances of a historical social formation, viz., the economic, political and cultural-ideological instances, each of which is regarded as 'an autonomously constituted theoretical field.' 'My fundamental argument, he writes' . . . is that an explicit conceptualization of the political instance of social formations (as also the ideological-cultural instance) is essential if we are to address ourselves to the problems of the *transition* from one mode of production to another' (Chatterjee, 1985: 59). In these transitions, what is central, in Chatterjee's view, is the *political* form of the class struggle over the definition of one's right to the means of production and to the products of social labour.

He argues that the transition of historical social formations from primitive communism to feudalism or from feudalism to capitalism can be fruitfully analyzed, not in terms of the 'techno-economic determinism' of orthodox Marxism, but in terms of the interplay of three modes of power, viz., the *communal*, the *feudal*, and the *bourgeois* modes, which are explained as follows.

Under the *communal* mode of power, individuals and groups have rights, entitlements and obligations only by virtue of their membership of the community. Authority resides in the community as a whole, and not in any of its functionaries. The *feudal* mode of power operates through the physical subordination of the subject population. In the *bourgeois* mode of power, the domination of the capitalists over the wage-labourers is secured, not through physical force, but through property rights and market mechanisms. The bourgeois state is separate from the civil society and is 'neutral' with respect to the real inequalities which exist in the society.

Applying this framework of the modes of power to the transition of Indian society under colonial rule to the capitalist mode of production, Chatterjee points out that it has been an *incomplete* transition and that this incompleteness is shown in the fact that the colonial state machinery continued for a long time as an *admixture of feudal and bourgeois modes* [emphasis added]: a simple appropriation of older forms and symbols of authority and methods of administrative practice with the object of establishing and holding a position of physical domination over a subject population, along with the introduction of bourgeois notions of rule of law, equality before the law, impersonal procedures of administration and justice, and the evolution of a political process in which the government dealt with bodies which claimed to *represent* in some way or other the citizens of the country (Chatterjee in S.S. I: 17).

According to Chatterjee, the introduction of new political institutions based on bourgeois law, bureaucracy and representation has had differential impacts on the pre-capitalist structures, which were sometimes destroyed, sometimes modified and sometimes reinforced or given new leases of life under the new system of surplus extraction and political governance (S.S. II: 347); see also Guha in S.S. VI: 226 *et passim*).

Drawing out two aspects of the incompleteness of the Indian transition to capitalism, Chatterjee mentions that (*a*) there were several instances of peasant communities struggling autonomously to protect their 'communal rights' against encroachments by feudal lords or the imperial bureaucracy; and (*b*) in subjugating and ruling over 'a population organized as communities,' the colonial state had to water down or occasionally abandon the bourgeois principles of equality before the law and of the neutrality of the state (S.S. I: 17–18). These aspects of the 'admixture of feudal and bourgeois modes of power' in colonial/post-colonial India lead Chatterjee to conclude that 'the dominance of the characteristically "modern" modes of exercise of power seem limited and qualified by the persistence of older modes' (S.S. II: 349). He goes on to note that it is through this combination of different modes of power that the present-day ruling classes are able to exercise their domination.

In his view, the Indian national movement had all the short-comings of a 'passive revolution' of capital in the Gramscian sense. It was, he says, essentially a movement for forming a politically independent nation-state that was to be in the service of capital. Accordingly, it entailed 'a series of alliances . . . between the bourgeoisie and other dominant classes and the mobilization, under this leadership, of mass support from the subordinate classes' (1986: 49). He notes that in this project, no attempt was made to break up the 'rational' authority set up in the period of colonial rule in the domains of administration, law, economy and education. There was also no full-scale assault on the dominant classes of the pre-capitalist order, who were in fact brought into the project as subsidiary allies. Hence, says Chatterjee, the dominance of Indian capital rests not on 'its hegemonic sway over "civil society" but on its control over the state apparatus.

According to Chatterjee, the incompleteness of the transition of the colonial/post-colonial Indian social formation to capitalism as manifested in the ruling classes having to rely on a combination of the modern/bourgeois and traditional/'communal' modes of power is not something that can be overcome—as the liberal political theorists think—through a full-fledged bourgeois assault on the feudal or communal modes of power. In his view, the hope for a full-scale bourgeois revolution is a *liberal illusion*. Following Marx, he maintains that capital is *not* a universal category that is destined to triumph over all obstacles. Rather, the incompleteness and retardations of the transition to capitalism in colonial/post-colonial social formations 'are precisely the expressions of the historical limits of capital, which it is beyond its power to transcend' (Chatterjee, 1983: 64).

In order to understand these 'historical limits' of capital and to see beyond them, we must, says Chatterjee, investigate the structures of the state and, more importantly, of 'community'. In his view, 'community' is in deep contradiction with 'capital.' This is the message he sees in Marx's mature theory and in the insurgencies of the peasant classes of colonial India who, time and again, rebelled against the intrusions of the feudal and bourgeois modes of political power into their communal mode of organizing and exercising political power. Therefore, in his view, in the present context of 'the historical limits of capital,' a political theory of social transformation has to be based on 'the opposition between community and capital.'

Such a project, he clarifies, is a project neither of Hegelian totality that would encompass antagonistic contradictions nor of Nietzschean politicism which disregards the economic level. Chatterjee claims that his political theory of the opposition between community and capital is fundamentally a Marxist project. In support of this claim, he points out that Marx, in 1881, reminded his Russian correspondents that the end of the crisis of modernity lies in 'a return of modern societies to an archaic type of communal property' in a superior form. Chatterjee reminds us, in other words, that the Marxist project, in a fundamental sense, is the rescuing of Reason from the clutches of capital. We are reminded that Marx, in his last years, saw the imperialistic stage of capitalism to be opposed to reason and science and that therefore even in the 'archaic' resistance of the subaltern classes in countries still not enslaved by capital, there is the possibility of a new beginning (Chatterjee, 1985: 60; and 1986: 170).

Chatterjee's *political theory* of the role of subaltern resistance in the *never-to-be-completed* transition of the Indian colonial social formation to capitalism is a brilliant elaboration of some of the political implications of the *subaltern historiography* of Indian nationalism. This historiography has been originally advanced and admirably defended by Ranajit Guha, the intellectual mentor and leader of the Subaltern Studies group. Some of his writings are now surveyed.

According to Guha (1983: 336), the task of historiography is 'to interpret the past in order to help in changing the world . . . [through] a radical transformation of consciousness,' which, in Marx's words, 'consists *only* in making the world aware of its own consciousness . . . in *explaining* to it the meaning of its own actions.' Guha and his colleagues point out that both the colonialist and nationalist varieties of liberal historiography are elitist in that they leave out the politics of the people or the subaltern classes. They also criticize liberal historiography and ideology for spreading the *illusion* that capitalism has the *universal* capacity to liberate and transform nature and society against all obstacles thrown up by the old or feudal order. Subaltern historiography is intended to radically transform these forms of false or ideological consciousness and thus pave the way for 'the conquest of power' by the subaltern classes for which it speaks.

In a major contribution, entitled 'Dominance without Hegemony and its Historiography' (S.S. VI), Guha shows that in the colonial/post-colonial situation, the rule of the dominant classes does not rest on the hegemony of liberal or bourgeois or 'modern' political culture; in this situation, which he sees as the moribund phase of the history of capitalism, the bourgeoisie has been experiencing the *insurmountable* limitations of capital. Accordingly, it has departed from its original universal mission of liberating, transforming, or modernizing nature and society and has entered into regressive compromises with its erstwhile enemies, namely, the lords of the feudal order. Guha finds affinities or continuities between this bourgeois regression in the colonial situation and that of the Prussian revolution of 1848, which has been commented upon insightfully by Marx.

Guha reminds us that while Marx saw the bourgeoisie playing a liberative and transformative role against the forces of feudalism in both the English Revolution of 1648 and the French Revolution of 1789, he regarded the Prussian Revolution of 1848 as a compromise of the bourgeoisie with the forces of feudalism against the interests of the people which actually lay in bringing about a transformation of nature and society. Marx, as Guha reminds us, brought out in a prescient manner the basic contradiction of capitalism between its promise of a universal tendency to destroy the 'slave-owning and feudal cultures' and the historical frustration of that tendency since the nineteenth century. Since then, the universalizing tendency of capital, says Guha, has remained only an 'illusion' or 'pretension' of liberal historiography and thought. By contrast, subaltern historiography and political theory, say Guha, Chatterjee and their colleagues in the *Subaltern Studies* project, is inspired by Marx's 'prescience' which *'envisages the development of capital's universalist tendency to a stage where it "will drive towards its own suspension"'* (Guha in S.S. VI: 225). Guha writes that the project of capitalism faces limitations which 'capital can never overcome' and that it is therefore a 'project predicated on the certainty of its failure to realize itself.'

Turning to the colonial situation, Guha says that the colonial project has *not* been an extension of any universalist mission of the European bourgeoisie to defeat the forces of the old or feudal order. On the contrary, there was a 'vast tolerance [by the imperialist bourgeoisie] of pre-capitalist values and institutions in Indian society.' Thus, in the colonies, the bourgeoisie did not free the people from the old order and lead them into a new or better social order. Hence the dominance which the bourgeoisie, in collaboration with the top layers of the old, feudal order, exercises over the society is not *hegemonic* in so far as it is based more on coercion than on the consent of the people.

Devoid of hegemony, colonial rule, says Guha, was based on a specifically colonial mix of the metropolitan (imperialist) and indigenous idioms of coercion (order and *danda*) and persuasion (improvement and *dharma*), collaboration (obedience and *bhakti*) and resistance (rightful dissent and *dharmic* protest). Guha notes that the specifically colonial structure of the relationship between these 'two very different paradigms of political culture . . . one of which is contemporary, British and liberal, and the other precolonial, Indian and semi-feudal' should not be interpreted *either* as the meeting of the dynamic modernity of the West with the inert tradition of India *or* as a mere mechanical coexistence of Western liberalism and Indian feudalism. In the colonial mould, says Guha, each of these elements or idioms has acquired paradoxical or double meanings such that what is long dead (in Indian tradition) appears as not defunct, and what is dynamic or progressive in metropolitan soil becomes regressive on colonial soil (S.S. VI: 270–71).

Guha's analysis of colonial rule as 'dominance without hegemony' leads him to the important conclusion that *'bourgeois culture hits its historical limit in colonialism,'* which he defines as the regression of an advanced bourgeoisie from the universalist project of capital to a compromise, through the mechanism of the colonial state, with pre-capitalist particularism. He concludes: 'None of . . . [the] noble achievements [of bourgeois or liberal culture]—Liberalism, Democracy, Liberty, Rule of Law, etc.—can survive the inexorable urge of capital to expand and reproduce itself by means of the politics of extra-territorial, colonial dominance' (S.S. VI: 277).

He therefore opposes liberal historiography and thought which retain the *illusion* of the universalist mission of capital. These he says must be criticized and attacked 'from a historic opposition invested with such ideals, values and ways of interpreting the world as constitute a challenge to liberalism.' He writes that such a critique, which will bring about the 'dissolution of the material basis of bourgeois dominance and the corresponding social and political structures,' will have to come from outside the universe of bourgeois dominance, that is, 'from another and historically antagonistic universe.' In his view, in other words, the critique of the liberal political culture or ideology can only come 'from an ideology that . . . is antagonistic towards the dominant culture [of liberalism] and declares war on the latter even *before* the class for which it speaks comes to rule' (S.S. VI: 222). Such a critique, he admits, anticipates 'the conquest of power by its [ascendant] class' from 'the moribund but still dominant' class.

Similarly, Asok Sen (whose earlier works have been referred to in the previous section) writes that subaltern historiography is a form of Marxist mediation in a 'wider historical outline of a non-capitalist transition,' in which he situates the revolutionary subject of *Subaltern Studies*. He finds 'the true self of that revolutionary subject' in the subaltern rebel who fought for a vision of community life that was 'irreconcilable with the life of the empire, and with the policies necessary to protect and perpetuate "England's work in India." ' Moreover, 'the cardinal protest of subalternity' was, in his view, autonomous from the liberal-nationalist movement led by the bourgeois class, which, he clarifies, was only a 'passive revolution' that was meant to 'appropriate the subjectivity of the working class to a consensus which perpetuates the subordination of labour to capital' (Sen in S.S. V: 230–31).

Sen maintains that in colonial India, the dominant classes 'had no feeling of community, no national bonds and no political organization adequate for the task of social transformation.' Even in the mass movements launched by Gandhi, whenever the potential for 'an unrelenting people's war' became clearly visible, he, says Sen, repeatedly 'monitored the ethic of the burgher to prevail over the revolutionary ethos of the peasant and the people.' Sen goes on to write:

> Modern India has now lost most of the ideological and practical means of revolutionary community that might have been available. The losses are critical for those who wish to move ahead of the capitalist order, and *Subaltern Studies* tries therefore to recover lessons which remain relevant. (S.S. V: 221)

The most important of such lessons, in Sen's view, is that the autonomous subaltern uprisings, which sought 'to turn the world upside down,' were an attempt to restore the network of community relationships which were ruptured by the colonialist combination of capital, pre-capitalist wealth and state power. What the autonomy of subaltern consciousness signifies to Sen, in other words, is the people's 'will to power' in a non-capitalist transition to socialism, i.e., a transition to socialism without waiting for the full maturation of capitalism.

The paper in which Sen advanced these ideas was presented originally at the second Subaltern Studies conference, held at Calcutta in January 1986. Reporting on that conference, one of its participants, David Hardiman (1986), writes that the project seemed to have come to a crossroads, from which one group of contributors seemed to favour further work along the deconstructive road, while another group (which included Sen) wanted the study of subaltern consciousness and action to foster the struggle for a socialist society in India. While the former was seen to be a road towards the relativity of all knowledge, the latter was seen to be a struggle for socialism on the basis of those aspects of subaltern consciousness and action which are opposed to feudalism and capitalism. This second road has been labelled by its detractors as a search for a 'Marxist Hind Swaraj.' Hardiman writes that he would accept this label as a complimentary characterization of a new quest, which, in his view, calls for a focus 'on the actual workings of the political process, seeing how the elite and subaltern domains of politics braid together and react against each other over time.'

Concerning the deconstructivist road, Dipesh Chakrabarty (1991) notes that it can be seen to be followed in his own book on working class history as well as in the recent writings of Guha, Chatterjee and Gyanendra Pandey. Chakrabarty points out that these works analyze the Indian experience of modernity as an experience of what Guha has called 'dominance without hegemony.' In these works, in other words, as Chakrabarty goes on to note, 'the conception of the nation loses the sanctity it once had for both imperialists and nationalists.' Hence, *Subaltern Studies* can, in his view, be seen to have affinities with the post-structuralist/post-modern critiques of the grand narratives of modernity, viz., the narratives of 'nation', 'progress,' 'freedom,' etc.

While sharing this post-modernist critique of the universalist theories of modernity, the *Subaltern Studies* project rejects the post-modernist denial of subjectivity and agency. Such a rejection is forcefully defended by Gayatri Chakravorty Spivak, one of the contributors to *Subaltern Studies*, who argues that the upholding of the strategically essentialized subjectivity of the subaltern rebels is necessary for the politics of resistance against imperialism.

In a paper published in the fourth volume of *Subaltern Studies* (1985), Spivak notes that one part of Guha's project, namely, the critique of the liberal-elitist historiography, seems to be a progress-ivist or evolutionist radicalization of the historiography of colonial India through 'a combination of Soviet and Barthesian semiotic analysis.' This aspect of *Subaltern Studies* is not attractive to Spivak. She however finds it meaningful to read the work of the subaltern historians 'against the grain of their theoretical self-representation' and to interpret their theoretical or methodological strategy as a strategy of 'affirmative deconstruction,' which, in her view, is a 'most useful' corrective to the anti-humanist post-Marxism of Western/Foucauldian post-structuralism.

Spivak notes that there is an affinity between the subject-agent of humanism and that of imperialism in the sense that they both stand for 'the sovereign subject as author, the subject of authority, legitimacy, and power.' It is, in her view, this 'hero' of humanism and imperialism who is questioned and undermined by both Western post-structuralism/deconstruction and post-colonial, subaltern historiography.

However, in so far as they remain committed to the subjectivity of the subaltern rebel, the subaltern theorists, says Spivak, do not fully share the anti-humanist post-Marxism of the Western post-structuralists. The former, she says, can be read as being moved by Marx's view that 'man must strive toward self-determination and unalienated practice and Gramsci's that the "lower classes" must "achieve self-awareness via a series of negations"' (S.S. IV: 336).

Spivak finds Western post-structuralism to be wanting or deficient in two interrelated respects. First, although some of the Western post-structuralists are genuinely critical of the ravages of contemporary neocolonialism in their own nation-states, they, writes Spivak, are 'not knowledgeable in the history of imperialism, in the epistemic violence that constituted/effaced a subject that was obliged to cathect (occupy in response to a desire) the space of the Imperialists' self-consolidating other' (p. 348). She notes that Foucault's otherwise brilliant analysis of the invention of a new mechanism of power in the West in the seventeenth and eighteenth centuries remains marred by his failure to point out that that new mechanism was 'secured *by means of* territorial imperialism—the Earth and its products— "elsewhere"'. According to her, in other words, Foucault's 'self-contained version of the West' ignores 'its production by the spacing-timing of the imperialist project.' To her, therefore, Foucault's clinic, asylum, prison and university seem 'screen-allegories that foreclose a reading of the broader narratives of imperialism' (Spivak, 1985 and 1988).

Second, according to Spivak, given their ignorance of the epistemic violence done to the 'other' of the imperialist subject-agent, the Western post-structuralist anti-humanists do not appreciate the strategic relevance of the affirmation of subjectivity by the decolonizing self, such as the subaltern rebel whose subjectivity gets restored in subaltern historiography. Spivak criticizes Foucault for his refusal to 'represent' the oppressed subject, who, he assumed, can speak for himself. This, according to Spivak, is an abdication of the 'representational' role of the theorist. By contrast, the subaltern theorists, says Spivak, are 'methodical trackers of representation' of the subaltern peasantry, who have been denied subjectivity in both colonialist and liberal-nationalist historiography. She finds in Guha's affirmation of the subjectivity of the subaltern rebel a useful corrective to Louis Althusser's notion of history as a 'process without subject.' She commends Guha's programmatic intention to focus on the consciousness of the subaltern rebel because, as he writes, 'it is not possible to make sense of the experience of insurgency merely as a history of events without a subject' (Guha as quoted in Spivak, 1985: 350).

Thus, the recovery, by the subalternist historians, of 'the peasant-rebel's awareness of his own world and his will to change it' is read by Spivak as 'a *strategic* use of positivist essentialism in a scrupulously visible political interest.' Using the terms of Derridean deconstruction, she equates the subaltern theorists' restoration of the subjectivity of the subaltern with the *affirmative* moment or phase of deconstruction, which she, following Derrida, believes must *strategically* precede the deconstructive moment or phase of *displacing* the oppressive or alienating sign-system or discursive field. So understood, the affirming of a *positive* subject-position for the subaltern can, according to her, be 'reinscribed as a strategy [of transformative intervention] for our times' (1985: 345).

Somewhat in line with Spivak's reading, Gyan Prakash (1992) too argues that in so far as it restores the subject-position of the subaltern rebel, not as a pre-given foundation or essence but as an 'effect of power-relations,' the *Subaltern Studies* project can be interpreted as a most prominent example of post-foundational/post-Orientalist historiography.

Some Critical Commentaries on '*Subaltern Studies*'

Dipankar Gupta, Rosalind O'Hanlon and Mridula Mukherjee have separately criticized subaltern historiography for its hidden or not-so-hidden elitism. Their criticisms are surveyed in the following passage.

According to Gupta (1985), Guha's attribution of an autonomous or separate mentality or mind to the subalterns (the peasantry and the tribals) amounts to *ethnicizing* their identity and history. Gupta notes that Guha considers the insurgent peasantry as an ethnic mass, having 'a relatively autonomous culture or mind of their own.' This ethnicization of the culture and consciousness of the subalterns is said to lead Guha to describe them through such 'harsh adjectives' or 'undiluted invectives' as 'less sophisticated,' 'inchoate,' 'immature,' 'disjointed,' etc. Gupta maintains that the use of such 'harsh adjectives' and 'undiluted invectives' amounts to suggesting that peasant consciousness, because of its 'backward- ness,' had still 'to progress up the evolutionary ladder.' Hence, Gupta contends that 'Guha's ethnic historiography cedes more territory to the elitists than perhaps do those whom Guha calls elite historians' (p. 16). Gupta's contention, in other words, is that Guha's ethnicization of subaltern consciousness 're-erects elitism on a sounder basis' by separating the peasantry and the tribals from the rest of the population 'on a mental and intellectual basis.'

Gupta makes a further contention that the ethnic explanation of subaltern insurgency is a *culturological* and not a *structural* explan- ation. In his view, we must go beyond the 'business of mentality' and pay close attention to the respective positions that the insur- gents and the elites occupy in the social structure, particularly in terms of their relative strategic access to power (p. 10). He suggests that from such a structural perspective, we would be able to appreciate the fact, for instance, that cultural and religious meta- phors can be used for purposes which they have never served before, e.g., the use of religious symbols for secular objectives.

Following to some extent Dipankar Gupta's critique, Rosalind O'Hanlon (1988) argues that the way in which the contributors to the Subaltern project represent the collective cultures and tradi- tions of the subaltern classes seems to undermine 'just that sense of power which it is the contributors' concern to restore.'

For instance, Partha Chatterjee's notion of peasant-communal ideology or the communal mode of power, says O'Hanlon, is a notion of unity and consensus, in which relationships of power seem to be absent. Concerning Chatterjee's claim that the distinc- tive feature of the communal mode of power is 'the conviction [of its members] that bonds of affinity *already exist* which then become the natural presupposition for collective action,' O'Hanlon says that since no peasant community can be thought to have a 'perfect equilibrium of material and political forces,' the imputed conviction that the bonds of affinity already exist and that they can therefore be naturally presupposed for collective action reflects a 'strategic weakness in the treatment of power.' 'The point,' writes O'Hanlon.

is that if the contributors are to maintain the radical impetus of their emphasis on power, it is vital that it should not be brought to a halt through a static idea of the subaltern collectivity: whether in the shape of this apparently 'natural' community, or in the unitary 'moral economy' of which many contributors speak, or in any other laying down of a preordained subject-position which can stand outside the fluctuations of human existence to impose an order of value or of narrative. (p. 212)

O'Hanlon argues that since subject-agent identities and histories do not exist as essences but are constructed or produced in discourses, the strategy of recovering the presence of the subaltern classes should not lapse into a search for essentializing, autonomous origins but should seek to reveal that presence 'to be one constructed and refracted through practice.' Such a strategy, she notes, will indeed entail the subversion or deconstruction of the self-constituted or self-determined subject-agents of elite historiography.

O'Hanlon however sees a problem in the elite-subaltern dichotomy employed by the Subaltern writers, namely, its 'tendency to assume that discourses have an existence which is prior to, and hence unsullied by, the interventions of those over whom they are to have jurisdiction.' In her view, hegemony 'does not spring fully-formed into being to be followed by a resistance which must always operate within its pre-given confines.' By this, she seems to mean that in its very construction, the discourse of hegemony faces or engages the discourse of resistance and *vice versa*. This would imply that the issue of the dichotomy/autonomy between elite consciousness and subaltern consciousness needs to be rethought.

In opposition to Gayatri Spivak's 'against the grain' reading of the restoration of subaltern subjectivity by the authors of *Subaltern Studies* as a most useful strategy of affirmative deconstruction, O'Hanlon (1988) criticizes it on the ground that what is restored is the mirror-image of the same classic figure of western humanism, who is the author of the subalternity or otherness of the subaltern.

O'Hanlon does indeed commend the authors of *Subaltern Studies* for their critique of both 'ethnocentric historicism' and 'the conventional genres' of colonialist, nationalist and Marxist historiography. She also finds that some aspects of the strategy employed by Guha and his colleagues for recovering subaltern consciousness (e.g., the investigation of the negation of the signs of elite authority by the subaltern rebel) have been 'strikingly fruitful.' Yet she feels that in the key area of power and resistance, the *Subaltern Studies* project has suffered from a 'slow theoretical paralysis' in so far as it has borrowed the key tools of the dominating discourse of Western humanism which, she suggests, has produced the subaltern *qua* subaltern. Among those borrowed tools, she singles out the notion of the unitary, self-originating, self-determining individual of liberal humanism. It is this 'classic figure of western humanism', which she finds is 'readmitted through the back door in the figure of the subaltern himself, as he is restored to history in the reconstructions of the Subaltern project' (p. 191). She explains this in the following words:

> Essentially, this consists in the recuperation of the subaltern as a conscious human subject-agent. We are to restore him, in the classic manner of liberal humanism, as a subject 'in his own right,' by reclaiming for him a history, a mode of consciousness and practice, which are *his own*: which are not bestowed upon him by any elite or external leadership, which have their origins nowhere else but in his own being (p. 196).

According to O'Hanlon, the adoption of this liberal-humanist notion of autonomous subjectivity by the authors of *Subaltern Studies* has contributed to their conceptualizing the issues of domination and resistance in a limited and distorted manner. In making this criticism, she, in opposition to Spivak, draws support from the 'formidable' and 'extremely fruitful and liberating' Western critique, by Marx, Nietzsche, Althusser and Foucault, of Western traditional philosophy's search for essentialist origins or foundations and of its product in humanism's self-constituting subject. Following Althusser's interpretation of Marx's theoretical anti-humanism, she warns us of the dangers of any attempt to root the explanation of social formations and their history in a 'concept of man as an *originating subject.*' She endorses Althusser's argument that when one begins such an explanation with a conception of man as an 'originating subject,' one would be led, step by step, to believing in the omnipotence of liberty, bourgeois ideology and capitalism. O'Hanlon also accepts the validity of Nietzsche's and Foucault's critique of 'origins' and of Man as a fixed, essentialized universal category. In particular, she endorses Foucault's genealogy, which rejects what he called 'the existence of immobile forms that precede the external world of accident and succession.'

Following Edward Said, O'Hanlon maintains that the Western post-structuralist critique of the discourse of liberal humanism is helpful in critically analyzing the Orientalist construction of the identities of the colonized peoples.[5]

Concerning the question of the autonomous origins of a social consciousness, she endorses Rashmi Bhatnagar's view (1986: 210) that the search for such origins becomes 'a longing for an impossible purity and a yearning for the fullness of meaning,' which is a fundamentally misguided move.

According to O'Hanlon, the Western post-structuralist critique of essentializing origins and of the self-constituted subject-agent of the discourse of liberal humanism gives us a correct understanding of the constitution of the coercive or hegemonic structures of domination and a liberating conception of resistance against it. She feels that even though none of the Subaltern writers would want to espouse essentialist humanism, their emphasis 'on the subaltern's action *on his own*' or, in other words, on the *autonomy* of the history and consciousness of the subaltern groups or classes makes it vulnerable to the post-structuralist objections to the liberal-humanist conceptions of the virile, self-constituted subject-agent and its other.[6]

---

[5] It is pertinent to note here that Said has written the Foreword to Guha and Spivak, *Selected Subaltern Studies* (1988).

[6] In a subsequent article, Rosalind O'Hanlon and her co-author David Washbrook, while continuing to be opposed to liberal humanism's 'undifferentiated and static' conception of subjectivity, develop a 'different' argument, namely, that what emancipatory political struggles require is not the post-structuralist conception of contingent, plural subject-positions but the Marxist notion of the universal class-identity of the underclasses of capitalism. They write that post-structuralism, as domesticated within American academia, by downplaying or screening off 'the identity . . . of class or material relations,' denies the underclasses 'the ability to present themselves as classes: as victims of the universalistic, systemic and material deprivations of capitalism which clearly separate them off from their subaltern expositors.' They therefore associate the post-structuralist view of subjectivity with political conservatism and implicit authoritarianism—O'Hanlon and Washbrook, 'After Orientalism: Culture, Criticism, and Politics in the Third World,' *Comparative Studies in Society and History*, 34 (1), January 1992. Cf. also Gyan Prakash's reply to them in 'Can the "Subaltern" Ride? A Reply to O'Hanlon and Washbrook,' *ibid.*, Vol. 34 (1992).

O'Hanlon also seems to suggest that when the discourse of resistance is counter-present within a discourse of hegemony or domination and *vice versa*, the strategy of resistance need not necessarily be centred on violent onslaught. Accordingly, she suggests, we should also look for 'forms of resistance more feminine than masculine.'

In a two-part article entitled 'Peasant Resistance and Peasant Consciousness in Colonial India: "Subalterns" and Beyond' (1988), Mridula Mukherjee has challenged the central thesis of the Subaltern school that there was a 'structural dichotomy' between the elite and subaltern domains of politics in colonial India or, in other words, that there was a binary opposition between elite consciousness and subaltern consciousness. In opposition to Guha's subalternist notion of an 'autonomous,' 'pure' domain of subaltern politics (in which the insurgent or rebel as 'the conscious subject of his own history' resists all elite attempts at leadership, manipulation or appropriation), Mukherjee endorses the standard Marxist view that the peasants cannot represent themselves and that they must be represented by revolutionary leaders, who should take socialist ideas and consciousness to them. According to her, it is *not* the case that revolutionary leaders cannot arise from 'elite' backgrounds.

She in fact adduces considerable historical evidence, some of it from the *Subaltern Studies* themselves, which show that, except occasionally, the subaltern classes did not throw up leadership from among themselves and that the initiative and leadership for mobilizing and organizing the peasantry for resistance came 'largely from "outsiders" or from "insiders" who had exposure to the world outside through travel or education or some other means.' Guha's *autonomous* model of the Subaltern domain, Mukherjee concludes, fails to recognize the role of *outside* leadership in transforming the consciousness of the peasantry and in mobilizing it for social change.

Focusing on the peasant movements in India during the late nineteenth and the twentieth centuries, she finds that agricultural labourers, most of whom were untouchable or tribal peoples, did not show any anti-feudal or anti-capitalist consciousness; their consciousness did not seem to have gone much beyond their right to subsistence. She points out that their struggles were not directed to secure the complete abolition of land revenue for the state or of landlordism. Following Irfan Habib (1983), she writes: 'Centuries of custom, sanctified by religion, had denied them the right, in most parts of the country, to even think of owning or cultivating their own land' (p. 2175).

In Mukherjee's view, this customary practice, from which the peasantry derived their notions of fairness, rights and legitimacy, did not belong to any 'pure,' 'autonomous,' subaltern domain of politics but was defined and redefined by the ruling or dominant classes during centuries of domination and subordination. So penetrated by elite ideas, subaltern consciousness, says Mukherjee, cannot be assumed to be autonomous or inherently revolutionary. It has rather to be transformed as part of a wider ideological and political struggle for a revolutionary transformation of the social system. 'In this context,' writes Mukherjee, 'the "subaltern" perspective, which postulates an advanced consciousness as inherent, impedes such efforts towards ideological transformation and is objectively reactionary' (p. 2179).

According to Mukherjee, the elements of feudal, communal and caste consciousness which are present in peasant consciousness have the potential of being used for reactionary and divisive politics. They must therefore be made to give way to 'more secular and modern forms and ideologies, such as those based on nation, class, culture, etc.' 'But this can be done,' she writes, 'only if they are not seen as inviolate and inherent parts of "subaltern" or peasant consciousness which should not be disturbed by the "elite" in "its" struggle for nationalism and socialism' (p. 2180).

She finds in Partha Chatterjee's contribution an indication of the failure of *Subaltern Studies* to provide a framework of ideas for transforming the communal and caste elements of peasant consciousness. She notes that Chatterjee is disinclined to regard 'communalism' as a basic problem and 'secularism' as its answer because he believes these were made into problems of politics by the communalist and secular 'appropriation' of subaltern actions which, to use his words, were 'neither "communal" nor "secular" . . . for those categories were quite irrelevant to the political world' of that domain of politics which lay outside the legal-political order upheld by the state (cf. Mukherjee, 1988: 2151). Mukherjee thinks that Chatterjee's views about the position of the Indian state vis-à-vis the various Indian nationalities fail to recognize the positive role of anti-imperialist nationalism.

Mukherjee also criticizes Guha's preoccupation with the *how* of insurgency or struggle to the exclusion of consideration of the *why* of it. 'This preoccupation with *forms* of struggle or protest to the exclusion of the aspects of *aims, of programme and ideology*' she writes, 'also leads to a romantic glorification of violent forms of struggle' (p. 2111. Emphases mine). She challenges the assumption, held at least implicitly by the subaltern school, that 'violent forms of struggle, which are the "subaltern" forms of struggle, are *per se* more revolutionary than non-violent forms of struggle, which are "elite" forms of struggle' (p. 2112). According to her, the choice between violent and non-violent forms of struggle is linked not so much to the elite/subaltern dichotomy as to the nature of the political structure of the state and to its administrative and repressive capacities. In her view, violent forms of struggle are relevant when directed against a non-hegemonic state, which is based primarily on force, whereas non-violent forms of struggle become relevant when it is directed against a hegemonic or semi-hegemonic state, which has an efficient administrative set up and considerable repressive force. She writes:

> Where the character of the state is hegemonic or semi-hege-monic, as in British India, the struggle against that state is also primarily a hegemonic one, and hegemonic struggles are usually characterized by peaceful mass movements and ideological-political struggle, rather than by violent rebellion or insurrec-tionary seizure of power. (p. 2113)

She goes on to point out that in hegemonic or semi-hegemonic situations, non-violent forms of struggles may be more viable and effective in mobilizing people and putting pressure on the govern-ment, whereas the violent method may 'perform an objectively counter-revolutionary role by exposing the movement prematurely to repression and demoralizing the participants.'

From the foregoing review of the *Subaltern Studies* project and of its several criticisms, I shall draw an admittedly oversimplified summary-conclusion: Though the *Subaltern Studies* project has made a most valuable contribution by reclaiming and affirming the subjectivity and politics of the 'subaltern classes' which have been ignored by elitist historiography, the perspective of subalternism, like that of elitism, is a partial or limited interventionist stand-point.

Its emancipatory-transformative impact seems to me to be limited or restricted to the *mere inversion* of the hierarchic, oppressive sign-system of the dichotomously essentialized subjectivities of the superordinate and the subaltern. No doubt, an *inversionary move* is indeed an emancipatory necessity. But it does not suffice by itself. Mere inversion only brings about the mutual substitution, often through violent, annihilatory means, of the superordinate and the subaltern within the same sign-system.[7] For reconstructing such a sign-system, the inversionary move has to flow into processes of *displacement* or transformation. This would seem to require what Gandhi referred to as new experiments with inter-subjective moral-political truth, in which the means and ends of emancipation merge into each other. I shall return to this idea in the next chapter as well as in the concluding chapter.

---

[7] In *Elementary Aspects of Peasant Insurgency*, Guha writes: 'By trying to force a mutual substitution of the dominant and the dominated in the power structure it [peasant revolt] left nothing to doubt about its own identity as a project of power' (p. 9).

4

Gandhi: *Swaraj, Sarvodaya* and *Satyagraha*

Introductory Remarks

In the literature of the social and political sciences, five interpretations of the Gandhian way of socio-political transformation can be identified. They are:

1. That Gandhian values and strategies are functional to the modernization of Indian tradition and to the traditionalization of (Western) modernity in India;
2. that Gandhian values and strategies contribute to the political appropriation of the peasantry by/for the passive bourgeois-national revolution, which *defers or deflects* the socialist revolution in India;
3. that the programme of Gandhian *sarvodaya* must be revised and extended into a strategy of Total Revolution.
4. that some aspects of Gandhian thought subserve the Hindu nationalist ideology; and
5. that the Gandhian programme of *sarvodaya* through parliamentary *swaraj* and *satyagraha* is superior to the liberal and Marxist-Leninist paradigms of development and governance.

Of these five interpretive positions, the fourth, which paves the way for the Hindu nationalist appropriation of aspects of Gandhism, will be reviewed in the next chapter. The literature on the other interpretations is reviewed here.

Gandhi and the Modernity of Tradition

Lloyd I. Rudolph and Susanne H. Rudolph (1967) draw a distinction between two aspects of Gandhi's transformative vision and programme of action, viz. (*a*) his 'postindustrial critique of industrial civilization' and the related espousal of spirituality, the self-sufficient village, and non-violence; and (*b*) his middle-level norms of modernizing conduct or this-worldly asceticism, which resembles the protestant ethic of modernizing Europe. Of these two aspects of Gandhism, the first (i.e., Gandhi's post-industrial critique), say the Rudolphs, 'no longer speaks to the needs of the politically active classes of the sixties.' Concerning the second aspect of Gandhi's thought and practice, the Rudolphs maintain that it is of continuing relevance to the social and political modernization of India (1967: 217–19).

By transforming the traditional values of his religious heritage from an other-worldly and fatalistic ambience into activist and this-worldly concerns, Gandhi, say the Rudolphs, made a unique contribution to the modernization of Indian society and policy. The Gandhian middle-level norms of modernizing conduct or this-worldly asceticism which they hold to be of continuing relevance are the economizing of time and resources, courageous and self-esteeming behaviour, the building up of modern, democratic political organizations and the promotion of national coherence and identity.

Like the Rudolphs, P.C Joshi (1979) too finds the Gandhian intervention as having reduced the gulf between tradition and modernity in India. Gandhi, we are told, preserved the vital elements of Indian tradition and at the same time brought about major reforms in it. By promoting a this-worldly, puritanical ethic at the elite level and an anti-fatalistic orientation among the masses, Gandhi, says Joshi, attacked traditionalism at its roots. In this way, Gandhi, for Joshi, became a 'far more powerful modernizer of Indian society than thousands of modernists who had dismissed him as a traditionalist.'

Gandhism as an Ideology for the Political Appropriation of the Subaltern Classes

Partha Chatterjee (1986) interprets Gandhi's intervention in Indian politics as constituting a crucial moment of manoeuvre of the subaltern classes, i.e., the peasantry, in the passive bourgeois-national revolution of India. His thesis, which I reviewed in the previous chapter, contains the following interpretation of Gandhi.

Because of the historical/colonial constraints on its path of development, India's indigenous bourgeoisie could not wage a full-scale political assault either on the old, pre-capitalist dominant classes or on the colonial power. It therefore had to resort to a 'passive revolution of capital', i.e., a bourgeois revolution in partial partnership with the old, pre-capitalist dominant classes and with the appropriated support of the subordinate classes, especially the peasantry. In this passive revolution, what the bourgeoisie sought was not the establishment of hegemony over 'civil society' but the securing of dominance over an interventionist national state. For this, the subaltern classes or the peasantry were not required to be culturally modernized; they had only to be politically appropriated by the bourgeoisie for its project of gaining domination over the new state. This, says Chatterjee, is exactly what Gandhism did; it served to mobilize the peasantry into the Indian national movement without either making them culturally modern or incorporating them as a class force into the structure of the new state. He writes:

> While it was the Gandhian intervention in elite-nationalist politics in India which established for the first time that an authentic national movement could only be built upon the organized support of the whole of the peasantry, the working out of the politics of non-violence also made it abundantly clear that the object of the political mobilization of the peasantry was not at all what Gandhi claimed on its behalf, 'to train the masses in self-consciousness and attainment of power'. Rather the peasantry were meant to become willing participants in a struggle wholly conceived and directed by others. (Chatterjee, 1986: 124)

In the overall Gandhian ideology, Chatterjee identifies two contradictory yet integrated/reconciled aspects, viz. (a) a traditional, peasant-communal *moral* critique of the political, economic and techno-scientific features of modernity or 'civil society'; and (b) a set of procedural or organizational norms for the formation and operation of the political and legal structures of bourgeois modernity. The former, he says, served to politically mobilize the peasantry (*for* the native bourgeoisie *against* the foreign bourgeoisie) without modernizing or revolutionizing them culturally, while the latter gave the indigenous bourgeoisie dominance over the state structure, from which the peasantry was kept distanced.

In Chatterjee's view, Gandhi's 'monumental significance' lies in his success in combining these two contradictory ideological strands into an effective 'moment of manoeuvre' in the 'passive revolution of capital' in India. Gandhi, says Chatterjee, did this by means of his *satyagraha* way of organizing or conducting mass political action and his *ahimsa* tactic of 'conflict-accommodation' (as contrasted with 'conflict-resolution' through class struggle). Moreover, *satyagraha* is interpreted by Chatterjee as a form of organizing/conducting mass political action, which involves the non-democratic imposition of the absolute moralism of Truth by the *satya-agrahic* leaders. Similarly, the 'experimental' politics of *ahimsa* is interpreted as a tactic, not of resolving, but of accommodating 'a potentially limitless range of imperfections, adjustments, compromises and failures.' According to Chatterjee, in other words, the *satya-agrahi's* 'experimental' politics of *ahimsa* is not a non-violent way of pursuing truth in political conflicts but an avoidance of 'politics' (by which he means 'the violent struggle between classes') with a view to securing the political acquiescence of the subaltern classes to their domination by the bourgeois-national state. Instead of preparing the peasantry for subaltern socialism through class struggle, Gandhi's moralism, says Chatterjee, bridged 'even the most sanctified cultural barriers that divided the people' and thereby 'provided for the first time in Indian politics an ideological basis for including the *whole people* within the political nation' (p. 110). That ideology, however, is, according to Chatterjee, an articulation of a traditional *moralism* which lies 'entirely outside' the political philosophy of the Enlightenment and which therefore is not relevant to the resolution of the historical contradictions of post-Enlightenment modernity (pp. 98–100). Moreover, according to Chatterjee, the *satyagraha* way of political action for *swaraj/sarvodaya* is neither democratic nor revolutionary.

Like Chatterjee, Ranajit Guha (1989) and Prakash Chandra Upadhyaya (1989 and 1992) too interpret Gandhian thought and strategy as having prevented the transformation of the Indian anti-imperialist struggle into a class struggle for socialism. According to Upadhyaya, Gandhi made a successful manipulation of the traditional idioms of *Ramrajya, satya and ahimsa* for subserving the interests of the propertied classes. Guha's thesis, which was reviewed in the previous chapter, contains the following assessment of Gandhi.

Departing from Antonio Gramsci's *antinomous* juxtaposition of dominance and hegemony, Guha maintains that dominance entails both coercion and persuasion/consent (i.e., hegemony), with the former *outweighing* the latter. Applying this idea to British colonial rule, he says that after its initial, 'conquest' phase, it operated through force *and* through 'institutions and ideologies designed to generate consent.' He further shows that while coercion was exercised through a combination of the Western idiom of Order and the Indian idiom of *Danda*, the idiom of Persuasion comprised two sub-idioms, namely, Improvement (of several aspects of the condition of the subject population) and *Dharma*. He takes *dharma* to be a conservative ideology, which preserved the organic unity of society by ensuring the performance of duties by all according to their fixed place in the caste hierarchy (Guha, 1989, S.S. VI, pp. 231–44).

According to Guha, during the *swadeshi* movement of 1903–8, Tagore made use of the idiom of *dharma* 'as a unifying (*aikya*) and harmonizing (*samanjasya*) principle of politics.' Similarly, concerning the Gandhian transformation of the Congress Party into a mass movement, he writes:

> . . . the idiom of Dharma continued to influence elite political discourse, especially that particular variety of it which refused to acknowledge *class struggle as a necessary and significant instrument of the struggle against imperialism*. Since Gandhism was, in this period, *the most important of all the ideologies of class collaboration within the nationalist movement*, it was also the one that had the most elaborate and most frequent recourse to the concept of Dharma (Guha, 1989, S.S. VI, p. 246. Emphases mine).

JP's Revision of the Gandhian Strategy for *Sarvodaya*

The ideology of peaceful total revolution, which Jayaprakash Narayan (JP) articulated in justification of the 'protest movement,' which he led in Bihar and Gujarat during 1974–75, is a revision of the Vinoba-line of the *sarvodaya* strategy of non-violent revolution, which JP too had been following until then. In a sense, it was also a revision of the transformative strategy of the Lok Sevak Sangh as envisaged in Gandhi's Last Will and Testament. In it Gandhi had written:

> Congress in its present shape and form, i.e., as propaganda vehicle and parliamentary machine, has outlived its use. India has still to attain social, moral and economic independence in terms of its seven hundred thousand villages as distinct from its cities and towns. (Pyarelal, 1956: 666)

Gandhi had proposed that the Congress be disbanded as a political party and converted into a Lok Sevak Sangh which should, among other things, guide political power without engaging directly in electoral and party politics.

This 'Last Will', which was rejected by the Congress on the ground that its dissolution would create a dangerous political vacuum in the country, eventually (i.e., during 1971–74) became the source of a split, within the Sarvodaya movement, between Acharya Vinoba Bhave and his followers on the one hand and JP and his followers on the other. While Vinoba Bhave remained committed to the idea that the *sarvodaya* workers or Lok Sevaks had to remain aloof from party/electoral politics while working to usher in a new, spiritualized, non-violent social order, JP made a revision of Gandhi's ideas on the Lok Sevak Sangh to justify its entry into party and electoral politics in order to transform it from within. Ostergaard (1985a: 160) sums up the differences between Vinoba's and JP's strategies in the following words:

> Vinoba was concerned to pursue what may be described as a purist alternative strategy, concentrating on building the new cells of the *sarvodaya* society, ignoring the old politics. JP, on the other hand, was pursuing a less purist strategy which sought to shape and reshape the politics into the new. In a sense, Vinoba was working 'outside' the existing system, endeavouring to develop a new system which would eventually replace the old, while JP was working in a non-partisan way 'inside' the existing system, endeavouring to transform it into the new.

JP also disagreed with Vinoba's thinking on the nature and role of *satyagraha*. While the latter stood for a 'gentle' and 'positive' conception of *satyagraha* as a form of non-violent *assistance* in right thinking, the former favoured a 'negative' and 'harsh' conception of *satyagraha* as a 'peaceful' and 'large-scale' mode of 'resistance' to, and transformation of, every sphere and aspect of society. JP believed that through 'peaceful' direct action the people could and should bring about a total revolution. The movement for 'total revolution' was to include (*a*) the enlisting of students and youth into the movement, (*b*) the enlargement of the arena of action to cover such areas as price rise, corruption and unemployment, (*c*) participation in electoral and party politics, and (*d*) the challenging of state power.

In his study of Jayaprakash Narayan's 'total revolution' version of the *sarvodaya* ideology, Ghanshyam Shah (1977) finds it to be deficient as a counter-hegemonic ideology of the oppressed classes. In his view, the *sarvodaya* emphasis on class collaboration and trusteeship is misplaced. He finds that even in places where *sarvodaya* workers have done intensive work, there has been 'an accentuation of the class conflict'. He also questions the realism of the *sarvodaya* stand that the existing state structures can be transformed into instruments of the common good without undermining their present class biases. As the Bihar movement matured, he writes, it failed to draw in poor peasants and agricultural labourers', whereas businessmen and rich farmers joined the students and the urban middle class in their protest against Congress rule. Shah concludes that being so deficient, the *sarvodaya* ideology did not uplift the Bihar movement into a revolutionary reform movement. He writes:

> Although the Sarvodaya ideology stands for revolution, in actual practice it has so far helped the perpetuation of status quo. The insistence on class collaboration and Sadhan Suddhi have so far helped the landed class, businessmen and other sections of the rich, and helped to nullify the struggle of the poor against the exploiters, though against the wishes of the Sarvodayites. (Shah, 1977: 156)

According to Shah (1979), JP's claim that his strategy of 'total revolution' is a synthesis of Gandhism and Marxism is untenable as there are unbridgeable contrasts between Gandhi's moralism and

Marx's materialism. The two, Shah maintains, do not meet on the crucial issues of violence, class war and the use of state power. He sums up the limits of JP's vision as follows:

> His ethical principle of giving primacy to individual morality over material forces comes in his way. His vacillations are also due to his hesitation in accepting the existence of classes . . . having opposed interests, and the dominance of certain classes over state power.

In his assessment of JP's conception of peaceful total revolution, Ostergaard (1985a) finds it to be a great advance over the *sarvodaya* strategy favoured by Vinoba Bhave; it did have a potential for bringing about a revolutionary transformation of the existing system. This potential, however, was in fact dissipated, notes Ostergaard, by a 'fatal error' on the part of JP, namely, his reliance on party and electoral politics. These, says Ostergaard, could only have served as instruments of legitimation or reform, and not of revolution. According to Ostergaard, in other words, JP's peaceful total revolution suffered from a 'fatal ambiguity' between reform and revolution. For a truly *revolutionary* rather than a *political* or *reformist* Gandhism, Ostergaard calls for a 'further revision of JP's revised strategy.' This further revision, he says, lies in the *exclusive* reliance on non-violent direct action, both combative and constructive, for replacing 'state power' with 'people's power' or 'self-managing direct democracy.'

Ostergaard's imposition of the conventional dichotomy between reform and revolution on the JP movement has been criticized by Selbourne (1985: Introduction). In his view, one should not look for 'success' in social transformation only in 'revolutions' and, in the process, fail to see any virtue in social-democratic movements which seek to bring about a radical reform of existing oppressive systems. The JP Movement, says Selbourne, *did address* some of the real issues of political struggle in India.

Similarly, Richard Fox (1989) maintains that JP did not make any simplistic choice between reform and revolution but viewed his movement as a permanent or continuous revolution, the objectives of which were not fixed once for all but had to be 'fixed and re-fixed' by the people in the course of the struggle.

An indirect endorsement of JP's revision of the *sarvodaya* strategy by making it rely on party and electoral politics may also be found in T.K. Oommen, 'Rethinking Gandhian Approach' (1979). He notes that while the goal of Gandhian *swaraj* (which he takes to mean just political freedom) has been achieved, the goal of Gandhian *sarvodaya* has not been achieved. He argues that unless the Gandhian approach to power politics and administrative leadership is radically altered, the latter objective cannot be achieved. According to him, social-structural transformation can be brought about, not through the change-of-heart approach which Gandhi advocated, but by managing or controlling the structures of power and authority, from which he and many of his followers shied away. *Satyagraha*, we are told, has been an appropriate means for securing *swaraj* but not for the tasks of nation-building and social reconstruction. Those who are committed to bringing about the Sarvodaya Samaj should, says Oommen, abandon the orthodox Gandhian attitudes towards positions of power and authority and try to occupy or control 'structurally strategic positions.'

The Gandhian Way as an Alternative to the Liberal and Marxist-Leninist Paradigms

In this sub-section, my focus is on those studies which, in opposition to the 'modernity of tradition' and 'subaltern-Marxist' interpretations, present the Gandhian approach as pointing, in some ways, beyond the liberal and Marxist-Leninist paradigms. Even though they could belong to this sub-section, the works of Rajni Kothari and V.R. Mehta are relegated to the chapter devoted to them (chapter 6).

According to Ravinder Kumar, Gandhi pursued 'class' politics in the struggles he led in Champaran, Kheda and Ahmedabad, but shifted to 'communitarian' politics in the larger national movement which he successfully led against British rule. Thus, starting with the 1919 Rowlatt *satyagraha*, Gandhi used 'moral issues,' rather than class-based economic issues, 'to cement a grand alliance of Hindus and Muslims, rich and poor . . . the working class and the industrial magnates . . . the zamindars and the peasants, in a great struggle against the British Government' (Kumar, 1983: 27). While admitting that this moral-political strategy was uniquely successful in winning national liberation from colonial rule, Kumar maintains that it at the same time failed to bring about any fusion of the different religious communities into a common national identity. He also notes that while Gandhi's *sarvodaya* ideal of the human person served to overarch the different social groups which characterized the Hindu social order, it was also responsible for entrenching the privileged position of the upper classes both during and after the freedom struggle (pp. 141–44).

The Gandhian phase of the Indian national movement was, to use Gandhi's own words, a struggle, a movement and a constructive programme. Using Antonio Gramsci's phrase, it may be interpreted as a 'war of position', or, in other words, as a counter-hegemonic struggle *against* colonial rule. Gramsci did in fact make a contemporary note of this character of the Gandhian movement as it was then evolving. In his *Prison Notebooks* (pp. 229–30), he wrote:

> . . . India's political struggle against the English . . . knows three forms of war: war of movement, war of position and underground warfare. Gandhi's passive resistance is a war of position, which at certain moments becomes a war of movement, and at others underground warfare. Boycotts are a form of war of position, strikes of war of movement, the secret preparation of weapons and combat troops belongs to underground warfare. (Quoted in Bipan Chandra, 1988: 23).

The Gandhi-led counter hegemonic struggle of the Indian people for *swaraj* or post-coloniality was not a conventional class struggle but a multi-class movement *against* imperialism/coloniality and *for* an anti-imperialist, post-colonial national identity. This is well brought out by Bipan Chandra in the following words:

> . . . as a popular mass anti-colonial movement it had to be open-ended, without a fixed class hegemony or a necessary class character. It had to be a multi-class movement rather than a mere alliance of different classes. It was not a movement of the bourgeoisie, national or otherwise, or led or controlled by it. Nor was the National Congress a class party of the bourgeoisie or a united front of the bourgeoisie and landlords, but was a party of the Indian people as a whole including peasants and workers, artisans, the bourgeoisie, the petty bourgeoisie, the

intelligentsia, and sections of landlords. Nationalism, or anti-imperialism, in a colony did not represent only the ideology of the bourgeoisie or express only the bourgeoisie's contradiction with imperialism. It represented the entire colonial society's contradiction with imperialism. (1988: 71)

In this struggle for decolonization, Gandhi's non-violent mass movement proved to be superior to the paradigms of constitution-alism, insurgency and communalism (Josh, 1992: ch. 2). Gandhi, it may be recalled, wrote his *Hind Swaraj* as an 'answer to the Indian school of violence.'

Both Bipan Chandra and Bhagwan Josh reject the communist categorization of the Gandhian phase of the nationalist struggle as merely a bourgeois movement all the way through. Chandra points out that Gandhi's overall programme contained very many radical, anti-bourgeois ideas and themes which were creating 'constant openings for any pro-poor, socially progressive ideology and for co-operation between Gandhi, Gandhians and the Left' (1988: 85). Chandra however admits that the national movement ended up, not in this radical direction, but 'under the hegemony of bourgeois or capitalist developmental perspective.' This, he adds, came about as a result of a 'complex of forces,' including, among other factors, the failure of the Left to grasp the nature of the Gandhian strategy and to relate to it in a creative manner.

Somewhat like Bipan Chandra, Bhikhu Parekh (1991b: 222) writes that 'though the Marxist commentators are right in pointing out that Gandhi did not provide a viable *alternative* to capitalism, they are wrong not to appreciate that his thought had enough resources to offer a coherent and practical *critique* of it.' Parekh goes on to indicate that Gandhi's ideas on 'legally enforced trustee-ship, nationalization without compensation, the minimum possible wage differential, a heavy death duty, rural uplift and a compre-hensive programme for leveling up the poor went a long way towards changing the inner structure of capitalism.' Parekh adds that the nationalist struggle constrained Gandhi from fully exploit-ing these radical themes.

Gandhi, according to Parekh, was engaged in the interlinked tasks of regenerating Indian tradition and reconstructing Western modernity. In his view, the Gandhian approach had some elements of continuity and some elements of change with respect to the four schools of pre-Gandhian Indian thought, viz., traditionalism, modernism, critical traditionalism and critical modernism. He writes that though Gandhi was very sympathetic to the critical traditionalists, he found them neither critical nor traditional enough; they too were dazzled by modernity and had not dug deep enough into the regenerative resources of the Hindu tradition. Gandhi, therefore, according to Parekh, mobilized the people into unconventional political action, directed against both traditionalism and modernism. Gandhi is shown to have done this by generating unconventional forms of *shakti* (energy) and *adhikar* (authority) in himself through his unconventional life-style, including his unconventional experiments dealing with sexual energy (Parekh, 1989b).

In another of his significant writings on Gandhi, Parekh (1991a) interprets Gandhian *satyagraha* as a new mode of revolutionary action. Gandhi is shown to have rejected the traditional theory of revolution, which neatly separates good and evil and which uses violence to suppress the latter. The Gandhian *satyagrahi*, in other words, refuses to regard the oppressors as totally evil and the oppressed as totally innocent. Gandhi, writes Parekh, gives us 'a new theory of revolution grounded in the three principles of the unity of humankind, the indivisibility of means and ends, and a non-Manichaean view of the world.'

According to K. Raghavendra Rao (1985 and 1986), Gandhi's *Hind Swaraj* has to be taken as 'a serious document in the technical mode of social science methodology and vocabulary,' which not only deconstructs the epistemological foundations of modern/ Western social sciences but also offers a 'transformational paradigm' of social and political life. Gandhi's *swarajist* conception of the self and of its relationship to society and state is, according to Rao, a studied departure from both the liberal and Marxist conceptions. While J.S. Mill's liberal theory regards the individual to be an *asocial* bearer of rights and Marx's socialist conception of the individual is cast in a materialist-naturalist mould, Gandhi takes the human person to be a self-limiting, self-disciplining, duty-accepting, truth-searching moral agent. In Rao's view, the *swarajist* is neither an individualist nor a statist, though both Gandhi and Marx are 'united against liberalism in downgrading the state in relation to society.' Highlighting the Gandhian departure from liberalism and Marxism, Rao writes:

Given the Gandhian transformational syndrome of low-level non-market productivity, limited minimal consumption level based on the ideals of limited wants and ascetic's restraint, and a highly decentralized structure of political power, it is not difficult to see that the Gandhian transformation postulates goals inconvenient to, and inconsistent with, both liberalism and Marxism, though to different degrees and in different respects. (1985: 141)

Rao concludes that Gandhi's *swarajist* theory of the self, society and state must be accorded 'enormous intellectual and theoretical respect, even if we may find ourselves departing from it partially or wholly.'

In an address delivered at the University of Oxford in October 1970, Professor V.K.R.V. Rao, the then Minister of Education in the Government of India, interpreted Gandhi's *satyagraha* and *sarvodaya* as a needed and effective alternative to the Marxist-Leninist model of scientific socialism or communism for which class war and proletarian dictatorship are the means. Even though there may be some superficial similarities in the ideal social order envisaged by Marx and Gandhi, the latter's vision and strategy are, according to Rao, 'quite clearly and categorically an alternative to Marx and Lenin, Stalin and Mao' (1970: 345). The crucial differences between them, says Rao, is that while Marx and the Marxists separate or dichotomize the means and the ends of human action and justify the use of violent means, Gandhi ruptures the means–ends dichotomy and maintains that only non-violent means can lead to non-violent ends.

Rao goes on to point out that the essence of Gandhi's alternative approach to social change is 'truth and non-violence, love in place of hate, service in place of self, and conformity by moral conviction in place of conformity by physical coercion' (p. 345). In Rao's view, the non-violent approach to social transformation is superior to the method of violence in so far as the former can transform oppressive social/class structures without destroying persons. The Gandhian approach, moreover, upholds the essential unity of mankind and the fundamental equality of all human persons, which are violated by the conventional or traditional revolution-aries; they destroy some persons for the·sake of others. Rupturing the conventional dichotomies between private morality and public/

political effectiveness or expedience, or between the means and ends of human action, Gandhi, writes Rao, 'brought religion, in its true sense of spirituality, into all aspects of life, including politics, and set before his people the ideal of social change through the conversion of the individual and his consequent better functioning in society' (p. 14).

Rao justifies Gandhi's conception of the moral-political individual, the *Satyagrahi*, as the primary agent of social change. Tellingly, he quotes Gandhi:

> Socialism begins with the first convert. If there is one such, you can add zeros to the one and the first zero will account for ten and every addition will account for ten times the previous numbers. If, however, the beginning is a zero, in other words, no one makes the beginning, multiplicity of zeros will also produce zero value. Time and paper occupied in writing zeros will be so much waste.

Rao concludes that what is unique to the Gandhian approach to social change is the demonstration that *satya* and *ahimsa* could be understood and appreciated by the masses and that embodied or articulated in *satyagraha* they could bring about fundamental changes in the political, social and economic spheres of our life. We are told that it is from such a line of thinking that Gandhi was led to his conceptions of trusteeship and Constructive Programme. Rao concludes that Gandhi's non-violent approach can be used on a generalized basis for conflict-resolution and social change.

Like V.K.R.V. Rao, Geoffrey Ostergaard (1977) too regards Gandhi's *satyagraha/sarvodaya* as a superior alternative to the Marxist-Leninist strategy of class war, which according to him, does not prevent the emergence of new ruling classes. Ostergaard also recognizes that the distinctiveness or originality of the Gandhian approach to social change is its rupturing of the dichotomy between the means and ends of human action; for Gandhi, but not for Marx or Lenin, truth and non-violence are both the end and the means of human action.

Among other writers, who interpret Gandhi's rupturing of the means–end dichotomy as his unique contribution to the theory of social and political change are Raghavan Iyer and Joan Bondurant. According to Iyer (1979), Gandhi stands 'almost alone among

social and political thinkers in his firm rejection of a rigid dichotomy between ends and means and in his moral preoccupation
with the means to the extent that they provide the standard of
reference rather than the ends.' He did not regard violence and
non-violence as mere alternative means (or techniques) to the
same end; they are morally different and must necessarily lead to
difference end-results. Iyer (1985) also maintains that while utilitarianism sacrifices the minority by/for the majority and communism
justifies violent methods, Gandhian *satyagraha/sarvodaya* respects
the fundamental equality of all persons and insists on non-violent
means.

Writing as a 'post-Gandhian,' Ashis Nandy interprets Gandhi as
providing us with a 'most creative' frame of critical-traditionalist,
decolonizing thought and action. That frame of thought and action,
says Nandy, includes bicultural elements from both tradition and
modernity. Gandhi, we are told, did not bypass modernity but
'carefully read and digested the relevant Western experience' as an
insider-outsider. His critique of modernity, in other words, was
done not from a traditionalist standpoint but from a standpoint
that was critical-traditional and post-modern/post-contemporary
at the same time. In Gandhi, thus, Nandy finds 'a critique of
traditions coupled with a critique of modernity' (1987b: 157). He
elaborates:

> . . . Gandhi's movement against the tradition of untouchabil-
> ity . . . [was] the other side of his struggle against modern
> imperialism . . . . Unlike Coomaraswamy, Gandhi did not want
> to defend traditions, he lived with them. Nor did he, like
> Nehru, want to mesmerize cultures within a modern frame.
> Gandhi's frame was traditional, but he was willing to criticize
> some traditions violently. He was even willing to include in his
> frame elements of modernity as critical vectors. (Nandy, 1987a:
> 240–41).

In Nandi's view, what may seem like Gandhi's 'primitive false
consciousness' was in fact a valid frame of ideas to assert the
autonomy, survival and creativity of 'the victims of the present
global system.' Thus Gandhi's language of spirituality (as opposed
to materialism), myths and self-abnegation (as opposed to 'history')
and self-realization (as opposed to social engineering) was, according to Nandy, a valid way of freeing the victims of 'history' from

Eurocentric evolutionism, historical-materialist determinism, scientism and technicism (1983: 55–63; 1987a: 243–45; 1987b: 135–62). He finds in Gandhi's emphasis on self-control and self-realization not an other-worldly message of escape from the politics of the real world but a valid, alternative, approach to social trans-formation. That is, while the modernists seek to bring about social change through the *control* or engineering of the external, objective world (including the not-self or the 'other'), Gandhi shows us an alternative way of social transformation through self-control and self-realization-in-being. The Gandhian approach is shown to oppose the scientism and technicism of both the liberal-utilitarian and Marxist-Leninist models of modernization, development and 'progress.' Gandhi, Nandy writes, 'always pushed social analysis to the level of personal life-style'; he did not want the historicist doctrine to be used as a substitute for one's political responsibility or political morality. He ruptured the private–public, means–ends dichotomies of the modernist theory of ethics and politics, and experimented with a novel moral-political mode of human action.

In Nandy's view, Gandhi's *satyagrahic/swarajist* conception of the self is a corrective to liberal-utilitarian individualism; the former, unlike the latter, overcomes the modernist dichotomy between the individual and the social. *Satyagraha*, however, should not be interpreted, notes Nandy, as amounting to any denial of individuality or democracy. On the contrary, it affirms individual conscience, dissent, negotiation, self-criticism and self-correction.

Nandy also argues that Gandhian trusteeship and *sarvodaya*, far from denying equality, espouses or promotes a non-violent, non-contractarian, non-hegemonizing equality of care and love and nurture. A particularly noteworthy feature of Gandhi's conception of emancipatory or transformative politics is shown to be its caring concern for the common humanity of both the oppressed and the oppressor. Moreover, according to Nandy, Gandhi's unconventional ideas on age, sex and history serve to deconstruct the modernist or imperializing/colonizing conceptions of time, adulthood and masculinity. Similarly, his advocacy of *khadi* or *charkha* is interpreted not as an anti-technological step but as an anti-technocratic move to reassert what is uniquely human to us, namely, our moral agency/responsibility.

In an article, entitled 'Thinking with Mahatma Gandhi: Beyond Liberal Democracy,' I have argued that Gandhi's *swarajist* critique of 'modern civilization' and his *satyagraha* way of transformative action have a post-liberal or trans-liberal character (Pantham, 1983). Gandhi seems to me to be responding to, and resolving, a basic contradiction in the public/private dichotomy of the liberal-utilitarian paradigm of modernity, namely, a contradiction between the affirmation of the natural freedoms and rights of the individual in the *private* sphere of morality on the one hand and, on the other, the curtailment of such freedoms and rights in the *public* or *political* sphere, which is supposed to be an amorally procedural or technical sphere, to be managed by experts and leaders, who would 'represent' the *political/public* (but not the *private or moral*) selves of the ordinary citizens.

Gandhi repairs/resolves this contradiction through a two-fold process of moral-political action for *sarvodaya* through parliamentary *swaraj* and *satyagraha*, viz.: (*a*) the *swarajist* struggle by the 'masses' for reclaiming their political selves or freedoms from the objectified, amoral state (this has been wrongly interpreted by some scholars as an assertion of Indian anarchism); and (*b*) the *satyagraha* way of extending the principles of morality or *ahimsa* from the private or personal level of human life to the public or political level.

Gandhi's *swarajist* project of redeeming the political freedoms of the people from the objectified amoral state should not be interpreted to mean that he is unconcerned with the problem of social order. I have tried to show that compared to the liberal-democratic theorists, Gandhi shows a greater concern for both individual freedom and social harmony, with the latter concern governing his conception of the interrelationship between politics and morality or ethics. On this, I have suggested that Gandhi has effected an inversion of the Hobbes-to-Lenin approach to political thinking and action: Gandhi has challenged their political paradigms based on the assumption that human persons are irreducibly brutish and 'atomistic' and that therefore their interests are to be taken by the political 'machinery' or 'system' as being morally neutral. Gandhian *satyagraha*, as I have tried to show, is based on the counter-assumptions that not all our interests are of equal moral worth and that we, *as isolated individuals*, are not the sufficient judges of the truth or moral worth of our interests, if they are to be embodied in socially binding norms; their truth or moral worth has to be tested or experimented with in *satyagraha*, which, I have suggested, has some interesting similarities *and* differences with Habermas's discourse ethics (Pantham, 1983: 176–78; and 1986a: 200–4).

Civil liberties and democratic rights are of central importance to Gandhi's conception of, and programme of action for, *swaraj* or decolonization. He writes: 'Civil liberty consistent with the observance of non-violence is the first step towards *swaraj*. It is the foundation of freedom.'

In this context, I feel that it is a failure to appreciate the central role of civil liberties and democratic rights in the Gandhian programme that has led Partha Chatterjee to conclude that Gandhism is a traditional, peasant-communal moralism or ideology that lay entirely outside the thematic of post-Enlightenment thought. Chatterjee's claim that Gandhi's moral critique of civil society did not 'emerge out of a consideration of the historical contradictions of civil society as perceived from within it' does not seem to me to be quite correct. Gandhi's *swarajist* intervention took place when 'the historical contradictions of civil society' were already becoming world-systemic. The *swarajist* struggle which he led was that of the victims of capitalist imperialist modernity, who cannot be said to have been located 'entirely outside' the world-systemic historical contradictions of post-Enlightenment modernity. And Gandhi's moral-political thought, which justified their *swarajist* or decolonising struggle was obtained partly by *inverting* the imperializing, binary logic of modernist thought and partly by adapting ideas and values drawn both from India's non-modern cultural traditions and from liberal-democratic modernity. The moral-political thought which he so constructed seems to me to have gone *beyond* the conventional 'isms' of political action. Gandhi himself claimed that he subscribed to no ism and that a new political vocabulary (*swaraj, sarvodaya, satyagraha, satya, ahimsa*, etc.) is required to express the meaning of the political struggle or *experiments* he was undertaking for *swaraj* or post-coloniality.

Gandhi, moreover, seems to me to have not only inverted some of the binary oppositions of Western modernist thought but also experimented with a mode of political action (i.e., *satyagraha*) based, in part, on a non-binary framework of ideas about the self and the other and, in part, on a post-relativist conception of truth. Far from regressing to any primitivist or organicist conception of the person, Gandhi experimented with a *post-liberal* or trans-liberal concept of the person or self, namely, a self not only of civil/political/economic liberties but also of *dharmic or satya-agrahic* qualities or potentialities. Gandhi also referred to the latter as the soul-force or love-force of the *satyagrahi*, namely, one who pursues truth through *ahimsa* (non-violence *and* love). The experimental subjectivity of the *satya-agrahi* seems to me to be going beyond the dichotomously essentialized subjectivities of the self *versus* the other, which are celebrated in Western post-Enlightenment thought.

It is because they are expected to act as trans-liberal persons that the Gandhian *satyagrahis* seek to realize their *swaraj*, not by inflicting annihilatory violence on their oppressors, but by aiding them too to realize their *swaraj*. This 'politics of *ahimsa*,' as I have tried to argue, rests on a *post-relativist* conception of truth, as contrasted with both the ethnocentric Reason of positivist/imperialist modernity and the historicist relativism of romanticism, traditionalism or nativism (Pantham, 1988, 1989 and 1991a). I would think that this is what Gandhi expresses in the following words:

> Whilst, with the limits that Nature has put on our understanding, we must act fearlessly according to the light vouchsafed to us, we must always keep an open mind and be ever ready to find that what we believed to be truth was, after all, untruth. This openness of mind strengthens the truth in us.

Fred Dallmayr interprets Gandhi as a marginalist *par excellence*, by which he means that Gandhian thought belongs to the border zone between Western and non-Western thought, between *polis* and cosmopolis, between modernity and post-modernity. Gandhi, writes Dallmayr, 'preferred to inhabit the margins of entrenched culture, seeking to energize their lacunae and untapped possibilities.' Dallmayr sees Gandhi as recovering the living core of Hindu tradition from beneath empty rituals and speculative doctrines and the *hidden* spiritual and humanist strands of Western thought from beneath its 'fascination with mastery and domination' (Dallmayr, 1989).

Some Gandhian Ideas on Economic Change

The studies surveyed thus far focus on aspects of Gandhi's transformative thought and action which emphasize the extension of
morality/spirituality from the private/personal sphere to the public/
political sphere. I shall now turn to some studies of the Gandhian
approach to economic change, which emphasize the extension of
the ethics of *ahimsa* (non-injury and love) into the economic
sphere from/through the political sphere.

In these studies, Gandhi is interpreted as providing an alternative
to utilitarianism and 'scientific socialism' by rupturing the dichotomy between economics and ethics. Some of these studies give
strong endorsement of Gandhi's views contained in the following
statements:

> If *dharma* and economic interest cannot be reconciled, either
> the conception of that *dharma* is false or the economic interest
> takes the form of unmitigated selfishness, and does not aim at
> collective welfare. True *dharma* always promotes legitimate
> economic pursuits. For imperfect man, this is a fine test of
> whether what 'purports to be *dharma* is true *dharma*.

> That economics is untrue which ignores or disregards moral
> values. The extension of the law of non-violence in the domain
> of economics means nothing less than the introduction of moral
> values as a factor.

J.D. Sethi, a former professor of economics at Delhi University
and member of India's Planning Commission, has interpreted
Gandhi as having *reconstructed* the positivist science of economics.
He sees Gandhian trusteeship as a non-violent and non-exploitative
alternative to capitalism, communism and the mixed economy.
Unlike these, trusteeship, Sethi writes, is based on the 'ethico-
economic principles' of non-possession, non-exploitation, bread
labour and equality of rewards (1986a: 92). In his view, trusteeship
is 'the hallmark' of the Gandhian approach to economic change
and 'the only non-violent path through which economic transformation should take place' (1978: 141–42). Sethi also criticizes those
who, in the name of Gandhi, falsify the problems of India's industrialization. Gandhi, Sethi argues, was not against industrialization

as such, but was against 'the spirit of Western industrialization which induced a dangerous acquisitive lust and also became an instrument of imperialism' (1985: 220).

Some of Gandhi's ideas on small-scale and labour-intensive industries have been used by Charan Singh (1978) to put forward what he claims is a Gandhian alternative to the Nehruvian model of development. In his view, no capital-intensive project should be allowed 'to come up in future, when a labour-intensive alternative is available,' no large-scale enterprises should be set up if the goods it seeks to produce can be produced by small-scale industries, and no small-scale industries should be developed at the expense of cottage industries. The existing mills and factories which produce goods which can be produced on a small or cottage scale, he says, should be made to sell their products abroad and not within the country.

Charan Singh's alternative to the system of private monopolies and public sector enterprises has been criticized by some economists and political scientists. Babatosh Datta has noted that in Gandhi's time the dimensions of the problems were smaller than those of today and that Gandhi 'relied on a type of human motivation which is nowhere in sight' (1977: 113). Datta also finds a contradiction between Charan Singh's attack on private monopolies and his advocacy of trusteeship. According to Brahmananda, Charan Singh is torn by a deep contradiction between his agricultural fundamentalism and his advocacy of labour-intensive production of non-agricultural consumption goods (1978: 115). Charan Singh's model, Brahmananda suggests is a supplement to the Nehru–Mahalanobis model. Similarly, Mohanty has argued that the focus on decentralization and rural development dissociated from an overall strategy of social-structural changes will only strengthen the forces of agro-capitalism in the countryside (1979: 52).

V.M. Dandekar of the Gokhale Institute of Politics and Economics has argued that the Gandhian economic system is not of relevance to the Indian people. In his view, the Gandhian economy prefers village self-sufficiency to economic efficiency, and produces no surplus over its daily needs. This, says Dandekar, cannot solve the chronic poverty of the Indian peasant. In his view, this path can only lead to an alternative goal of human life and existence than the one which India has been and still is pursuing. The Gandhian economic goal, Dandekar concludes, is not acceptable or relevant to the common man (Dandekar, 1978).

Some writers, like Sethi, Das and Lutz, find Gandhi to be advancing an alternative economic order in supersession of capitalism and communism. The Western paradigm of capital-intensive, urban-based, dependent development, they find, is responsible for our structural unemployment, reduction of investible resources, ecological crisis and the reproduction of underdevelopment and poverty. This is especially so in a poor backward country, where there is a large number of unemployed people. If such a society uses its scarce investible funds exclusively or predominantly for capital-intensive technologies of production, there will be an increase in unemployment from year to year. Even if such a country were to launch a successful programme of population control, be it of the voluntary or forced variety, the problem of structural unemployment will continue to deepen until about 15 years after such a programme. According to Amritananda Das, the Gandhian way to break out of this structural unemployment and poverty is by increasing the share of labour-intensive activities in the investment mix. This is not to suggest that there should be no investment in the modern, capital-intensive sector. What the Gandhian approach demands is not the total neglect of socially useful capital-intensive activities but the making of those activities complementary to or supportive of labour-intensive activities (Das, 1979).

Detlef Kantowsky, a German sociologist, notes that the Western materialist paradigm of development, which seeks to bring about economic growth through capital-intensive technology, individual competition and/or centralized planning, has reached a point of self-destruction. He sees Gandhian *sarvodaya*, which embodies 'an altruistic ethic for self-realization', as constituting a first step in an alternative direction. Its value system, he notes, differs fundamentally from modernist thinking; while *sarvodaya* seeks a maximum necessary for the well-being of all, the modernist technocrats are concerned with providing 'the minimum energy input required (by those below the poverty line) to keep individual labour intact and craving for material acquisitions growing' (Kantowsky, 1980: 180).

In a significant theoretical article on Gandhian economics, Mark Lutz, Professor of Economics at the University of Maine, presents it as a political economy of *ahimsa* (social affection), the validity of which he finds to be comparable to, and in considerable measure derived from, that of John Ruskin's legitimate assault on the utilitarian political economy of Jeremy Bentham and J.S Mill.

According to Ruskin, the Bentham–Mill tradition of constructing a deductive science of economics from the abstract axioms of self-interest and utility (abstracting from love or social affections) was a one-dimensional reduction of a multidimensional human activity. In his view, the notion of a purely rational economic man without any social affection is an untenable abstraction. Hence social affections too must be included in any meaningful or comprehensive theory of economics.

Inspired by Ruskin, Gandhi, says Lutz, reconstructed the science of economics by reintegrating it with *ahimsa* (non-violence and love or social affection). Lutz points out that Gandhian economics takes into account 'the total person with body, mind, and heart rather than the fragmented abstraction: insensitive economic man' (Lutz, 1983: 951). Finding utilitarian economics to be 'a heartless doctrine' that has done great harm to humanity, Gandhi redefined the science of economics as the science of *sarvodaya* (the welfare of all).

After highlighting the place of *satya* and *ahimsa* in Gandhi's philosophy of life and the premises of his socio-economic thought, Lutz singles out the following principles of Gandhian economics, which he finds to be of relevance for an alternative to classical and neoclassical political economy:

1. Non-violent Ownership   – Trusteeship
2. Non-violent Production   – Appropriate Technology
3. Non-violent Consumption   – Non-possession
4. Non-violent Work   – Bread Labour
5. Non-violent Allocation   – Cooperation
6. Non-violent Distribution – Equality
7. Non-violence in Reforming Economic Systems (Lutz, 1983: 41–43).

Like Lutz, Ramashray Roy too brings out the significance of Gandhi's Ruskin-inspired 'humanization' of economics by integrating it with moral values. Roy points out that the partitioning of life-activities into autotelic water-tight compartments, each governed by its own laws or principles, militates against Gandhi's philosophy of human self-realization or truth-realization through *ahimsa*. Since, according to Gandhi, *satya* and *ahimsa* govern 'the whole gamut of man's activities', any science of economics, which abstracts it from them, would be a reduction of life to a 'maze of sound and fury signifying nothing'. Gandhi therefore rightly maintained that 'true economics' and 'true ethics' or 'true *dharma*' must go together. Roy endorses this conception of the desired economic order, which, he notes, is based on such principles and values as minimization of wants, bread labour, equality, decentralization and co-operativisation (Roy, 1985: 129–41).

As a concluding note to this chapter, it may be observed that the Gandhian approach, which differs from the liberal and Marxian approaches, also differs from that of Hindu nationalism, to which I turn in the next chapter.

5

The Ideology of Hindu Nationalism

Introductory Remarks

'**Among the visible** strands in the political ideology of contemporary India,' writes Romila Thapar, 'is the growth and acceptance of what are called communal ideologies' (1989: 209). And among them, the Hindu communal ideology is, in her view, of major importance as 'it involves the largest numbers and asserts itself as the dominant group.' Similarly, in his book on the construction of communalism in colonial North India, Gyanendra Pandey notes that we today face 'an increasingly strident demand for recognition of what is called the essentially Hindu character of India, Indian civilization and Indian nationalism' (1990: 259–60). According to Gail Omvedt, 'the ideology of identifying *India as Hindu and Hinduism as nationalism* has gained increasing weight and power—at the cultural, social and political levels' (1990: 724). In the opinion of Dileep Padgaonkar (1990), the advocacy of *Hindutva* by L.K. Advani, the BJP president, has 'altered the terms of political discourse and perhaps also laid the ground for the creation of India's second republic.'

The votaries of *Hindutva* see the past, present and future of India differently from those of liberal, Marxian and Gandhian persuasions, even though the BJP claimed from 1980 to 1985 that 'Gandhian Socialism' constituted its official statement of policy.

In what follows, I shall survey some of the literature of the political and social sciences as well as some commentaries by journalists on the nature of the *Hindutva* ideology and on how it differs from the liberal-secular, socialist and Gandhian approaches to social reconstruction.[1]

Hindutva

In the literature on religious communalism in Indian politics, we can see a major distinction being made between what may be called the *communitarian* politics of the pre-1920 period and the *communal* politics of the post-1920 years. Bipan Chandra refers to the former as 'liberal' communalism and the latter as 'fascist or extreme' communalism, while Gyanendra Pandey refers to them as 'community-based nationalism' and 'citizen-based nationalism,' respectively.

Until the 1920s, Hindu religious revivalism took the form of 'liberal communalism' or 'affirmative Orientalism' which, in opposition to the 'pejorative Orientalism' and 'civilizing mission' of the imperialists, *imagined* a future independent India in terms of Indian cultural values. It was 'liberal' in the sense that it was opposed to imperialism, and *not* to the non-Hindu minority communities living in India (cf. Bipan Chandra, 1987: 323–30; and Richard Fox, 1989: 126).

Thus, in 1909, in his important book, *The First Indian War of Independence: 1857*, V.D. Savarkar wrote: 'our idea of *swadharma* is not contradictory to that of *swaraj*.' By this he meant that the *swadharma* of both the Hindus and the Muslims was compatible with their collective or common, national *swaraj*. 'The sepoys,' he

[1] In this chapter, I have surveyed only those writings which help to explain how the ideology of Hindu nationalism compares with, or differs from, the liberal, Marxist and Gandhian models of social transformation. Obviously, for a historical and politico-sociological understanding of the ideology and politics of Hindu nationalism it would be necessary to analyse them in their interrelationship to the ideology and politics of minority communalisms, especially Muslim communalism, and of the 'social movements' of the 'backward classes' and the *avarna Hindus/dalits*. This would of course be done in other surveys being undertaken under the sponsorship of ICSSR. However, on the ideology of Muslim communalism, see, among others, Smith (1963), Shakir (1986), Engineer and Shakir (1985), Engineer (1989), Bjorkman (1988), M. Hasan (1988 and 1991) and Z. Hasan (1989). Some of the works on the ideologies of the social movements of the backward classes and the *dalits* are: Shah (1990), Doctor (1991), Vora (1986), Zelliott (1986), Punalekar (1988), O'Hanlon (1985), Omvedt (1971), Kavalekar and Chausalkar (1989), Chandramohan (1987) and Malik (1977).

went on to state, 'would take the water of the Ganges or would swear by the Koran that they would live only to achieve the destruction of the English rule.'

During the nineteenth and early twentieth centuries, the Indian nation was thought of as a *composite* body of several communities; Hindu + Muslim + Christian + Parsi + Sikh, and so on. This community-based or, in other words, communitarian conception of Indian nationalism reflected the *limits* of the relevance of liberalism to the Indian society of that period; at that time, service to Community was not seen to be opposed to service to Country (Pandey, 1990: 210–11).

During the early 1920s, the community-based conception of nationalism was increasingly challenged by a new, individual- or citizen-based conception of nationalism, with the liberal-secular nationalists insisting that religious identities and attachments had to be confined to the *private* sphere and kept *separated* from the public, political sphere. However, the entry of the masses into the Indian national movement, the politics of the Non-cooperation and Khilafat Movements and the politics of electoral numbers accentuated the tension between secular nationalism and communal politics. Pandey lists the religious reform movements, the administrative demands of the colonial government and the pressure of census operations and 'representative' politics as factors that made the elite groups among the Hindus, Muslims, Sikhs, etc., to appropriate or incorporate their marginalized sections and to purify and strengthen their own religious communities in an aggressive, exclusivist or separatist manner (Pandey, 1990: 204, 233 and 239. Cf. also Raghavan, 1983).

Tapan Basu et al. (1993: 10–11) interpret the ideology and politics of *Hindutva* as an effort of the upper castes to regain their hegemony, which was slipping out of their hands in the wake, for instance, of the anti-Brahmin movements of the backward castes and the *dalits* led by Jyotiba Phule and B.R. Ambedkar. It is pointed out that in Maharashtra, which played a central role in the formation of the ideology and politics of *Hindutva*, the Muslims were in a rather insignificant minority.

The ideological articulations of the extreme form of Hindu nationalism have been given by V.D. Savarkar, K.B. Hedgewar, M.S. Golwalkar and Deendayal Upadhyaya. Their ideologies find organizational expression in the Hindu Mahasabha, the Rashtriya

Swayamsevak Sangh (RSS), the Vishwa Hindu Parishad (VHP), and the Bharatiya Janata Party (BJP). According to one of its leaders, the BJP is the 'political' wing, while the VHP and RSS are the 'social' and 'organizational' wings, respectively (cf. Basu et al., 1993: 47–48).

In his celebrated book, *Hindutva or Who is a Hindu* (1923), V.D. Savarkar wrote that 'Hinduism is only a derivative, a fraction, a part of *Hindutva*,' which, he pointed out, was broader than a religious or theocratic notion. According to him, *Hindutva* or the essence of being a Hindu is determined by 'the tie we bear to our common fatherland, and by the common blood that coursed through our veins and also by the tie of a common homage we pay to our great civilization or Hindu culture' (p. 74). *Hindutva*, so defined, was meant 'to draw the line of distinction and mark well the position it occupied so as to make it clear to themselves where exactly they stood and how they were unmistakably a people by themselves' (p. 23). *Hindutva* stood for the totality of the Hindu individual's racial, geographical and cultural (including religious) identities and it was meant to unite all sections and all 'sister communities' of the 'Hindu civilization' (i.e., Buddhists, Jains, etc.) and to mark them off 'as a people by themselves.' *Hindutva*, in other words, is what makes a person accept Hindusthan or 'the land of the Hindus' not only as the *Pitrbhu* or fatherland but also as the *Punyabhu* or holyland. According to Savarkar, the Hindu converts to Islam and Christianity do not share *Hindutva* because their 'holyland is far off in Arabia or Palestine.' They can however regain *Hindutva* by recognizing Hindusthan 'both as their father-land and their holyland.'

In *We, or our Nationhood Defined* (1939), M.S. Golwalkar wrote:

> The non-Hindu peoples in Hindustan must either adopt the Hindu culture and language, must learn to respect and hold in reverence Hindu religion, must entertain no idea but those of glorification of the Hindu race and culture . . . in a word they must cease to be foreigners, or may stay in the country, wholly subordinated to the Hindu nation, claiming nothing, deserving no privileges, far less any preferential treatment—not even citizen's rights.

The votaries of *Hindutva* believe that Indian culture is safe in the custody of Hindus alone and that non-Hindu Indians, *qua* non-Hindus, have not and cannot make any contribution to it. Golwalkar maintains that each nation has a 'unique national genius,' while Deendayal Upadhyaya speaks of a nation's *chiti* or essence (Golwalkar, 1966: 1–10; Upadhyaya et al., 1979: 34ff. Cf. also Bipan Chandra 1987: 217–18). They identify two cultural essentials in the Hindu tradition, viz.: (*a*) a deep spirituality in contrast to the crude materialism and consumerism of the West; and (*b*) an organic conception of society in contrast to an individualistic conception. In the light of these postulated essentials of Hindu culture, both individualistic liberalism and the materialistic, class-war-oriented socialism of the West become suspect in the eyes of the votaries of *Hindutva*. They however favour a hard, militarized modern state, large-scale industrialization, the development of science and technology and the manufacture of modern weapons and bombs.

The Hindu nationalists maintain that the weakness of the Indian nation is due, in considerable measure, to the failure of the non-Hindu Indians to recognize their *Hindutva* and the resultant yielding, by the state, to their political demands at the expense of the just demands of the majority community. Accordingly, the votaries of Hindu nationalism favour such policies as: (*a*) stopping or curtailing the policy of reservations for the Scheduled Castes and Tribes and for the Other Backward Classes; (*b*) restricting the state's welfare programmes; (*c*) a programme of decentralization and voluntary agencies to replace Russian-style socialism; (*d*) the reclamation of the Hindu temples which the Muslim rulers had captured and made over into mosques; (*e*) the prevention of conversions of untouchables, tribals, etc., into non-Hindu religions; and (*f*) legislation of a common civil code for all Indians (cf. Fox, 1989: 242–45).

The Integral Humanism of Deendayal Upadhyaya

In January 1965, the working committee on the Jana Sangh Party adopted Integral Humanism as its official statement of fundamental principles. These were formulated by Deendayal Upadhyaya, a lifelong RSS *pracharak*, who was then the party's General Secretary and who later became its President. According to him, the Western political ideologies of liberalism and socialism are based on partial, atomistic conceptions of the human person and hence they promote materialism, individualism, or economism, all of which can only lead to exploitative competition, class war and social anarchy. He blamed India's leadership for its proneness 'to ignore the nation's real "self" and to adopt recklessly foreign patterns.' He noted that while Western thought emphasizes the inevitable *conflict* between the individual and society, the Indian philosophical tradition of *Advaita Vedanta* emphasizes the *social nature* of the individuals. In his view, therefore, India needs a model of development based on cooperation and interdependence. In place of foreign ideologies, he proposed an *integral-humanist* approach to the 'realization of National Self' by catering to the needs of the body, mind, intelligence, soul and emotions. According to him, an *integral* conception of the human person recognizes not only the needs of the body, mind and soul but also the requirements of *social harmony* or, in other words, the imperatives of the 'social nature' of the human person.

Deendayal Upadhyaya also endorsed the Gandhian type of non-violent popular agitations. He attacked those who favoured the crushing of all popular movements, in which they saw nothing but the hidden hand of the communists. He urged his partymen to actively participate in popular movements which he said are 'the medium of expression of social awakening.' He stated: 'Those who are keen to preserve the status quo in economic and social spheres feel threatened by these movements and are wont to create an atmosphere of pessimism. We are sorry we cannot co-operate with them' (cf. Andersen and Damle, 1987: 174). Somewhat like Gandhi, Upadhyaya also favoured small-scale industries, cooperative ownership of large firms, decentralization, uplift of women, removal of untouchability, abolition of dowry, etc. He also called for a narrowing of the gap between the rich and the poor by keeping a ratio of no more than 20: 1 between the highest and lowest incomes.

Some commentators have argued that Upadhyaya's integral-humanist approach and programme marked a 'populist,' 'revolutionary' turn within the ideological current of Hindu nationalism and that it facilitated the ideological appropriation of 'Gandhian Socialism' by the BJP in 1980 (Fox, 1989; Andersen and Damle, 1987).

The Spiritual Humanism of V.P. Varma

In 1978, in the Deendayal Upadhyaya Memorial Lecture which he delivered in New Delhi, Professor V.P. Varma of Patna University propounded a manifesto for the political, administrative, social and economic reconstruction of India on the basis of his political philosophy of spiritual humanism, which he presented as an elaboration of Upadhyaya's concept of 'integral humanism.' Those lectures have been elaborated into a book: *Philosophical Humanism and Contemporary India (1979)*.

In this book as well as in some of his earlier writings, Varma has been arguing that India's political institutions should be based on an idealistic-philosophical-humanist conception of man, i.e., a conception of man as a 'moral and spiritual subject.' In his view, such a model of man is contained in the 'perennial stream of Indian culture.'

According to Varma, spiritual humanism is a philosophy of 'realistic absolutism,' which considers the phenomenal universe as 'real' in the sense that it constitutes 'an organic component of the Absolute.' 'The philosophy of idealistic humanism,' writes Varma, 'accepts the possibility of the development of the powers of man to know at least partly the Absolute Real' (1979: 16). He writes:

> Idealistic humanism starts with the notion of a spiritual Existent, or an absolute indeterminate-determinate substantial subject. Existence is common to the different existing particulars. The existence within space and time implies a spaceless and timeless *Being* because there can be no specific terminal point beyond which it can be stated that there is nothing. The vast eternal Reality is the great foundational concrete universal but without any internal differences (Varma, 1979: 13).

Spiritual humanism, we are reminded, adheres to the Vedic/ Vedantic idea of 'divine humanity', according to which the *atman* cannot be reduced ultimately to the qualitatively differentiated notion of matter or energy. The 'spiritual Absolute' is immanent in 'man'. 'Man is significant but he derives his significance from being part of God or an appearance of the infinite spiritual Consciousness or as a mode of the transcendent-cosmic Reality' (Varma, 1979: 189).

Varma maintains that the 'cultural continuity' of the Vedic-Buddhistic tradition is the fundamental basis of the organic unity of the Indian nation and that the aim of his political philosophy of integral-spiritual humanism is to secure 'loyalty to the organic nation which is the vehicle for the preservation of the cultural heritage.' In his view, the spiritual-humanist view of man calls for a political order that can enable all its members to realize themselves. It cannot be used to legitimize the pursuit of egoistic, parochial or sectarian interests; it cannot sanction exploitation of the weaker sections of the society; it will not call for the 'violent liquidation of the expropriators'; it will not overemphasize the 'maximization of appetitive satisfaction'; it will pursue the method of 'uncoerced consensualism'; it will favour judicial review and the decentralization of power. It will also, among other things, regard Kashmir as an 'integral organic part' of India as it 'has been the land of some of the prime exponents of Indian cultural values.'

Varma maintains that philosophical humanism is a vital alternative for India and, 'to a certain extent,' for the rest of the world, both to the 'West-European-American tradition of liberal, constitutional, polyarchical representative democracy with its stress on individual freedom' and to the 'East-European-Soviet philosophy of dialectical and historical materialism' with its 'gospel' of atheism and violence. This political philosophy of spiritual humanism, he claims, can serve to liberalise both capitalism and communism. He writes:

A philosophy of freedom for man as a moral and spiritual subject can alone be the antidote to the excesses of nationalistic chauvinism, ethnocentric imperialism, totalitarian materialism and the fascist cult of racialism, controlled economy and power politics. (p. 197)

Varma distinguishes his political philosophy of idealist or spiritual humanism from the 'materialistic new humanism' of M.N. Roy and the 'agnostic humanism' of Jawaharlal Nehru. Both of them, Varma says, were uprooted or alienated from India's cultural heritage, especially from the Vedic and Vedantic tradition, which upholds 'the supremacy of a primordial archetypal spiritual Reality which is simultaneously transcendent, cosmic and individual.' According to him, this indigenous tradition or cultural heritage is the source of the vitally relevant political thought of Vivekananda, Dayananda Saraswati, Tagore, Tilak, Aurobindo, Gandhi and Deendayal Upadhyaya. They are said to 'sponsor humanism because they consider the human body and the embodied human self as manifesting an immanent trans-mechanical teleology' or a 'super-temporal being.'

Inspired by Deendayal Upadhyaya's attempt to 'reincorporate the spiritual *elan* of the old Hindu culture into the fabric of contemporary civilization,' Varma reads the tradition of Upanishadic Vedantism, the Bhagavad Gita and Buddhism as yielding a 'positivistic and world-affirming gospel.' This is claimed to be constituting one of the sources of philosophical humanism. Its two other sources being modern, Western science and the poetic spirit of the romantics.

He claims that the spiritual or moral humanism he propounds is a 'scientific' and 'realist' position; *satya/dharma and science* are said to enter into its definition. He writes:

> . . . a humanism deriving sustenance from the spiritual and moral traditions of the sanctity of Satya as formulated in Indian culture and corroborated by the conclusions of contemporary natural and behavioural sciences can provide an alternative to bourgeois capitalism and coercive communist totalitarianism. (pp. 197–98)

He presents philosophical humanism as an alternative to 'communist totalitarianism' and says that the 'ontological absolutism' of the former does entail an 'ethical absolutism,' which he defends against the relativism of the 'exponents of poly-culturalism.' He maintains that there are some ethical prescriptions (liberty, equality, justice, etc.) which are absolute and relevant to all mankind. He notes that a philosophical humanist would not like that communist teachers be permitted to teach their students lessons which would weaken nationalism or glorify anti-democratic methods.

In his view, although non-violence is a 'profound goal' for humanity, there can neither be any total abjuring of violence nor any unilateral disarmament at the present time. Philosophical humanism, he states, is not a philosophy of 'Unadulterated Ahimsa,' but a realist political theory. He maintains that given the stockpiles of bombs and intercontinental ballistic missiles that could be used against India, 'for safe-guarding the precious heritage of the civilization and culture of this land, it is essential in self-defence to manufacture atom, hydrogen and neutron bombs.'

Turning to the economic sphere, Varma calls for a 'revised Gandhism,' which would recognise the role of heavy industries, centralized planning, an interventionist state, a mixed economy, a two-party system, a tolerance of limited violence by the exploited classes, etc.

Varma's thesis of philosophical humanism seems to me to be deeply contradictory. He claims on the one hand that philosophical humanism is an antidote to 'ethnocentric imperialism' and 'totalitarian materialism' and on the other hand he affirms that philosophical humanism upholds an 'ethical absolutism', which is based on a foundational, realist ontology of the unified and organic Absolute Reality. According to him, a philosophical humanist would want to 'universalize the foundational ethical and spiritual principles of Indian culture for the redemption of humanity'. He also characterizes the cultural tradition of Upanishadic Vedantism, the Bhagavad Gita and Buddhism as 'positivistic and world-affirming' and that it is oriented, not to iconoclastic rejection, but to the 'absorption of vital, sociological, aesthetic and ethical symbols in a spiritual frame of universal reference' or 'global universalism.' He does not clarify why the 'ethical absolutism' and 'global universalism' of his constructed model of the perennial stream of Indian cultural tradition is preferable to the 'ethnocentric imperialism' of 'totalitarian materialism' of the West.

A second major problem with Varma's political philosophy is that while he does grant that there are different strands or 'sections' within the Indian cultural tradition, he does not give reasons for his choice of one of those strands or 'sections,' namely, what he calls the 'positivistic and world-affirming' strand. We are also not told if the Indian tradition of positivism and world affirmation differs from similar traditions in the West and, if it does, why the former is preferable to the latter.

The BJP's Appropriation of 'Gandhian Socialism'

The RSS, the Vidyarthi Parishad and the Bharatiya Jana Sangh were active participants in the 1974–75 mass protest movement in Bihar which was led by Jayaprakash Narayan (JP). In the general elections held immediately after the 1975–77 Emergency, the Janata coalition consisting of the Hindu nationalist, centrist and social democratic parties adopted a manifesto which, by and large, contained a statement of JP's Gandhian vision. It promised decentralization, subsidy for cottage industries, promotion of rural development, honesty and simplicity of public servants, equality of opportunity, etc. Soon these came to be called a programme of 'Gandhian Socialism.'

When the Hindu nationalists withdrew from the Janata party and formed the BJP in 1980, the new party claimed itself to be heir to the legacies of JP and Deendayal Upadhyaya. It adopted 'Gandhian Socialism' as its basic philosophy and gave an honoured place in it to Upadhyaya's 'integral humanism.' Atal Behari Vajpayee, the party's first president, said that its Gandhism was socialist because it would regard 'the poor man to be the centre of all economic activity.' According to him, moreover, its socialism was Gandhian, and not Marxian, because it rejected materialism, violence and centralization.

According to the RSS weekly, *Organizer* (25 October 1981), 'Gandhian Socialism' means 'socialism with a human face and a moral tone,' and not communism or the governmentalization of industry. Concerning the belief of many people that Gandhi appeased the Muslim community, the *Organizer* article clarified that he had faced an 'intractable problem' and that he tried to solve it peacefully and honourably by being 'soft as a flower' at times and at other times 'hard as a diamond' towards the Muslims. The *Organizer* article also claimed that the RSS/BJP and Gandhi were 'closer in their basic thinking than is often realized'; both of them, it was claimed, stood for Hindu Rashtra, the difference in their idioms being due only to the fact that 'Gandhiji was dealing with political affairs and RSS was dealing with socio-cultural matters.' Even so, we are reminded, 'the whole content of Gandhian thought was Hindu.'

The adoption of 'Gandhian Socialism' as the BJP's basic philosophy did not go unchallenged from within the party. In fact, a faction opposed it vehemently and, in 1985, 'integral humanism' replaced 'Gandhian Socialism' as the party's statement of basic philosophy.

The adoption and subsequent abandonment of 'Gandhian Socialism' by the BJP have been commented upon, among others, by Richard Fox. According to him, its adoption by the BJP in 1980 marked an ideological reduction and appropriation of Gandhi's transformative utopia, which was thereby made to subserve the ideology of Hindu nationalism. Fox goes on to note that by the mid-1980s, the Congress too came to make 'Hindu appeals' to the electorate in north India. Consequently, the BJP realized that it was no longer the sole representative of Hindu nationalism. Hence it decided in 1985 to abandon 'Gandhian Socialism,' which had been causing some embarrassment to it and which, it felt, was no longer needed as a special means of legitimation (Fox, 1989: 234 and 259; Andersen and Damle, 1987: 236).

Some Arguments for and against *Hindutva*

Some recent arguments in support of the *Hindutva* ideology have come from, among others, Swapan Dasgupta (1991) and Gopal Krishna (1991). The latter sees some virtues in semitic religions, viz., religious seriousness, a healthy self-regard and a spirit of religious fellowship. These, he says, can help Hinduism to overcome its weaknesses and vices. A semitized Hinduism, he suggests, would be better placed to fight its 'just wars.'

Swapan Dasgupta too defends the semitization of Hinduism. Rejecting the view of colonial and Marxist historians that India had been a mere notional aggregation of separate nationalities, he states that 'there are adequate grounds for insisting that India was a civilizational entity tied together by a common ritual language (Sanskrit), a pan-Indian Brahminical elite and a common adherence to what can loosely be described as the *Sanatan Dharma*.' He however grants that India had lacked a 'systematic commitment to a nation-state' and that therefore, with the steady advance of Islam, India suffered 'physical contractions'—first with Afghanistan (which had Shaivite kingdoms) going out of the orbit of Indian civilization during the tenth century and second with the 1947 Partition. At the present time, the Punjab and Kashmir problems, says Dasgupta, present threats of further vivisection. In his view, therefore, a political agenda is now needed that can preserve India both as a civilization and as a nation-state. In this, he regards as relevant Savarkar's (agnostic) *political* concept of *Hindutva*, which he deliberately distinguished from the purely religious or spiritual dimension of Hinduism.

Dasgupta (1990) also maintains that since the numerically preponderant community will be 'an effective watchdog of national unity and integrity,' Mr. Advani's recent movement for *Hindu Rashtra* provides 'a post-partition view of Indian nationalism that challenges all forms of separatism—cultural, ethnic and religious.'

The ideology of *Hindutva* has been criticized by Marxist, liberal-secular and Gandhian commentators. Some of their works are surveyed here.

According to Bipan Chandra (1987: 348–50) and Sumanta Banerjee (1991: 97), the proponents of the extreme version of Hindu nationalism define Hindu culture and nationhood in such a way as to preclude their rational, logical or historical assessment. The former finds them to be relying on the language of war and enemy, appeals to irrational impulses and exaltation of virility and violence.

According to Christophe Jaffrelot (1993), Hindu communal nationalism is an ideology of 'strategic syncretism,' whereby the cultural values of the dominating or threatening 'other' (the Muslims and the British) are assimilated into or appropriated by Hinduism for the purpose of vindicating itself. Some of the values so appropriated are monotheism, individualism, egalitarianism and semitic solidarity. Jaffrelot concludes that the Hindu nationalist identity which is constructed through such a strategic syncretism turns out to be not very Hindu.

In a useful introduction to a good collection of essays on communalism in contemporary India, K.N. Panikkar points out that the recent trend of appropriating *cultural practices* for communal mobilization, viz., the equating of the right to worship as the right to culture, has pernicious implications. He notes that though culture and religion do intermingle during the evolution of any society, cultural practices go beyond the religious domain. He goes on to point out that the new form of communalism which, among other things, reduces cultural practices and traditions to religious worship, militates against the cultural, social and political *reconstructions* for which we waged our anti-colonial struggle. 'What is at stake,' writes, Panikkar,

is democracy, secularism, rule of law, nationalism and culture; in essence all that Indians fought for and held dear during the last two hundred years. The idea of democracy is being replaced by majoritarianism, the concept of secularism is interpreted in religious terms, the rule of law is subverted by public coercion,

Indian nationalism is equated with *Hindutva* and Indian culture is described as Hindu culture (1991: 15).

The assumption of the *Hindutva* ideologues that religion and culture coincide in a particular way for the Hindus is not a valid assumption because culture does cut across religious boundaries. This has been argued by Sarah Joseph (1993), who points out that by equating Hindu religion with Indian culture, the *Hindutva* theorists seek to forcibly include within the Hindu tradition those groups which would prefer to be left out, e.g. the tribal groups and the *dalits*.

Praful Bidwai (1991) argues that the doctrine of majoritarianism which the militant Hindu nationalists advocate, is not directed against the minority religious communities alone; it is equally directed against 'pluralism, multiplicity of theological conceptions, notions of sacredness, cultural traditions and rituals within Hinduism itself.' Bidwai goes on to note that the doctrine of majoritarianism is not only 'a retreat from the great Indian project' of multi-ethnic, multi-lingual, multi-religious living but also a perversion of democracy, which is based on a framework of *universal* rights and obligations, including those of the minorities and the dissenters.

In Randhir Singh's view, the ruling classes use the ideology and practice of communalism as a tool to dominate over the subordinate classes. According to him, the structural inequality and unevenness of capitalist 'underdevelopment,' with a massive feudal-colonial inheritance and deep religious divisions, has brought India to the 'deepest-ever crisis of legitimacy since independence.' Hence, the ruling classes, he notes, are increasingly turning to an authoritarian or even fascist model of nationalism and governance. In this, they see the functionality of the aggressive assertion of an identity based on religion. 'With the older bases of their power and hegemony weakening, they,' writes Singh, 'are increasingly turning to communalism in general and to Hindu communalism in particular, to win votes, fragment and divide the people and, above all, secure their continued political and ideological dominance over them' (1991: 114).

Following Marx, Singh points out that communalism has an irreducible basis in religion itself and that therefore the criticism of the former has to be extended to a criticism of the latter, which, in its turn, has to be made into a criticism of the society that makes religion and religious communalism necessary and possible. In his view, given the interconnection between communalism, under-developed capitalist economy and class domination, the struggle against communalism has to be understood and waged as part of an overall revolutionary struggle by the people 'against the ruling classes, against their economy, politics, ideology, culture, etc., a struggle *against* the present economic and social order and *for* socialism' (Singh, 1991: 123).

In an examination of the discourse of secularism in India, Sudipta Kaviraj writes that 'under the conditions of small-scale unencum-bered communities' of the bygone days, the discourse of religion produced 'nice, peaceable humanistic forms of religiosity,' whereas under the present-day conditions of bourgeois modernity, religious communities have been constructed for the politics of majorities, minorities, elections, concessions and reservations. This largely 'deethicalized religion,' he says, is a furious, terrifying religion, whose adherents can be 'in a sense very modern and very cynical people.' In his view, secularism requires that the people cease to be religious at least in the long run. He writes:

> To go beyond communalism . . . is to go beyond religious dis-course; for as long religiosity remains an active alphabet, but is used to interpret a different type of world from the one to which it was suited, there will always be the possibility of its suddenly breaking into a communal conjugation. To ask people to cease to be communal in the short run need not mean asking them to cease to be religious. But in the longer term it must (Kaviraj 1990: 206).

That the hidden agenda of *Hindutva* is directed against socialism, which is doctrinally more disturbing for *Hindutva* than the ideology of Islam, is argued by Tapan Basu et al. in their book, *Khaki Shorts and Saffron Flags: A Critique of the Hindu Right* (1993). According to them, the notions of *angangibhava* (organic theory of society), 'integral humanism,' etc., which are emphasized in the *Hindutva* ideology serve to occlude the theme of exploitation or oppression and to discredit the values of individual freedom, civil rights, democracy and the struggles (conflicts) by oppressed castes, classes, women, etc.

Concerning the contrasts between the Hindu-nationalist and Gandhian frameworks, I would suggest that the latter, unlike the former, has within it an important liberal component, which respects religious freedom, religious pluralism, the principle of minority rights and the composite character of Indian nationalism. Thus, Krishna Kumar (1991) writes that the Gandhian phase of India's freedom struggle brought about 'a fresh starting point in Indian history,' namely, a participatory process of dialogue and deliberation, in a spirit of tolerance, for shaping the future of the Indian people as a whole. In contrast, the Hindu revivalists maintain that India's future was shaped once and for all in some distant past. They however favour the revival of the past only at the 'symbolic level,' i.e., in the sphere of culture or religion, while at the 'material level,' they accept modern science, technology and technical organization. Such cultural revivalism, Kumar says, is a means of deluding the ordinary people into a sense of togetherness in what is actually a divisive, ideological project of imitative, colonial/neocolonial modernization.

According to Gail Omvedt (1990), Gandhi's vision of a reformed Hindu community which he, in opposition to Ambedkar, thought would keep the untouchables as part of the 'Hindufold,' has been appropriated by the Hindu communalists. She however recognizes that the 'liberal' Hinduism which Gandhi practised can resist being appropriated by/for militant Hindu nationalism and that it can serve as a secular force in India.

In Ravinder Kumar's view (1983), Gandhi was the first nationalist leader who understood the crucial importance of 'existential communities' to the lives of the Indian people and who built up an all-India movement on the basis of an alliance among the Hindu and non-Hindu communities. Gandhi's 'orthodox plural' model of secular nationalism (in contrast to both the 'liberal plural' model of the moderates and the 'radical socialist' model of Nehru and the Marxists) had, according to Kumar, both great merits and serious flaws. Its chief merit was that it was eminently successful in winning national liberation from colonial rule. It was flawed in that it left two bad legacies for post-independence India, namely: (a) the heightened gulf between the different religious communities, associated with the fact that religious and communitarian solidarities often masked class domination; and (b) the domination of the polity by the rich and the powerful who had been brought into the national movement on terms which more than protected their interests (Kumar, 1983: 43).

Concerning the semitized, intolerant *Hindutva* ideology of

colonial modernity, Kumar (1991) notes that it is a departure from the tolerant existential Hinduism of Indian tradition and that, if unchecked, it can generate ferocious conflicts between different religious communities.

In a paper entitled 'The Politics of Indian Secularism' (1992), Prakash Chandra Upadhyaya grants that Gandhi's conception of secular nationalism, centred on the principle of *'sarva dharma samabhava* (let all religions prosper)' (*sic*), is an advance over Hindu communal nationalism in so far as it (i.e., the former) upholds the principle of minority rights and the idea of composite nationalism. Upadhyaya however feels that the *'sarva dharma samabhava'* model of secular nationalism falls short of the secular-socialist model of politics and that therefore it lends itself to be appropriated by the communalist forces. He argues that by merely trying to *accommodate* the interests of the different religious communities rather than to *separate* religion from politics, the *'sarva dharma samabhava'* model serves to traditionalize present-day India by giving a 'new and rigid juridical status' to religious customs. In his view, the politics of religious communities when played out on communitarian lines rather than on class lines will inevitably throw up communal politicians. Moreover, the use of non-class metaphors (*Ramrajya, ahimsa*, etc.) by Gandhi for his 'moral' or 'communitarian' politics, says Upadhyaya, served to legitimize inequality and class exploitation.

According to Devdutt (1981), the BJP's adoption of 'Gandhian socialism' is 'an unusual case of ideology transplant.' He notes that the BJP's commitment to Hindu nationalism is in clear opposition to Gandhi's concept of *composite* nationalism, which, he adds, is of the utmost relevance to India today. He also notes that Gandhian non-violence is not generally subscribed to by the leaders of the BJP. Hence, in the absence of any 'crash programme of a sort of de-ideologisation and a programme of effective internalization of Gandhian ideology, the BJP seems to him to be undertaking a non-viable, mechanical ideology-transplantation.

Some of the differences between the Gandhian and the Hindu nationalist approaches to shaping the future of India are brought out by Andersen and Damle (1987). They point out that the Hindu revivalists opposed Gandhi's 'ascetic non-kshatriya style of leadership, his definition of *dharma* as the non-violent pursuit of "truth", and his assimilationist conception of the Indian nation, which he saw as a brotherhood or a confederation of communities.' They also saw Gandhi's *ahimsa* as going against the 'energism' and militancy they favoured.

According to Richard Fox (1989), although the Hindu communalists shared Gandhi's commitment to Indian independence and to discipline and simplicity in personal life, they found his non-violence cowardly, his commitment to Hindu-Muslim unity traitorous, his conception of God as Truth apostate and his democracy anarchic. There was a clear hostility on the part of the Hindu communalists towards the Gandhian utopia. Whereas Gandhi challenged both the colonial regime and aspects of the indigenous social order, the ideologues of Hindu nationalism used their ideology to legitimize 'the superiority of Hindu traditions and the superior place of the high castes, which served as custodians of those cultural traditions' (Fox, 1989: 222). Fox also points out that although Hindu nationalism is presented as the political philosophy 'for all Indians in the future,' it is in fact a conservative political ideology that serves the interests of the urban, lower-middle class 'forward' castes.

According to Ashis Nandy, Gandhi's religion was a faith, a way of life, a life of religious tolerance, while the religion of the Hindu nationalists is an ideology, a 'text'. While Gandhi's religious/spiritual politics resisted traditionalism, modernity and colonialism, the *ideology* of Hindu nationalism is a pathetic and pathological by-product of colonial modernity. The RSS ideology, Nandy notes, has always and systematically drawn doctrinal and organizational forms from the semitic religions and the modern-Western ideology of the nation-state. Nandy adds that it is in the name of such an ideological or instrumental conception of religion that Gandhi was assassinated; the tolerant Hinduism which he practiced, like the tolerant Buddhism which Asoka practiced and the tolerant Islam which Akbar practised differed sharply from the semitized, Westernized Hinduism of the militant Hindu nationalists (Nandy, 1988: 183–88; 1991).

Contrasting the Ram of the Hindu fundamentalists with Gandhi's Ram, T.N. Madan (1991) writes that the latter, also called Allah, 'was the God of inter-religious understanding, love and non-violence, God of all India, and not a Hindu God imposed on others, confined to a temple' (cf. also Madan, 1987).

Chaturvedi Badrinath argues that the political notions of

Hindutva, 'nation-god' and *rashtra-bhakti* and the claim that the Hindus are the 'chosen people' of Indian nationalism are all borrowed from European romanticism and the Semitic religions and that they result in discord, ironies and violence. In his view, the Marxist alternative too is limited by its anti-national temper arising out of its Enlightenment faith in the rational, universal, dialectical laws of the historical development of all societies. He favours the *dharmic* approach to the resolution of conflicts, which, he says, can overcome the dualisms or dichotomies of European Enlightenment and Romanticism (Badrinath, 1990 and 1992; cf. also I. Rothermund, 1990).

According to Paulos Gregorios, the Western/modern secular-rational approach to politics relies on mechanisms or structures of external controls, which, in their turn, depend on a logic of dualism between the self and the other. He argues that a better framework of social life can be found in the Indian conception of enlightenment, which both the Buddhist and the Vedantic traditions took to mean an inner illumination that dispels the illusion of the centrality of the ego and sheds light on the Buddha-nature or dharmic-unity of all reality (Gregorios, 1989 and 1990).

That the 'dialogical religiosity,' which Gandhi practised, is what is needed against both militant religiosity and Western secularism is the argument of Ishanand Vempeny (1990 and 1990a). He points out that the Western idea of secularism could mean either atheism or the separation of religion or religiosity from politics. Under the secular states of the liberal-democratic or Marxist systems, he writes, 'a person may be a good citizen before the state but may be an evil man before his fellowmen. You remain a good citizen before the state provided you commit your crimes and evils in such a way that you are not caught. In such a situation, hypocrisy and duplicity would be the accepted norm in human relations.' In Vempeny's view, this Western conception of the secular state contrasts with the idea of *dharma*, which, as a principle of unity and harmony, differentiates human beings from animals. Hence, a state which is separated from *dharma* is a state of 'nature' or of the animal world.

Vempeny goes on to argue that since *dharma* is defined differently by the different religions, social life should be organized on the basis of *sarva-dharma-samabhava*, which he translates as 'dialogical religiosity' and which he takes to mean one's commitment to one's own religion, openness to and love and respect for other religions and commitment to the welfare of all. Gandhi, according to Vempeny, practised such a religiosity, which, he suggests, is the needed alternative to both religious militancy and the secular disregard of *dharma* in political conduct.

A brief defense of Gandhian secularism is also provided by K. Raghavendra Rao in the following words:

> In a multi-religious and multi-caste society, secularism is a dire necessity for society's survival. If a plurality of groups is to function as a minimally interrelated society functioning on the basis of minimal trust, the political system has to generate a frame of reasonable parity between the groups. In a society where 'religion' is an everyday mode, not a sociological dramatisation, secularism cannot mean a structural separation between the religious and the secular, but an arrangement in which all group identities, contingently 'religious', enjoy a fair deal (1990: 43).

Following Gandhi, Rao goes on to argue that what is required for secularism in India is 'not an abolition of the religious category in politics but a religious parity within the political framework' (p. 44).

It must however be noted in conclusion that the principle of *sarva-dharma-samabhava* does not, by itself, serve either to promote or to prevent religious communalism. What would seem to make the crucial difference is the nature of the principle of equality that is sought to be realized through the politics of *sarva-dharma-samabhava*. This principle can be understood and pursued *either* in a formal, anti-democratic sense, which would amount to denying the basic liberties and rights of the minorities *or* in a democratic and truly egalitarian sense, which would respect and uphold the basic liberties of the minorities against even the most formidable of majoritarian claims and which would grant that special provisions to ensure the protection of minority rights may be necessary for the sake of non-pseudo equality (cf. Mohanty, 1989; Bhargava, 1991; Panikkar, 1991; Sheth, 1992; Kapur and Cossman, 1993). In the case of Gandhi, certainly, his conception of *sarva-dharma-samabhava* was meant to realize the latter concept of equality, i.e., *swaraj* and *sarvodaya* through the politics of *satya* and *ahimsa* (cf. chapter 4 *supra*).

6

Theories of 'Integral Pluralism' and 'Alternative Democracy'

Introductory Remarks

Two contemporary Indian political theorists, V.R. Mehta and Rajni Kothari argue that neither the liberal-capitalist nor the Marxist-Leninist path of political modernization can find legitimation in the cultural values of the Indian people. They however differ from each other in interpreting the Indian cultural tradition and in constructing a culturally sustainable indigenous alternative to the liberal-capitalist and Marxist-Leninist paradigms of politics and development. Mehta interprets the Indian cultural tradition in terms of an 'integral-pluralist' framework of individual–society relationships. By 'integral', he means 'organicist' and by 'pluralism' he means the idea of 'wholes existing within wholes.' Kothari sees the Indian cultural tradition as containing such values or ideals as social pluralisms and tolerance of value-ambiguity (rather than theological dogmatism), which, in his view, can aid us in working out an Indian version of a 'post-modern, post-secular society'.

The Integral Pluralism of V.R. Mehta

According to Mehta, both the liberal paradigm of modernization and the Marxist-Leninist approach to overcoming underdevelopment are teleological and Westcentric. They are incongruent with the socio-cultural values and identity of the Indian tradition.

The liberal-democratic ideology of modernization, which is based on 'principles of market rationality and unbridled economic competition', has brought about a process of change in India that is imitative of, and subordinated to, the industrial modernity of the West. In this process, some traditional structures have been reinforced and some new structures or forces of domination have been created. Under the rights-centred atomism or competitive individualism of liberal democracy, political institutions have become too weak against the powerful vested, sectional interests.

Turning to the Marxist-Leninist model, Mehta finds that while Marx's humanism is to be welcomed, the economism and State-centric, bureaucratic authoritarianism of the Marxist-Leninist systems are to be rejected. He admits that Indian Marxist scholars have produced 'some brilliantly insightful socio-historical analysis' of the rise of capitalism and the inequalities and contradictions it has brought in India. In his view, the considerable merits of the Marxist approach to social theory and political change should not make us overlook its crucial shortcomings; its overemphasis on the 'economic base' has resulted in the de-emphasis of the 'socio-religious' in Indian life, namely, the importance of 'caste, religion, untouchability, tribal problems, problems of nationality and ethnic groups.' Marxist analysis of Indian society, we are told, has underrated the conflicts 'between upper castes and the lowest ones, Hindus and Muslims, rural middle classes and the urban classes, the cohesive socio-religious centre and the artificially created political centre' (1983: 107). This inadequate understanding of Indian society has been responsible for the inadequacy of the Marxist strategy of social change. He writes:

> . . . the gravamen of our argument is that in pinning their hopes for revolutionary transformation in society on peasantry and workers the Marxists have largely ignored the scheduled castes, the agricultural labourers and unorganised workers who alone have revolutionary potential in the situation in which the country finds itself . . . (1983: 100).

Moreover, the Marxist-Leninist model of social and political change, says Mehta, shares in the Eurocentrism of the liberal paradigm of modernization; the former straitjackets India into 'the Western stream of historical development' from feudalism to communism through capitalism—a process of world-historical change, in which British imperialism is credited with a regenerative or progressive role vis-à-vis India. India, he argues, should adopt a political framework of change that is not Eurocentric but nativist or indigenous. Such a framework, he claims, is available in India's socio-religious or socio-cultural tradition of integral pluralism.

He finds earlier formulations of 'integral pluralism' in Vivekananda's notion of Vedantic socialism, Aurobindo's ideas of 'complex communal freedom' and 'integral humanism' and in Gandhi's conception of 'oceanic circles' and *sarvodaya*. Mehta prefers the rubric of 'integral pluralism,' in which 'integral' means 'organicist', while 'pluralism' conveys the idea of the 'wholes existing within wholes: at each level there is a certain amount of autonomy in relation to smaller wholes and a certain amount of subordination to the bigger ones' (1983: 23 and 28). He writes that the framework of integral pluralism incorporates: (*a*) a theory of multi-dimensional existence, which recognizes the integral or wholesome nature of the several dimensions of life, viz., *dharma* (ethics), *kama* (sensual enjoyment), *artha* (wealth) and *moksha* (liberation); and (*b*) a theory of developing wholes, which views the individual–society relationship 'in terms of concentric or oceanic circles in which each circle is almost complete in itself and yet exists within a larger circle' (1978: 30–52). Integral pluralism is also said to uphold the principle that different individuals and societies 'ought to be able to fulfil themselves in terms of the dimension of life they consider necessary for their fulfilment' (1978: 39).

Mehta presents his model of 'integral pluralism' as a modified version of Gandhi's 'oceanic circle' model of *sarvodaya*. Gandhi, somewhat like Vivekananda, Tilak and Aurobindo, had brilliant insights into the cleavages that had developed between India's socio-religious or socio-cultural tradition on the one hand and the production relations and politico-juridical forms of the colonial system on the other. Gandhi pioneered a strategy of political action based on the former (i.e., the socio-cultural tradition of 'oceanic circles,' as contrasted with dichotomies or dualisms) and used it to resist and transform the latter (i.e., the colonial political economy). Mehta praises Gandhi's socio-religious wisdom in making the issue of social justice for the Harijans a central part of his transformative programme. Summarising his own Gandhi-inspired transformative framework, Mehta writes:

> Only in terms of the model of 'oceanic circles' as seen through the perspective of 'integral pluralism' can the nation discover the strategy of action consonant with enduring elements in the national life and only in the agricultural labourers and the scheduled castes under a strong leadership can it discover the active agents of its transformation (1983: 219).

He goes on to point out that one of the major imperatives of the integral-pluralist framework is that the cohesion of the socio-cultural or socio-religious sphere has to be ensured (*a*) through the uplift and integration of the scheduled castes and tribes and the agricultural labourers; and (*b*) through the fostering of Hindu-Muslim unity in terms of 'oceanic circles.'

While praising the Gandhian model of oceanic circles for encompassing the baffling complexity of Indian society as no other model has done thus far, Mehta feels that in some important ways, Gandhi's 'efforts were narrow and dated.' The shortcomings of the Gandhian approach, according to Mehta, are:

1. that it does not provide for a strong political centre that can resist the challenges of other states and powerful, domestic forces;
2. that the economic order and fiscal policies favoured by it seem to be meant for 'paupers and sanyasins'; that Gandhi's economic thought has, by overrating the altruism of human beings and the redistributive efficacy of trusteeship, contributed to the increase of the economic *and* political power of the wealthy;
3. that it overstates the principles of non-violence, which has thus far been accepted by only a very small number of people, whereas (men) have remained, for the most part, adherents of Machiavelli and Kautilya.

Given these shortcomings, the Gandhian model, says Mehta, should be modified in the light of such 'logistics of the present situation' as: (*a*) the creation of strong political centres at all levels of the federal polity, especially at the central level; (*b*) greater diffusion of political economic power; (*c*) agricultural and industrial development both for generating full employment and for increasing the strategic and defence capability as required by a modern state; and (*d*) a national policy of 'appropriate technology' with a 'high science content.'

Concerning Mehta's thesis of integral pluralism, I have argued that it is an important, original, nativist articulation that needs to be taken seriously by Indian political scientists (Pantham, 1980). His theory seems to have some serious flaws. I shall discuss them as issues for further inquiry. This I shall do in the concluding chapter.

The 'Congress System' of Political Modernization: The Early Works of Rajni Kothari

There have been two distinct phases in the development of Rajni Kothari's political theory of social transformation in India and the world. His works of the first phase (up to about 1975) are informed by a 'modified structural functional' framework, which has some affinities with the theory of 'modernization revisionism' (cf. section 2.5 of chapter 2 *supra*). I shall review those works in the present section under the rubric of 'The "Congress System" of Political Modernization.' In the next section, I shall take up the second phase (roughly since the mid-1970s), the focus of which is on alternative democracy, development and world order.

In the first phase, Kothari has been concerned with providing a justificatory explanation of the autonomous role of liberal-democratic political institutions in penetrating into and modernizing/transforming the rigid and growth-inhibiting structures and ideologies of the traditional order. Going beyond structural-functional 'frameworking' or 'typologising', he *theorized* the autonomous role of the national political elite and the state in building national and democratic political institutions and in pursuing social transformation and economic development.

In order to prevent this process of democratic-political transformation/modernization of the Indian society from lapsing into Westernization or teleological evolution towards West-centred modernity, he advanced the thesis of the two-way process of the modernization of tradition and the traditionalization of modernity in India. In this vein, he provided theoretical justifications of electoral democracy, left-of-centre ideology, caste associations, Indian political culture and the nation-state. According to him, the keystone of the polity was the 'Congress System,' in which the Congress Party represented within it almost the entire political spectrum of the country, with the opposition parties acting as mere parties of pressure on the balance of forces within the ruling Congress Party.

In Kothari's view, the philosophy of the Indian Constitution and the left-of-centre ideological consensus of the Nehru era constituted the beginnings of a viable 'model of political development that was in some ways peculiarly Indian and peculiarly suited to Indian conditions' (1976a: 52). The Western-educated national political elites, who inherited political power at the time of independence, were autonomous from the social and economic elites and were committed to the values of national autonomy and integration, liberal democracy, economic development, social justice and non-alignment. As creative agents of change in India, they have created a new political centre, which has penetrated into the periphery through the uniquely Indian 'Congress System' of political mobilization, integration and democratic consensus-building.

On the nature of the relationship between the institutions of modern parliamentary democracy and India's traditional social structure and culture, Kothari has many grounds of agreement with the critique which Lloyd Rudolph and Susanne Rudolph have made of the ethnocentric, teleological model of modernization. Somewhat like their thesis of the modernity of tradition, he advances the thesis of the traditionalization of modernity. He feels, however, that the Rudolphs have somewhat overemphasized the role of traditional institutions and norms in the process of change and underemphasized the transformation that has been brought about by modern democratic values and institutions. In his view, Indian tradition had justified such evils as rigid hierarchy, gross disparities and inequalities, and intense parochialism. The major stimuli for changing these, he says, came from Western modernity. Distancing himself from the position of the Rudolphs, he writes:

> In stressing the strength and flexibility of tradition it would be misleading to think that the sources of change (as distinct from

support for it) came from tradition itself. The few who have stressed the role of tradition in modernization have sometimes given such an impression; we would like to explicitly deny such a romantic view of tradition (1970: 97).

Rather than regard political institutions as mere superstructures of more basic relationships in society and economy, Kothari takes them to be 'the great creative force'. He writes:

. . . a country as vast and pluralistic as India can be effectively united only through a participant and accommodative model of politics . . . A concomitant of such a model is the autonomous and creative role of politics, and its penetration all the way down to the social infrastructure. The integrative capabilities . . . owe a great deal to such autonomy and creativity though no doubt they have been greatly helped or hindered by the persistence of (certain) cultural themes (from the past) . . . At any rate it is in terms of the performance of such a 'political model' of development, instead of any reductionist view of politics as found in both the 'social origins' and the 'prerequisites' models, that we have approached the subject of integrative outputs . . . (1970: 337).

The values which Kothari (along with his colleagues on the World Order Models Project) seeks to maximize are: autonomy, non-violence, peace, justice, decentralization, participation, etc. Of these, the central value is individual autonomy and self-realization, which is bound to the cultural autonomy of communities, which in turn sustains and is sustained by the autonomous nation-state. In his view, without the realization of the autonomy of the individual on the domestic plane, the autonomy of the nation-state on the international plane cannot be realized, and vice versa. This means that there must be genuine democratization of political and economic structures at the national and transnational levels so that the 'periphery' gains autonomy from the 'centre'. Accordingly, Kothari proposes a restructuring of the world into some politically autonomous and economically self-reliant culturally based federations of nation-states.

While supporting the transformation of the evil features of India's traditional order through the values and institutions of modern Western democracy, he maintains that certain other features of Indian civilization are of contemporary relevance in that they can contribute to a vastly improved model of democracy in India today. Accordingly, the Indian tradition is seen to be providing us with a sense of cultural unity and identity cutting across political, linguistic and ethnic divisions. It is also seen to be containing an ethic of the limitation of wants, a preference for value-ambiguity rather than theological dogmatism, a spirit of tolerance, 'agglomeration more than segmentation, accommodation more than segregation, consensus more than confrontation' (1970: 82).

By welding these progressive values and norms of Indian civilization with the progressive values and institutions of modern Western democracy, we can, he says, form an appropriate Indian model of social democracy. A good beginning in that direction has been made, he says, by the national elite of the Indian freedom movement; guided partly by modern values drawn from the West and partly by certain values from the Indian tradition, that elite penetrated into the 'periphery' of our society and mobilized it into participation in nation-building.

Critique of Kothari's Early Works

According to Bhambhri (1973), Kothari's *Politics in India* has been approached from the perspective of structural functionalism, which, he says, has a bias for consensus and stability and which therefore precludes the raising of issues pertaining to the contradictions and struggles between the poor and the entrenched classes. These issues, Bhambhri says, could have been raised, had Kothari adopted the historical-materialist theory rather than structural-functionalism. Bhambhri writes:

> Kothari's framework inhibits him from raising such basic questions in Indian politics as the class character of the state, location and distribution of political power, subordination or autonomy of the political system from the dominant and entrenched classes, and the actual performance of the system in terms of the benefits and advantages it brings to the dominant classes (Bhambhri, 1974: 186).

According to Ashok Mitra (1977), Kothari's Nehruvian model

would have been relevant if ours was a one-party system in a monoclass society. The present crisis of the Indian economy and polity, Mitra says, is the outcome, not of the politicians' deviation from the left-of-centre rhetoric, but of basic class conflicts. Refuting Kothari's claim that the fragmentations of the masses make any revolutionary class movement impossible, Mitra maintains that such fragmentations are created and maintained by the ruling groups to slow down a historical process. Taking class war to be inevitable, Mitra rejects Kothari's model as it fails to recognize the historic role of a party of the property-less and deprived classes. Chopra (1972) and Khaliq (1978) have also criticized Kothari for not advocating class war and for not regarding politics as being determined by economics.

S.D. Gupta (1976) argues that Kothari's radical Weberianism 'exhibits very subtle anti-Marxist theoretical twists' which has 'counter-revolutionary ideological implications.' For Gupta, the political restructuring or Gandhian decentralization advocated by Kothari does not amount to any transformation of class relations. It also renders irrelevant the question of choice between socialism and capitalism or between socialist and capitalist-imperialist allies. For Gupta, the rise of the transnational class of bureaucrats and technocrats has not invalidated the relevance of class struggles and hence Kothari's model of 'abstracted relations' between centre and periphery is a clever justification of the international and national-level status quo.

Kaviraj (1981), unlike most other Marxist critics, is appreciative of the fact that Kothari's theory of electoral politics fills a gap in Marxist political theory. The former also recognizes the latter's originality in giving a theoretical alternative to the ethnocentrism and ahistoricism of the functionalist theory of political modernization. But Kothari's thesis that India's traditional socio-cultural sphere is now serving as a suitable under-structure to democratic political institutions is, according to Kaviraj, a thesis of double romanticization; it romanticizes both the past and the present of Indian politics, which, according to Kaviraj, was/is 'deeply aristocratic, repressive and massively violent towards the oppressed.' Attributing democratic virtues to such a traditional culture, according to Kaviraj, has large implications for political practice as it will lead to 'confusion about the allies and enemies of the democratic process.' Instead of characterizing the Nehruvian model as consensual or pluralist-democratic as Kothari does, Kaviraj would rather characterize it as a model for the co-existence of partial democracy with a 'non-aggression pact between the bourgeois and the feudal interests.'

Iqbal Narain (1970) has two notes of dissent from Kothari. First, the latter's advocacy of traditionalization of politics does not appeal to the former, who would rather stress the need for the 'creation of a secular loyalty structure which cuts across the primordial network and provides the much needed secular input to the process of nation-building in India.' Kothari, according to Narain, seems merely to rationalize the interaction between caste and politics and does not stress 'the basic failure of the political elite to create a secular loyalty structure which can be treated as an alternative to the infrastructural loyalty structure.' Narain's second and more important critique of Kothari's book is that it does not resolve 'the dilemma of ideology versus consensus.' Kothari, Narain points out, 'shudders at the prospects of ideological polarisation which to him would spell chaos' (p. 1609). Narain insists that democratic politics in a developing country needs an ideological utopia.

V.R. Mehta thinks that Kothari's alternative democratic model of socio-political change is based on an assumption that the liberal-democratic political centre, represented by the consensus system of the Congress of the Nehru era, was autonomous from and strong vis-a-vis the social and economic systems. This assumption, according to Mehta, is not valid; the liberal section of the political elite had a weak support structure in the society and a non-hegemonic ideology. 'As a result the political centre created by it in the form of parliamentary democracy on the Westminster lines is too weak to reorient the existing social and economic institutions to the direction of its own value framework' (Mehta, 1983: 32–33).

Kothari's vision of a restructured world of culturally linked and economically self-reliant federations of nation-states has been criticized as an utopian vision, lacking any historical or philosophical basis (Swarup, 1977; Thakurdas, 1975: Chittick and Steiner, 1982). His scheme of Gandhian decentralization is disliked by Swarup, who fears that in it the society would become a greater tyrant than the state. Swarup, like Daya Krishna (1976), also feels that Kothari has overemphasized the role of the international political and economic structures in the denial of personal freedoms in the Third World countries.

Chittick and Steiner (1982) point out that the model of the just world envisioned by Kothari entails the cultural withdrawal and autonomy of the Third World countries from the present world system. This, they say, is neither desirable nor feasible in the present context of the globalization of production and transportation, which promotes inter-cultural contacts. Rather than trying to form a world of autonomous, self-reliant, culturally grouped federations of states, Chittick and Steiner would attempt to develop a 'pan-culture, a stock of widely shared ways of feeling and thinking appropriate for a global age.' For the development of such a panculture, they say, we must overcome not only the homogenizing or universalizing assumptions of Enlightenment, but also the Romantic conception of the incommensurability of cultures.

Kothari's argument for strengthening the states of the Third World against the core states of the world system has been criticized by his co-director on the World Order Models Project, Saul Mendlovitz (1981), who maintains that the states-system is itself the major obstacle to a just world order. Mendlovitz fears (wrongly, in my view) that strengthening the states of the Third World will strengthen the state-*system*. Therefore he would rather 'search for alternative political, social and cultural processes that embrace all of humanity.'

In a paper published in 1988, I have examined Kothari's interpretation of Indian politics, as contained in his writings up to 1986 (Pantham, 1988). In it, I have pointed out that he has tended to overemphasize the autonomous and progressive role of the national political elite during the Nehru era and the personalized nature of the political distortions brought about by Nehru's successors, especially Indira Gandhi. In so doing, he seemed to have underplayed the historical-materialist or class-related and internationalstrategic determinants of the actions and non-actions of political actors.

While suggesting therefore that his theoretical model needed to be strengthened by a historical-materialist analysis of states, classes and masses as these have been historically formed and as they continue to act and react in the present phase of the internationalization of production, I have maintained that his deft use of the relative autonomy of the political and the cultural for launching a theoretical and praxiological movement against the prevailing world-wide structure of domination must be seen as an original and relevant transformative or emancipatory move. I have argued that given the prevailing over-exploitative 'articulation' of the capitalist mode of surplus appropriation (i.e., through 'economic' means) with the pre-liberal (or illiberal?) modes of surplus extraction (i.e., through political and ideological control), the relatively autonomous political and cultural domains do provide a legitimate and realistic launching space for a transformative struggle and movement by the 'masses.' Kothari's view that 'the transformation of the state must be achieved through the transformation of the civil society, not the other way around' seems to me to be of considerable validity.

Concerning a certain theoretical or methodological fuzziness that is discernible in Kothari's search for a pluralistic alternative by drawing out elements from liberalism, Marxism, and Gandhism, I suggested that conventional notions of theoretical or methodological rigour cannot be applied to cases of partisanship with those whose struggles for survival and autonomy under perilous conditions depend on finding radical alternatives to the very normalities and 'rationalities' of the prevailing dominant modes of thought (cf. also Nandy, 1983: 107–12; Mazrui, 1975).

According to Baldev Raj Nayar (1989), Kothari's *Politics in India* is a work of *modified* structural functionalism (S-F) in that it 'supplemented the S-F approach with an emphasis on the autonomy of the political process, institution-building and system performance.' Such an approach, says Nayar, gave an 'eminently appropriate' account of Indian politics in the first two decades after Independence. 'After all,' he writes, 'during this period the outstanding feature of India's development was, indeed, the establishment of an institutional framework and there could be no question that this was the handiwork of a national elite that was largely autonomous, and so the attention to the top rather than the bottom was apparently justified' (1989: 65). Nayar also appreciates Kothari's commendation of India's ability to set up and operate a liberal-democratic framework under conditions of poverty.

According to Nayar, however, Kothari's modified structural-functional analysis of Indian politics had several limitations, viz.: (*a*) it exaggerated elite autonomy; (*b*) it ignored class conflicts; and (*c*) it did not seek to resolve the tension between democracy and development, namely, the tension between the sacrifices expected of the people for generating the resources required for development on the one hand and on the other the democratic requirement of consent from the same people (Nayar, 1989: 66).

Alternative Democracy and Humane Development: The Recent Works of Rajni Kothari

In the first phase of the development of his theoretical position, Kothari's focus, as we have seen, was on the democratic, nation-building and developmental initiatives of the national political elites. His concern in the second phase, as we shall now see, is with the politics of mass struggles for social transformation at the local, national and global levels.

His argument is that through an 'alternative' approach to democracy, development, and world order, we must try to transform the prevailing authoritarian, state-centric system of governance, technocratic and economistic model of development and the militaristic and iniquitous world order in the direction of a humane India in a humane world. According to him, in the present historical situation, the democratic process is likely to find its new bearings only if a comprehensive response to the shrinking of the space for the politics of the people is launched 'from a variety of vantage points of an "alternative movement."' While a part of that movement would have to come from conventional political struggles, the bulk of it must come 'in the form of independent citizen initiatives, of voluntary and non-party formations, of the struggle for civil liberties and democratic rights, in short, of *people's action*' (1989b: 397). 'The marginalised,' he writes, 'hold the promise for a recovery of the human, the good, and the just' (1988a: 2). Accordingly, the struggles by the oppressed classes and castes, by women and the tribals, by the populations of marginalized regions or endangered ecological areas, etc., are seen as constituting a broad social movement for change.

Kothari sees the post-Nehru era of Indian politics as facing an economic crisis and a deep contradiction between the democratic surge of the masses and the growing centralization and authoritarianism of the state, whose operators adopted, for some time, a populist posture and socialist rhetoric. The origins of this contradiction are seen to lie in certain initial errors and certain operational aberrations of the Nehruvian model of democracy and development. The initial error of the Nehruvian model was its pursuit of the capitalist model of economic modernization, which is characterized by centralization of political and economic power. He regards the Westminster model of liberal democracy (which he would presumably regard as a shade better than the presidential system) to be a centralizing model, which moreover places the ministers and the MPs above the party leaders. It also assigns a greater role to the bureaucracy than to the party system in economic planning. This bureaucratic model of governance favours the capital-intensive technologies of production, which exacerbates structural unemployment.

As operational failures or distortions on the part of Nehru's successors, he cites the erosion of party democracy, the decline of local and national autonomy and the rightist departures from the left-of-centre policies. Over the years, the national political elite has lost its autonomy and is increasingly becoming unable to resist the pressures of powerful social and economic interests both at the national and transnational levels. A decline in the role of the state as an agent or instrument of social transformation and social justice is going on in tandem with an increase in the coercive functions of the state apparatus, whose relationship with civil society is thereby vitiated (1986: 10). There is the real danger of the state becoming 'a militarized, communalized and upper class and caste dominated fortress.'

Thus, instead of development and the democratic-socialist transformation of the state, what has come about is 'the rise of a managerial and technocratic version of political democracy, based in turn on liberalization and privatization of the economy, opening up to transnational interests and recipes from the World Bank and the IMF conditionalities, and a process of recolonization of the rural peripheries . . .' (Kothari, 1988c: 277).

Kothari believes that in this situation, 'the forces being unleashed at the bottom of society can be garnered to generate a truly democratic, federal and decentralized polity that pursues an alternative model of development that is ecologically sensitive and truly pluralistic, and that at the same time allows civil society to find its bearings once again' (1988c: 277). He also argues that the economy must be restructured to make it serve such alternative goals as mass employment and the fulfilment of human needs rather than the multiplication of wants. Accordingly, lower ceilings on the ownership of the means of production and inheritance taxes directed against hereditary capitalism are advocated.

Development, he suggests, must be redefined as social transformation. Correspondingly, democracy must be operative not only at the political level but also at social and economic levels. A plea is made for 'an Indian version of social democracy' that can 'avoid the extremes of capitalism and communism, . . . of liberal democracy on the Western model and democratic centralism on the Soviet or Chinese model' (1976a: 51–52). Besides drawing support from aspects of India's culture, such a model of social democracy must, according to Kothari, take into account the 'linkages between national and international levels of state- and nation-building on the one hand and between political and economic factors, on the other' (1976b: 11).

Kothari criticizes the capitalist model of industrialization for its exploitation of labour and the colonies. It also brings about and sustains a dualist economy and centralizing state, which pushes increasing numbers of people 'not only to the peripheries of economic and political systems, but also to the peripheries of our consciousness' (1986: 3). He writes that our present-day human predicament is made up of 'the rampage of technology, the severe dualism of the human species, the sacrifice of life-chances of future generations, and the destruction of other species and other sources of life and sustenance' (1988b: 47).

As for the communist model of revolution and development, Kothari gives several reasons for its undesirability and/or non-feasibility. First, he finds the communist models of development to be dependent on a party bureaucracy that remains committed to heavy industrialization and global power. Second, the fragmented nature of our society makes it impossible to mount a united revolutionary attack on the system. Third, our polity has not yet exhausted the democratic-political mode of bringing about radical changes in our society. Fourth, the orthodox Marxist theory of class conflicts between the capitalists and the proletarians is inadequate to explain the major contradictions of our times. 'For, it is neither the world bourgeoisie, nor the world proletariat that has become a world class, but, instead, a world middle class which, strictly, cuts across capitalism and socialism, and which in effect undermines the autonomy of all but a handful of nation-states' (1976a: 23).

In the wake of the techno-bureaucratic distortions of the production process in the terminal phase of the capitalist world system, instead of the working classes of the world uniting, it is the world middle classes that are becoming conscious of their 'inter-dependence,' while more and more segments of the masses are getting marginalized and becoming 'a disorganized and "doomed" non-class' (1984: 217, 221). Due to a combination of rural economic stagnation and a type of technology which inhibits employment and causes ecological destruction, the rural poor are deprived of any means of livelihood.

This model of development is managed by a transnational techno-bureaucracy, which depoliticizes the public realm and prevents class solidarity among the poor on a national or global level. Accordingly, the state is 'perceived as an agent of technological modernization with a view more to catch up with the developed world and to emerge on the world and regional maps as a strong state (hence the vast sums spent on armaments) than to cope with pressing, often desperate, needs and demands of the poor' (1984: 217–19).

Sections of India's new middle class, Kothari says, are integrated into the transnational managerial class of the world capitalist system. India's bureaucratic-technocratic forces have become a powerful vested interest in a dual structure of dominance and dependence. They are the conduit of the subjection of the Indian people to *external* domination by the leader societies of the ethnocentric paradigm of industrial modernization. Subjection to such external domination can be maintained only on the basis of an *internal* structure of dominance and dependence (1976b: 22–23). Such a bureaucratic-managerial model of socio-political change has undermined the democratic process and the institutions of nation- and state-building, viz., the party system, the electoral process and the institutions of local self-government.

The bureaucratic-managerial model of change is based on Western, ethnocentric theories of modernization which foreclose the options of the newly independent Third World countries. Kothari writes:

> The operative model . . . is one in which the centre (or super-centre) is located in the territory of a dominant political power, the sub-centre in the national capital (with occasionally one or two additional sub-centres located in some other large-sized cities), and then, through a few inconsequential gradations, all the rest is reduced to a vast periphery. The emphasis of the model is on political autonomy, and aggregate economic growth,

at the cost of almost total neglect of the issues of distributive justice and democracy. (1976b: 12–13)

He goes on to argue that if we do not reject such theories and resist the actions based on them, 'the nation-state will lose its relevance as a principle of political organization, and the guardians, operating from a few metropolis, will work for the good of all mankind' (1976b: 5).

One of the transformative strategies advocated by him is the combative assertion of national autonomy by the dominated nation-states. He writes: 'It is by investing nation-states with autonomy and self-determination that freedom and justice for men and social groups can be possible' (1976b: 19).

A denial of the autonomy of the nation-states, Kothari maintains, results in the denial of the freedom and justice of the people of the newly independent states of the Third World. What is needed immediately, he says, is that in India and other Third World countries the democratic political forces must reclaim from the globally integrated managerial class the policy-making roles over the direction of socio-economic changes and the choice of techno-logical alternatives. This *political* alternative to the bureaucratic-managerial model of social change can succeed only if it is based on the struggles and democratic participation of the people. The demand for an end to democracy, he notes, has come not from the poor but from the rich as well as from the bureaucracy and the inane intellectuals. The poor and dispossessed, he maintains, have more to gain than the rich from the participatory model of politics. According to him, democratic politics which has been 'the creative force behind India's historic transformation' has been eroded since the mid-1960s and must now be restored and refurbished as an alternative to both capitalism and communism. 'Neither justice nor non-violence (our major operational values)' he writes, 'can be realized without an adequate distribution of power—between men and states' (1974a: 39).

In addition to the combative assertion of national autonomy, the Third World countries must also, according to Kothari, pursue a collective or cooperative programme of dealing with 'the threat of pre-emptive measures held out by the status quo powers. The exploited stratum of the states system, he says, must unite in the struggle against its privileged and exploiting stratum (1980: 22). Thereby the states system, he believes, will get restructured in a progressive direction.

A third strategy is domestic reform or transformation of the dominated countries; without putting its own house in order, no Third World state can succeed in initiating any effective movement for global transformation. Fourth, the emancipatory leaders of the Third World must attempt to form transformative alliances with those social forces within the Western nations which are also actual or potential supporters of a just and equitable world order. A novel feature of the present situation is that the local, national and international levels of politics are so interconnected that grass-roots movements even in the remotest villages of Third World countries have to address global issues such as development, ecology, peace and human survival.

Kothari also assigns great importance to theoretical work on the 'civilizational values of Asia and Africa,' which can enable us to envision an alternative world order, viz., an alternative to Western post-Enlightenment thought and to its related ideology of developmentalism and the 'totalistic impact of the modern state.' He maintains that both the bourgeois-liberal and Marxist-Leninist models are 'offshoots of the same philosophic pedigree of the enlightenment and nineteenth century (mechanistic) humanism' (1988a: 151). In his view, those theories are complicit in the construction of our present predicament. He writes: 'The stock of theories and models of social change and progress that have shaped the modern industrial civilization, its colonial expansion and its subsequent even larger expansion through the paradigm of modernization and development has created the world we live in.' (1988: 205)

As to the inspiration for his 'alternative' conception of democracy, development and world order, he claims that 'the moral imperative of treating people as a source in the recovery of a humane order' can be found best expressed in the Gandhian theory and practice of *satyagraha* and social reconstruction (1988a: 2). Although very greatly inspired by Gandhian ideas, he clarifies that he is pursuing a pluralistic style of theoretical analysis which also draws upon other existing theoretical traditions, without being wholly bound by any of them.

He believes that India has a distinctive role to play 'in working out a transition towards its own version of a post-modern, post-secular society'. He writes:

> Steeped in the tradition of social pluralism . . . (as distinct from the mere political pluralism as found in Western democracies) and in a conception of unity based on dispersed identities and shared values, endowed with a non-theological religious pedigree without a fixed doctrine or an official clergy, and given its high tolerance of ambiguity and a deeply ingrained tradition of skepticism, India may be better placed than most societies to carve out a niche for itself in a world undergoing great transformations. Its real test lies in its capacity to contain the centralizing impacts of the modern positivist age and especially moderate these impacts in the political sphere where the spectre of populism threatens the very survival of institutions and values. (1983: 45)

To initiate these strategies for socio-political transformation at both national and global levels, Kothari looks up to the progressive intellectuals of the Third World. He maintains that by trying to act as Marx's de-classed, world-changing intellectuals, Mannheim's free-floating intelligentsia or as the Gandhian *satyagrahis*, they can play a catalytic role in global transformation (1980: 35). Such intellectuals would be expected to aid the *politics* of global transformation by guiding the needed mode of intervention in the states system by the political leaders of the Third World (1980: 42).

An important role of such leaders and intellectuals is to lead the struggles of the poor through grass-roots movements and non-party political formations. He has himself been playing a leading role in organizing *Lokayan* (dialogue of the people), a macro-level forum of grassroots activists and academics. He notes that growing numbers of people are getting 'marginalized both from the organized economy and from organized politics.' As parties are declining and as the nation-states are getting 'sucked into the global status quo,' the non-party political formations can be a 'part of a larger movement for global transformation in which non-state actors on the one hand and non-territorial crystallisations on the other are emerging and playing new roles, taking up cudgels against imperialist forces' (1984: 220). To confine the politics of human emancipation through social transformation either to the politics of representative institutions or to the mere capture of state power is, according to Kothari, to acquiesce in the depoliticization design of the world middle class. Grass-roots movements and non-party political formations can, he says, rejuvenate and repoliticize the nation-state and liberate it from 'the stranglehold of imperialism,' thereby ushering in a *swaraj* mode of development.

While his alternative movement is based on, as well as upholds, the basic freedoms and rights of the individual, it goes beyond the rights-centred conception of democracy. He writes: 'Human rights movements, ecology movements, women's movements, the peace movement are all about restoring the first principles of the "good" and "good life" in the conduct of human affairs' (1988a: 3). Again:

> 'My preferred world is one in which the individual enjoys *autonomy* for his self-realisation and creativity—what is generally known as freedom. This is my principal value . . . . The primary condition of freedom is sheer survival, a protection against violence,—local, national and international violence, as well as violence tending towards either annihilation of the properties of life or towards a deadening uniformity of all forms of behaviour and social structure'. (1988: 173)

Some Critiques of Kothari's Theory of Alternative Democracy and Development

T.V. Sathyamurthy (1991: 2091) introduces his well-informed and extremely useful review of Kothari's five recent books with an apt characterization of the several dimensions of his contribution in the following words:

> Of all the academic political scientists in India since independence, Rajni Kothari has earned a unique reputation for generating a perspective for understanding and analyzing political change at once national and local, global and regional, concrete and theoretical, institutional and spaced outside the realm of formal structures, and above all, rooted in a method of approach that has enabled him to focus on the 'political' dimension without shutting out the light cast on it by other social science disciplines.

After giving a detailed examination of the several phases and dimensions of Kothari's contribution, Sathyamurthy commends its 'remarkable fusion of intellectual engagement and activist intervention.' He also places it in 'the mainstream of Gandhian socialist orientation deeply rooted in anti-colonial Indian nationalism.' Kothari's critique and reconstructive proposals however seem to Sathyamurthy to be suffering from a lack of a proper class analysis of the Indian state and society as well of imperialism. He feels that a focus on the problems faced by the different *classes* under the 'Congress System' and 'world order' could have yielded a well-rounded understanding of the problems of India and the world.

According to Prakash Karat, *Lokayan*, the grass-roots movement initiated by Kothari, is a 'factor in imperialist strategy' as it is among several Indian voluntary agencies and action groups that are financed by, and politically and ideologically oriented towards, the Western imperialist countries. 'By providing funds to these groups,' Karat writes, 'imperialism has created avenues to penetrate directly vital sections of the Indian society and simultaneously use this movement' (1984: 20). In a response to Karat, Harsh Sethi (1985) maintains that the oppressed strata and classes hardly have enough to survive and that they need support. In his view, funds from outside do not *per se* make *Lokayan* anti-national or counter-revolutionary. In his rejoinder to Sethi, Karat (1985) has pointed out the dangerous implications of imperialist funding of voluntary action groups.

Alluding (if I am right in saying so) to Kothari's thesis of grassroots movements/non-party political formations, Randhir Singh (1991) writes that it is an 'escape route' from the deepening crisis of Indian politics for the liberals and Gandhians, who, he notes, operate on the right of the political spectrum. He finds it to be providing 'too narrow and fractured a base, ideologically and organizationally,' for any kind of alternative politics in India. While appreciating the commendable work done by these 'formations' in the cause of the people, Singh hopes that the best of them will find their way to a radical or even revolutionary practice of politics such as the one favoured by 'the old communists'.

According to Pratap Bhanu Mehta (1991–92), Kothari's preferred model is that of a Gandhian social democracy which is founded on a critique of European modernity. Mehta feels that Kothari, like Gandhi, is inattentive to the kinds of institutions that could replace those of Western modernity. Like the 'colossal historic failure' of Gandhism, Kothari's model, writes Mehta, 'may only exacerbate India's practical predicament.'

In a stimulating review of Kothari's recent books, Manoranjan Mohanty (1991) finds in them 'a fairly comprehensive framework for an alternative political theory reflecting upon the human condition of our age in its essential dimensions.' In those books, Mohanty sees an expanded notion of both democracy and humanism, which question the conventional ideas of social change and development. He also sees in Kothari 'a serious blend of the theory and practice of political reflection and political action.'

Giving a correct location of Kothari's position in the history of political thought, Mohanty writes: 'Kothari's critique of the state and his advocacy of a decentralized self-governing polity, his repudiation of the modernization paradigm and plea for autonomy and justice in a non-acquisitive economy, and above all the stress on peace and non-violence, represent the Gandhian outlook to a very large extent' (pp. 158–59).

Mohanty, however, feels that Kothari is not simply a Gandhian but a 'modern' and a 'liberal' as well. The former therefore finds the latter's political theory to be that of a democratic humanism, which is more radical than that of Rawls. After commending several aspects of it, Mohanty points out two of its limitations, viz. (*a*) its neglect of the role of the productive forces in the process of development; and (*b*) its being permeated by elements of liberalism. Concerning the latter, Mohanty notes that the critique that Kothari provides is not of capitalism and imperialism but of 'the West, modernization, science and state.' Such a critique and the alternative that is based on it, writes Mohanty, only amount to 'permissible dissidence within capitalism, nationally and internationally.'

Concerning Kothari's idea that through the transformation of the civil society, the state can be transformed from being an instrument of domination to becoming an instrument of liberation, Mohanty notes that it is a romantic and ahistoric idea in that it asks 'for a new political organization of society without . . . taking full cognizance of its roots in social structure.' He goes on to add: 'The aggressive reassertion of the capitalist political economy in recent decades underlines the fact that democratic transformation of the capitalist state can be achieved only to an extent' (p. 155).

In the next chapter, I shall suggest that Mohanty's insightful critique of Kothari's transformational model brings up some important issues for further research. For instance, it raises the question of the relevance of pursuing the hitherto unrealized liberative potentials of the democratic movement of our times.

In bringing the present chapter to a conclusion, it is pertinent to note that the two largely indigenous political theories that have been surveyed here differ from each other in the nature and extent of their distantiation from the cultural essentialism of the religious revivalists. While their common emphasis on pluralism and on such liberal-Gandhian values as tolerance and communal harmony do mark their positions off from the *Hindutva* ideology, the organicist, conservative and essentialist features of Mehta's *socio-religious* alternative to the liberal-democratic and Marxist-Leninist models of the modern state can be seen or appropriated as supportive ideas for the ideology of 'religious' nationalism. By contrast, in Kothari's *democratic-political* approach to social transformation at the local, national and transnational or global levels, there is a pronounced emphasis on the need to go beyond both the Western capitalist-imperialist path of 'development' and the crudely relativist or essentialist versions of 'cultural' or 'religious' nativism (Kothari, 1992: 2696–97). In his view, the semitization of Hinduism, which is being pursued by the votaries of *Hindutva*, is not simply undermining India's indigenous cultural tradition (which, he notes, is 'the most non-semitic of all cultures') but is rather undoing the political institutions of modern democracy through which alone the Indian people can continue their struggle against the forces of the capitalist-imperialist world order *by* preserving and nourishing their pluralist, composite, living civilization.

7

Political Theorizations of Indian Society: Some Notes in Retrospect and Prospect

I.

As we have seen in the previous chapters, important contributions to political theorizations of social transformation have come from both the academic discipline of political science and from the other social and human disciplines. What this reflects is the fact that the sphere of politics is not the exclusive field of study by a narrowly conceived discipline of political science, just as the fields of the other social and human disciplines cannot be thought of in apolitical terms. As the society and economy have become politicized to a very great extent, both nationally and transnationally, those political scientists who take into account the 'findings' or 'insights' of the other social and human disciplines are better able to make *socially relevant* theoretical contributions than their professional colleagues who remain confined within narrow disciplinary contours, just as those members of the 'other' social and human disciplines, who are sensitive to political questions, are better able to make socio-politically relevant contributions than their discipline-bound fellow professionals.

In the case of Indian political science, as documented in the previous chapters, significant theoretical contributions have come from those scholars who have reached out from within the conventional boundaries of their discipline and gone into such other fields as international relations, psychology, history, philosophy, economics and literary criticism. Hence, it can be expected that significant political theorizations of the Indian society or of the contemporary world will be forthcoming more from the *trans-disciplinary* work of political theorists than from the narrowly conceived, within-the-discipline work of political scientists, though such work would indeed continue to have its own value.

While the specialized work of each of the social sciences and of the sub-disciplines within them is indeed indispensable for the growth of social-scientific knowledge, it is not sufficient by itself to provide any general or overall knowledge about the *present history* of any given society—about how a society is doing or ought to be doing *on the whole*. The dangers of mindless disciplinary special-izations are well brought out by Kaviraj (1990: 106) in the following words:

> Social scientists seem to have irretrievably divided the social world that ordinary people inhabit into discrete cognitive zones each complete with its own internal logic, rules of procedure, methodological orthodoxies, and sometimes not even easily translatable languages. Each works out generalizations running parallel to those of others, and indifferent to works coming from across these frontiers. Thus the problem in social science discourse is not so much one of paradigmatic or disciplinary competition as of paradigmatic indifference, the easy ability of theories internal to single disciplines to carry on without much curiosity about, or challenge from, the theories of others.

For understanding Indian society, we need to have not only the fragmented knowledges of the social science specialists but also, to use Kaviraj's words, the 'knowledge of the predisciplinary, unfrac-tured Indian society,' which the ordinary people, who inhabit it, must be assumed to have to some extent. I tend to think that one of the main reasons for the poverty of Indian political theory is the institutionalization of a variety of disciplinary and subdisciplinary separatisms in our programmes of teaching and research in the social and human disciplines.

For overcoming its theoretical sterility and enhancing its socio-historical relevance, Indian political theory therefore needs cross-fertilizations with history, philosophy, international relations studies, economics and literary criticism. Those who either *exclude* political theories from their considerations or adopt an *exclusive* preoccupation with political theories will not be able to engage themselves in the political theorizing of social reconstruction.

II.

Regarding the literature on the liberal models of democracy and development (chapter 2), I shall make the following general observations with a view to indicating some lines of further research

1. India's constitutional framework is a combination of *communitarian* moralities and *liberal* democracy. By this I mean that while we have a common or uniform set of *criminal laws* applicable to all members of all ethnic and religious communities, we do not have a uniform body of *civil or personal laws*; such minority communities as the Muslims, Christians and the tribal communities are governed by their own traditions of personal laws.

Pointing out that India's constitutional framework is 'a liberal democracy of a very peculiar kind,' Bhikhu Parekh writes:

> The Indian state . . . is both an association of individuals and a community of communities, recognizing both individuals and communities as bearers of rights. The criminal law recognizes only individuals whereas the civil law recognizes most minority communities as distinct legal subjects (1992: 171).

I would say that our constitutional framework can be appropriately referred to as communitarian-liberal democracy; it is *liberal* in the sense that in some respects it takes the individual to be prior to the community, and it is *communitarian* in that in some respects it takes the community to be prior to the individual.

The writings of Indian political theorists on liberal democracy, which have been surveyed in chapter 2, are silent on the question of the relevance or otherwise of communitarian-liberal democracy to the contemporary Indian society. Hardly any Indian political theorist has provided any major justification *or* critique of the combination of communitarian moralities and liberal democracy. This to me is one of the *most* glaring lacunas or absences in the literature of Indian political theory.

A brief illustration of what such a political-philosophical analysis can do has been suggested by Bhikhu Parekh, who, in an article, entitled 'The Cultural Particularity of Liberal Democracy' (1992), argues that liberalism is in some ways subversive of community and that therefore a multi-communal polity such as India can avoid inter-communal violence by recognizing or accepting the traditions, values and levels of development of its constituent communities.

2. In the literature on liberal democracy as surveyed in chapters 2 and 6, a very important distinction is being drawn between a 'wrong' kind of democracy, which is manifested in the authoritarian deinstitutionalization of the organizations, procedures and norms of democracy, and a 'right' kind of democracy, which calls for a reconstruction of political organizations and procedures with a view to making them embody the basic democratic ideal of freedom and equality of all.

A most striking and, in my view, happy development in post-Emergency political theory in India is a growing support to the civil liberties component of liberal democracy among sizable sections of the liberals, Marxists and Gandhians. Unlike in the pre-Emergency period, there has come about, in the post-Emergency years, a convergence of conviction on their part that the *civil liberties and democratic rights* are an indispensable and precious part of any framework of good governance. Among the contributory factors to this *democratic convergence* were the National Emergency (1975–77), the J.P. Movement, the return to power of the leaders of the Emergency regime with a massive mandate in the 1980 elections and the abortive outcome of the Naxalite Movement. As noted by Aswini Ray (1986: 1202), these developments 'helped in sharply underscoring the permissible contours of postcolonial India's developmental politics in the foreseeable future, strictly within the potential parameters of the liberal-democratic framework' (cf. also de Souza, 1992). The ensuing democratic movement has found organizational expression in the People's Union for Civil Liberties (PUCL), the People's Union for Democratic Rights (PUDR), the Public Interest Litigation movement, *Lokayan*, and several other organizations such as the Committee for the Protection of Democratic Rights (Bombay), the Andhra Pradesh Civil Liberties Committee and the Association for the Protection of Democratic Rights (Punjab). The role that these organizations have been playing has been confined to upholding the civil liberties and democratic rights component of liberal democracy. Though this is only a *first step* in a long-term liberative-transformative movement, they are of the utmost importance in present-day India. This is well brought out by Aswini Ray (1986: 1204) in the following words:

> Its modest success till now has been in keeping the democratic movement alive within a section of urban, middle class, intel-ligentsia . . . . It has also contributed to the widening of the social base of democratic consciousness in the country by opti-mizing the benefits of democracy to a section of the socially oppressed, and providing some marginal relief to such sections bypassed by the democratic process till now. More than that, it has contributed to the continuing social commitment of the democratic movement to the nationalist goal of social transform-ation of India's oppressive traditional hierarchy.

I would say that teaching and research in democratic theory with reference to India can no more be restricted to the *texts* of the Locke-to-Rawls tradition of political philosophy (though they are of *indispensable* value) but must also include the work of the *decolonization*, civil liberties, democratic rights, public interest litigation and grassroots movements in India. These movements, as suggested by Mohanty (1989), are bringing about a change in the terms of discourse from those of domination/subordination to those of real democracy.

3. A third general observation on the literature on the politics of development or modernization is that some of the Indian parti-cipants in this debate have highlighted the need to view develop-ment from a *moral-political* perspective rather than from the perspective of mere 'economic efficiency' or 'new political eco-nomy'. Thus, in his critique of the theory of political development, Daya Krishna writes:

> The crucial question which . . . remains to be answered is whether the realm dealt with by the science of politics is of such a nature as to permit the application of the concept of 'devel-opment' to itself. And our answer to this question is in the negative, for the simple reason that the only relevant distinction

here is between 'good government' and 'bad government,' and not between a 'developed polity' and an 'undeveloped polity,' as many contemporary political scientists seem to think (1979: 201).

I take the message of Daya Krishna's critique to be that the theory of political development and modernization is lacking in an acceptable moral-political theory of the good life. This, we may recall, was the central critique which Mahatma Gandhi had made of modern civilization. Although operating from a different social and philosophical context, Jurgen Habermas too, in his more recent writings (1990), is looking at modernity from the vantage point of what he calls 'discourse ethics.' However, some similarities notwithstanding, there are important differences between the Gandhian and Habermasian moral-political critiques of modernity and modernization. This is briefly discussed now.

Habermas is the most important contemporary defender of the universal validity of the principle of modernity, namely, the principle of the authority of reason, rather than religion, tradition or culture, in human affairs. Influenced by Piaget's and Kohlberg's theories of cognitive and moral development, he takes the highest stage of cognitive/communicative/moral competences attained by modern Western man to be the telos of development of human competences as such. By this reasoning, the 'development of a Western scientist' is posited as the ideal or standard of human development in all cultures.

Some of Habermas's post-structuralist, deconstructionist or post-modern critics find his evolutionary-teleological theory of modernization/rationalization to be 'dovetailed too neatly with the progressive ascendancy and domination of Western science and technology around the globe' (Dallmayr, 1992: 437). Rejecting what they call the universalizing or homogenizing 'metanarratives' of modernity, the post-structuralists write in favour of heterogeneities, differences, micro-powers and local resistances/struggles. These 'preferences' of the politics of post-modernization are described by Cornell West (1991: 19) in the following words:

Distinctive features of the new cultural politics of difference are to trash the monolithic and homogeneous in the name of diversity, multiplicity and heterogeneity; to reject the abstract, general and universal in light of the concrete, specific and particular; and to historicize, contextualize by highlighting the contingent, provisional variable, shifting and changing.

How the political theories and practices of post-modernization mark a departure from the 'philosophical discourse' of modernity is brought out by Dallmayr (1992: 439) in the following words:

In opposition to universal categories derived from Western modes of discourse, postmodern antiholism seeks to give voice to local or vernacular idioms and thus to empower the marginalized, in particular the poor masses in Third World countries trying to resist Western global control.

Dallmayr goes on to note that some 'largely salutary' Indian versions of post-modern thinking can be seen in the works of Ashis Nandy and Rajni Kothari. (I shall make a reference to the post-modern feature of the Kothari model in section VII.) Nandy, whose works have been surveyed in chapter 4, is regarded by Dallmayr as advancing a post-modernizing strategy through his 'critical-traditionalist' framework of social transformation, which challenges modernity's concepts of development, growth, history, science and technology in so far as they have become 'not only new "reasons of state" but mystifications for new forms of violence and injustice.' Dallmayr commends Nandy's critical-traditionalist view, namely, that 'living traditions' have within them liberating potentials and that these are not the monopoly of Western modernity. Following Nandy, Dallmayr (1992: 444) also regards Gandhi 'not as a modernizing nation-builder but rather as a critical traditionalist,' who 'has lessons to teach not only to India but to the world at large.'

Although in some ways Gandhi shares the post-modernist critique of modernity's metanarratives, in some other ways he departs from its relativism and nihilism. Both the Gandhian and Habermasian positions seem to me to be jointly opposed to post-modernist relativism in that they uphold the universality of the Kantian deontological morality of Right and Justice as being necessary for the peaceful resolution of conflicts. But, whereas Habermas takes such a deontological moral theory to be the whole of political morality under the conditions of modernity, Gandhi maintains that the universal, deontological morality of Right/Justice must merge with context-sensitive ethics of loving and caring responsibility (cf. Pantham, 1994).

I will bring the present section to a conclusion by suggesting that an increased participation by Indian political theorists is called for in the critical discourses of post-modernism and post-structuralism. This can help in explicitating dimensions or aspects of development and modernization that may remain unnoticed and unattended in the conventional techno-bureaucratic surveys and projections.

III.

I now turn to making some concluding observations on the Marxist writings on the transformational problems of Indian society and politics.

As we saw in chapter 1, in his review of the Marxist literature on Indian politics as of 1971, Sudipta Kaviraj noted that Indian Marxist scholars tended to be preoccupied with mere negative criticisms of the theories of non-Marxist writers rather than with providing positive, alternative Marxist theorizations of Indian society and politics. In the period surveyed for the present report, i.e., the years since 1971, Indian Marxist scholars *have* made impressive, positive theoretical contributions on such themes as the mode of production, the state, underdevelopment and, especially, on the struggles and insurgency of the subaltern classes.

An important development of potential significance for Indian Marxist political theorizing is what I have referred to as a 'democratic convergence' among the various schools of Indian Marxism. One of the long-standing controversies among them has in fact been about the emancipatory relevance or otherwise of parliamentary democracy. As we remarked earlier, almost all schools of Indian Marxism are now acknowledging the crucial importance of the civil liberties and democratic rights component of liberal/parliamentary democracy.

Extending the foregoing consideration, I would like to refer to a recent comment made by Bhikhu Parekh on 'Marxism and the Problem of Violence' (1992a). He argues that the collapse of Soviet communism enjoins upon Marxism the necessity to undertake a radical self-critique of its position of violence. In his view, 'although Marx's humanism and commitment to the free, full and non-coercive development of all human beings are genuine, his thought has several features that give some theoretical support to state terrorism' (p. 118).

In chapter 3, I have also attempted a brief review of what has been referred to as 'the most robust theory of India's political economy,' namely, Pranab Bardhan's analysis, which combines the methodologies of Marxism and neoclassical rational choice political economy. Bardhan's theory has the merit of emphasizing both the class-configuration of the Indian state and the autonomous interest (e.g., in ruler's rents) of the state elite. However, as pointed out by Sridharan, Kohli, and Nayar, Bardhan's rational choice Marxism needs to be further extended to include the role of such specifically political variables as leadership ideology, regime types and institutional-procedural frameworks.

Two other major developments in recent Indian Marxist scholarship are: (*a*) the continuing, productive debate between Indian nationalist-Marxist historiography and subaltern-Marxist historiography; and (*b*) the Indo-Marxian explanatory framework which has been developed by Arun Bose and commended, in an important review article, by Sudipta Kaviraj. These two developments or trends, both of which derive considerable inspiration from Gramscian Marxism, will, in my view, continue to shape future Marxist theorizations on Indian politics.

These 'schools' of Indian Marxist scholarship have already produced works of such importance that even the non-Marxists among Indian political theorists will have to take them into account. Turning to the Indo-Marxian paradigm, which has been developed by Arun Bose and commended by Sudipta Kaviraj, I feel that it can be regarded as opening up a course of 'creative transaction' between Marx's class-centred political economy paradigm and Louis Dumont's caste-centred socio-cultural explanatory framework (cf. Kaviraj, 1990: 111). This is now explained.

According to Bose, unlike Immanuel Wallerstein's economistic model of the capitalist world system, which reduces the underdeveloped economies to a 'faceless homogeneity,' Piero Sraffa's model of the international economy recognizes the authentic cultural specificities or autochthonous identities of the national or country-level economies which make up the world capitalist system.

From the Sraffian perspective, Bose finds that Marxian political economy can be integrated with Dumont's 'Indo-centric' socio-cultural theory of the caste system.

Adopting Marx's three-tier conceptualization of society in terms of 'economy,' 'civil society' and 'state', Bose argues that 'civil society' in India cannot be understood except in terms of the logic of the caste system as it has been analyzed by Dumont. Extending Dumont's idea of the *asymmetry* between power-hierarchy and status-hierarchy (based on notions of ritual purity), Bose arrives at 'an Indo-Marxian social paradigm in terms of a multiplicity of contending/colluding civil societies interacting in relation to one state and one economy.'

In a perceptive commentary on Bose's Indo-Marxian paradigm, Sudipta Kaviraj has shown that by integrating the Marxian model with the socio-cultural categories of ethnocommunities, civil societies and popular religions, Bose has brought about a commendable methodological innovation. Kaviraj however finds Bose's equating of the concepts of regional cultural formations, civil societies and ethnocommunities to be of questionable validity and explanatory utility. Yet Kaviraj maintains that Bose's Indo-Marxian paradigm does constitute a methodological prolegomenon for any Marxist analysis of the social history of India, which, he adds, must be viewed not merely as a political-economic entity but also as a socio-cultural tradition of multiple ethnocommunities, popular religions, etc.

When Indian society is so conceived, its transformation has to be attributed, in Bose's view, to its *inner* dynamics rather than to *outside* forces. This, as noted by Kaviraj (1990: 114), marks an interesting departure from earlier Marxism. The nature and implications of this departure will have to be further explored.

Concerning *Subaltern Studies*, I would single out Ranajit Guha's chapter, 'Dominance without Hegemony and its Historiography' (1989), Partha Chatterjee's *Nationalist Thought and the Colonial World* (1986) and Gayatri Spivak's 'Subaltern Studies: Deconstructing Historiography' (1985) as extremely important contributions, which deserve to be critically studied by all students of modern Indian political thought.

As pointed out by Sumit Sarkar (1984: 273), the term 'subaltern' has the merit of emphasizing 'fundamental relations of power, of domination and subordination.' By restoring their 'historical being' to the subaltern classes, the subalternist historians have contributed, in an inspiring way, to an emancipatory understanding of them (cf. Veena Das, 1989: 314).

Yet, the *Subaltern Studies* project seems to me to be limited by its confinement within a theory of the dichotomously essentialized subjectivities of the self and the other. Such a theory seems to me to be responsible for making some of the members of the project to resort to an essentialist privileging of violent methods of struggle over all other methods of resistance, including, in particular, the Gandhian *satyagraha*.

In my view, the subaltern theorists' extremely negative reading of the Gandhian intervention needs to be re-examined. One line of re-examination is contained in Mridula Mukherjee's (cf. chapter 3 *supra*) and B. Josh's interpretations of Gandhi's paradigm of peaceful mass movement as an appropriate, effective strategy of counter-hegemonic nationalist struggle against the semi-hegemonic and repressive colonial rule. According to Josh (1992: 45–67), the Gandhian strategy was a superior alternative to the strategies or paradigms of constitutionalism and insurgency/violence. Equating left-wing politics with the strategy of insurrection, the Indian communists, writes Josh, failed to comprehend 'the specific nature of . . . [Gandhi's] uniquely distinct paradigm' and wrongly labelled him as an arch right-winger.

It seems to me that Gandhian *satyagraha* is *an* extremely important emancipatory innovation in that its post-relativist conception of moral-political truth (between the *satya-agrahis* and their opponents) can be thought of as overcoming some of the limitations of political strategies based on the theory of dichotomously essentialized subjectivities, which are celebrated in both the elitist and subalternist varieties of historiography. Hence, I feel that the different 'schools' of Indian historiography need to initiate and pursue a course of interactive inquiry in which Marxian and Gandhian concerns and methodologies could get interrelated in a critical-creative manner. Is it such a project that is intimated in David Hardiman's reference to the notion of a 'Marxist Hind Swaraj' (cf. chapter 3)?

IV.

In this section, I shall attempt a few additional observations on the literature on the Gandhian way, which has been surveyed in chapter 4.

In a paper presented to a seminar on 'Gandhi and Our Times,' held at the Centre for the Study of Developing Societies, Delhi, in December 1981, Professor Raghavendra Rao of Mangalore University observed that while generations of scholars and commentators have worked to provide us with 'the basic groundwork and supergroundwork' of the contributions of Plato, Hobbes, Marx, etc., 'we have to contend with *an absence of an established intellectual tradition of coping with Gandhi*' (Rao, 1986: 128). *Today*, I cannot make a similar observation. In the recent literature surveyed in chapter 4, there is considerable evidence of a serious concern on the part of social and political theorists to come to grips with Gandhi. This, in my view, is a most welcome development.

I feel that the liberal moment or dimension of Gandhian thought and praxis has not been sufficiently researched into (cf. Conrad, 1987). Such work is, in my view, necessary if we are to understand how Gandhian thought differs from the ideologies of 'primitive, peasant-communalism' and *Hindutva*. Gandhian communitarianism, as I see it, was far from being anti-liberal or illiberal. Gandhi, as pointed out by Ashis Nandy (cf. section 5 of chapter 4 *supra*), provides a framework of social transformation that is critical-traditional and post-modern at the same time.

I would also suggest that Gayatri Spivak's observation (1985: 331) that the 'meticulously documented account' of the 'far from subaltern' character of the Gandhian intervention in Indian politics is 'one of the most stunning achievements' of the Subaltern Studies project needs to be *reassessed* in comparison with the contrary view held by the nationalist-Marxists (e.g., B. Josh), namely, that many sections of the left wing of the Indian political spectrum have misunderstood the 'complex position between the left and the right fringes,' which Gandhi occupied. Similarly, Partha Chatterjee's and Ranajit Guha's interpretation of Gandhi's politics of *satya, ahimsa and dharma* as a class-collaborative, conservative strategy also seems to me to require *re-examination*. In my view, there is a failure on their part to see the emancipatory-transformative significance of Gandhi's experiments with *satya-agrahic* subjectivity, which seeks to rupture the essentialist dichotomy and dialectical teleology between means and ends and between the superordinate and the subaltern.

I would also suggest that the trans-liberal character of Gandhi's communitarianism and the post-relativist or post-colonial character of his conception of moral-political truth point towards an alternative to the politically debilitating relativist versions of post-modernist thought (cf. Pantham, 1991).

V.

The literature surveyed in chapter 5 reveals that the *Hindutva* ideology, which, to use Dileep Padgaonkar's words, has 'altered the terms of political discourse and perhaps also laid the ground for the creation of India's second republic,' has not led to any major research publications by Indian political theorists. With the exception of some useful articles (e.g., by Mohanty, Kaviraj, Bhargava, Kothari, R. Singh, Sheth, Upadhyaya, etc.) there is no major treatment of the political philosophy or political theory of *Hindutva*. The academic discipline of political science still continues to rely on D.E. Smith's *India as a Secular State* (1963), which, despite its admirable scholarship and continuing relevance, has been outdated to some extent by the recent developments. While the history and sociology of these developments are being researched upon (e.g., by B. Chandra, G. Pandey, T.N. Madan, Tapan Basu et al.), their political-philosophical assumptions and implications are not being looked into to the extent required. Present-day Indian political scientists, with very few exceptions, do not seem to be continuing either the Locke-to-Rawls line or the Rammohun Roy-to-Jawaharlal Nehru line of political theorizing on the political unity of religiously plural societies under modern conditions. Among the crying needs of contemporary Indian political theory, in my view, are inquiries into the relative merits and demerits of the liberal-pluralist-just state, the *Hindutva* state and the moral-political framework of *Hind Swaraj*. In inquiries into these issues, Indian political theorists will have to pay attention to the rival conceptions of *swadharma* upheld by the votaries of *Hindutva* and by those who would call themselves *Hind Swarajists*.

In chapter 5, I have also suggested that Professor V.P. Varma's model of 'philosophical humanism' and 'ethical absolutism' which is based on an *essentialization* of Indian cultural tradition, cannot serve to emancipate the Indian people from 'ethnocentric imperialism' or 'totalitarian materialism.' This too is an issue that will have to be further inquired into from different political-theoretical perspectives. I would suggest, for instance, that a political theory of cultural traditions, which overemphasizes 'origins' at the expense of subsequent 'constructions,' is an anti-democratic theory which denies any creative role to the progeny of the originators.

As we saw in chapter 5, one of the participants in the debate on *Hindutva* has argued that the Gandhian notion of 'dialogical religiosity' is the needed alternative to both militant religiosity and Western secularism which does not recognize the role of *dharma* in political conduct (cf. I. Vempeney, 1990). The case of this 'dialogical religiosity' and its affinities with, and departures from, Jurgen Habermas's model of 'discourse ethics' need to be explored (cf. Pantham, 1986). I have also suggested that the idea of equality underlying the Gandhian principle of *sarva dharma samabhava* is not that of any pseudo-equality, which, in the name of a mechanical or formal equality, denies the basic human liberties of all those who hold a minority view or belief but is that of the genuine equality that rests on the twin principles of *satya* and *ahimsa*.

VI.

Turning now to the model of integral pluralism, which as we saw in chapter 6, is advocated by V.R. Mehta as an appropriate, nativist framework of development for India, I shall raise some critical notes, which I hope will serve as issues for further inquiry.

Mehta's so-called nativist thesis does not seem to me to be based on an appreciation of the underdevelopment of India that has been brought about by its incorporation in the capitalist world system (cf. Pantham, 1980 in chapter 6).

Mehta constructs Indian tradition as a socio-religious/socio-cultural tradition of 'integral pluralism' and uses that construction as a normative basis for criticizing the imported political theories and institutions of liberalism and Marxism. Concerning his logistical modification of the 'Gandhian model,' Mehta writes:

> Such reconstruction does not exclude some parts of the Western heritage as it does not mean an uncritical acceptance of our own national inheritance either. There is much good in Mill's *Liberty* and Marx's *Das Capital*, and there is something abominable in *Manusmrti* and the debased versions of the *Puranas*. (1983: 228)

However, the 'strong polity' or the 'modern state' which Mehta in fact borrows from European post-Enlightenment modernity and which he says must subserve the cause of 'an organic process [of change] in terms of a society's distinct personality and style' can, in my view, contribute to an authoritarian and conservative political order. Mehta's thesis raises a major question which will have to be addressed in future research, namely: What are the practical implications, for *swaraj* and *sarvodaya* or for freedom and democracy, of a combination of a theory of the 'strong political centre,' an integral-pluralist theory of individual-society relationship and an organic theory of social change?

After pointing out that the Indian cultural tradition has a distinctive 'personality,' 'peculiar genius,' or 'peculiar individuality,' Mehta argues that only that model of socio-political change will be appropriate which will either emerge from or conform to that 'personality' or 'genius.' At the same time, he calls for the uplift and integration of the Harijans and the agricultural labourers who, he grants, have been the victims of the politico-economic life of the same 'personality or 'genius' of the Indian socio-cultural tradition. What is problematic about this formulation and what will have to be inquired into by future researchers is the question of the fit between an organic theory of social change and the uplift of the Harijans. Relatedly, the biases or assumptions of the 'personality' theory of cultural traditions and of the 'organic growth' model of social change will also have to be further investigated.

In the light of the 'critical' points raised here, I cannot accept Mehta's thesis of integral pluralism. It however seems to me to be raising and attempting to answer some basic questions of political theory with reference to the transformation of Indian society. Particularly admirable is his attempt to interrelate the theories of selected Indian and Western political thinkers and to make them bear on problems of socio-historical change in India.

VII.

Concerning the 'alternative' approach to democracy, development and world order which is advanced by Rajni Kothari in his recent writings, which have been reviewed in chapter 6, I would like to make the following observations with a view to highlighting some issues for further research.

First, I see in Kothari's recent writings an inspiring espousal of a whole lot of liberative-transformative objectives or goals from the standpoint of the 'exploited stratum of the states system' and the oppressed peoples within the Indian nation. Those objectives, to use his words, converge on 'the problem of freedom in human affairs and of democracy in the institutions that sustain it.'

The rightness of Kothari's objectives however does not seem to be matched by a rigorous methodological or theoretical argumentation of how they can be achieved. I am inclined to think that this methodological or theoretical 'weakness' is reflective of what is nowadays referred to as the post-modern incredulity towards all meta-theories and meta-methodologies or, in other words, of the post-modernizing replacement of philosophical theories with political theories and political struggles. Kothari addresses his fellow social and political theorists not merely as academicians but also as citizens of a working democracy. A central concern of Kothari's Gandhi-inspired programme, as we saw in chapter 6, is with people's actions or struggles for filling the vacuum in *democratic-political* space that is caused by the *bureaucratic-technocratic* version of political democracy and by the coercive state. In my view, future research and writing for the further democratization of the Indian polity will benefit immensely from the line of thinking opened up and movingly presented in Kothari's idea of the *democratic-political* alternative to the *bureaucratic-technocratic* model of democracy. Future research in this area will also have to pursue his claim that his alternative conception of democracy is inspired by the Gandhian theory and practice of *satyagraha, swaraj and sarvodaya.*

While recognizing the crucial role of different forms of people's struggles, especially for civil liberties and democratic rights, Kothari does not regard the nation-state as having exhausted its emancipatory role altogether. Singly and cooperatively, the exploited states, he argues, can resist further exploitation by the privileged states and by powerful transnational agencies. This idea of the hitherto unrealized liberative role of the nation-state and of the largely untapped liberative potentialities of regional cooperation will have to be further explored.

Among Kothari's other ideas which I find to be stimulative of further inquiry are: (*a*) that we need to launch a theoretical and activist response that goes beyond both the neo-realist and economistic theories of the inter-state system; (*b*) that some of India's civilizational values are of unique relevance to the project of finding an alternative to the capitalist and communist models of industrial modernity; and (c) that while his alternative democracy is deeply committed to the civil liberties and democratic rights of the individual, it seeks to go beyond the Rawlsian-type, rights-centred conception of democracy towards restoring the 'first principles of the "good" and "good life" in the conduct of human affairs.'

With a view to indicating an important line of further inquiry, I shall now make a brief comment on Mohanty's criticism (cf. chapter 6 *supra*), namely, that Kothari's alternative theoretical and activist movement is permeated to a considerable extent by *liberal* values and that it constitutes *only* 'permissible dissidence within capitalism, nationally and internationally.' This criticism, I feel, can be accepted, with certain modifications/clarifications, as a *favourable* characterization of the Kothari strategy of transformative struggles.

One clarification that seems to me to be required is to indicate that the capitalism which now operates 'nationally and internationally' is a 'late' variety, in which, through transnational subcontracting, production has become globalized (cf. Frobel et al., 1980; Cox, 1981; Offe, 1985; Pantham, 1988; Ahmad, 1992). In this new phase, global capital has come to assert a greater degree of freedom from the political controls of particular nation-states. In this situation, whatever 'relative autonomy' is still available to the states-system is of crucial importance for reformist political actions and for transformative social movements. In particular, some of the values or ideals of the *liberal* political culture, e.g., civil liberties and democratic rights, will have to be seen to be having hitherto unrealized potentialities for the *swaraj* and well-being (*sarvodaya?*) of those who are marginalized or excluded by transnational capitalism.

Hence, when speaking—as Mohanty does—of the capitalist world system's 'permissible dissidence,' we must keep in mind the fact that there are sections, classes, elite groups or techno-managerial groups of that system, which, far from permitting such dissidence, are totally opposed to it. They would not hesitate to blame the worst-off victims of global capitalism 'for their own faults' and to exclude them from it altogether. Moreover, in negotiations for the re-location of certain industries from the metropolises into Third World countries and for loans from international financial institutions, some of the 'conditionalities,' which Third World countries try to resist are the 'illiberal' ones. In this context, an 'alternatives' movement such as Kothari's, which, as Mohanty notes, is permeated by certain *liberal* values, may *for that very reason* be a *part* of a relevant emancipatory strategy.

Moreover, those within the core countries of the capitalist world system who 'permit' or favour the universalization of such liberal values as civil liberties, democratic rights and social justice, should be seen as allies of those in the peripheral countries who are engaged in struggles for a world order of *swaraj and sarvodaya*. The deft use of the political and normative space (relative autonomy?) that is available *within* semi- or demi-democratic regimes as a legitimate starting point of liberative-transformative movements may have to be seen as having considerable strategic or realistic advantages from the point of view of those who are excluded or marginalized by the present 'system' of global capitalism. The liberal and Gandhian values of these movements put them on a trajectory that is different from those of communalism, authoritarianism and fascism.

VIII.

In this concluding section, I shall attempt a few overall observations on the problems and prospects of Indian moral-political theorizations of social reconstruction.

In their trend-reports on theorizations of the course of Indian politics as of 1970–71, both Rajni Kothari and Sudipta Kaviraj had observed that original and significant contributions had been made much more by the thinker-leaders of our national/freedom movement than by the academic social and political scientists of the first two-and-a-half decades following independence (cf. chapter 1). This situation has remained more or less unchanged in the years since 1971, which have been surveyed in the present study.

To date, the most original political theorizing of the Indian society can be found not in the writings of the academic social and political scientists but in the praxiological works of such thinker-leaders of our national/freedom movement as Rammohun Roy, Bankimchandra Chatterjee, Rabindranath Tagore, Lokmanya Tilak, Mahatma Gandhi, Aurobindo Ghose, Jawaharlal Nehru, M.N. Roy, Mahatma Phule, V.D. Savarkar, B.R. Ambedkar and Jayaprakash Narayan. Each of them brought a new voice into the political discourse and praxis of change and continuity in the social life of the people of India as they struggled for *swaraj* from the dead-weight of tradition and from the oppression of the imperialist system of Western modernity. As part of the moral-political movement which they led for the reformation and decolonization of Indian society, those thinker-leaders rejected the political vocabularies of both Indian traditionalism and Western modernism and brought forward such new ideals or terms of moral-political discourse and conduct as *satyagraha, Hind Swaraj, swadharma, swadeshi, Hindutva* and *sarvodaya*.

During the first quarter of the century following Indian independence, Indian political scientists, as noted by Kothari and Kaviraj, did not maintain any creative or critical relationship with the *swaraj–sarvodaya* discourse of the freedom movement (cf. also Mohanty, 1991). The terms or concerns of that discourse hardly figured in the teaching or research of Indian political *scientists*. The 'political theory' which was taught in Indian universities and colleges included the works of Plato and Aristotle, Machiavelli and Hobbes, Mill and Marx, Bentham and Oakeshott, Lasswell and Easton, but it did *not* include the critique or deconstruction which some of the thinker-leaders of our freedom movement had made of those theories. This situation did not contribute to any decolonization of the Indian mind. I think this is what Kaviraj had in mind when he wrote that there was a certain process of re-colonization of the discipline of political science in post-independence India.

Unlike in the years surveyed by Kothari and Kaviraj, in the period since 1970 which is surveyed in the present study, a considerable amount of scholarly attention has been given to the concerns of the *swaraj–sarvodaya* discourse. This is discernible not only in the works of political theorists but also in the contributions of scholars belonging to the other social and human disciplines.

There are indeed sharp differences among these writers in the interpretations and uses they make of the *swaraj–sarvodaya* discourse of the freedom movement, with some of them (e.g., Bipan Chandra, Ashis Nandy, K. Raghavendra Rao and the present writer) emphasizing its continuing relevance and others (e.g., Partha Chatterjee and Ranajit Guha) rejecting its central terms. I would still say that those who take seriously the *swaraj–sarvodaya* discourse of the freedom movement, irrespective of whether they eventually endorse or reject its values or ideals, are able to make more significant or socially relevant contributions to Indian political theory than those who, even when they theorize on such topics as 'post-colonial democracy in India,' *ignore* it altogether. Writings of the latter kind wrongly assume that Indian post-coloniality was born suddenly and fully formed in a midnight in mid-August 1947.

Let me rephrase and re-emphasize the foregoing consideration. I am suggesting that to be socially and historically relevant, future theorizations of Indian politics will have to be critically and creatively related to the *swaraj–sarvodaya* discourse that was initiated in our freedom movement. For, as perceptively noted by Manoranjan Mohanty, it is the protagonists of capitalist modernization who would have us believe that *swaraj* is a historically dated objective which has already been fulfilled and that our new objectives lie in the paradigm of capitalist modernization. This 'elite discourse' is, in Mohanty's view, fundamentally divorced from the *swaraj* or freedom discourse which is kept alive in numerous social struggles at the grassroots level, e.g., the emancipatory-transformative struggles of the poor, the *dalits*, the tribals, the oppressed nationalities, etc. To quote Mohanty:

> Class inequality, caste domination, ethnic alienation, gender exploitation and above all political authoritarianism at several levels make freedom the central category. Self-determination and liberation from multiple forms of domination and exploitation are still and will continue to be the main demands of people. (1991: 28)

Mohanty suggests that by re-linking ourselves with the freedom discourse of these social movements, we, as social theorists, can contribute to 'participative knowledge,' as contrasted with the 'derivative knowledge' that is presently being 'diffused.'

In addition to endorsing Mohanty's observation, I would go on to claim that a critical-creative relationship with the *swaraj–sarvodaya* discourse initiated by the Indian people in their world-historic struggle against imperialism/colonization would be a necessary, though far from sufficient, constitutive part of any post-colonial and post-relativist moral-political theory (cf. Pantham, 1994). I feel that in so far as they ignore the moral-political theory of decolonization or post-coloniality, which was initiated and 'experimented with' in the Indian freedom movement (especially in its

Gandhian phase), such leading contemporary political philosophers as Rawls and Habermas are missing out on the moral-political articulation of an important turn in world history. Habermas seems to admit that his theory of the cognitive and moral development of humanity does not escape a certain form of ethnocentrism. In the case of Rawls (1971: 364), his theory of civil disobedience is silent on the innovativeness of the Gandhian *satyagraha*. Moreover, his recent 'political' conception of justice marks a pragmatic, West-centric retreat from the earlier universalism of his moral philosophy (cf. Rawls, 1985).

My intention in referring to Habermas and Rawls in this manner is neither to underestimate the significance of their theories nor to set any agenda for them but to indicate a special role that Indian political theorists can and should play. I shall do so by turning to the following ideas of Alasdair MacIntyre and Bhikhu Parekh. The former writes:

> The Indian political theorist has a harder task than his Western counterpart. He first of all has to be a good deal more learned, for he is required to know the history of Western political thought as well as the history of Asian thought . . . .
>
> Second, he has to sustain a relationship with his Western colleagues in which he takes their concerns with a seriousness that they rarely, unless they are among the very few Western specialists in Indian politics, reciprocate. Thus, a genuine dialogue is for the most part lacking. It is we in the West who are impoverished by our failure to sustain our part in this dialogue. (MacIntyre, 1983: 623)

In a recent article, entitled 'The Poverty of Indian Political Theory' (1992b), Bhikhu Parekh points out that the critique which the scholars of the non-Western countries have made of the ethnocentrism of Western political theory has not been matched by the formulation of alternative, original, non-Western political theories. He goes on to argue that one of the important reasons for such an underdevelopment of political theory in India is that for historical reasons, the contemporary Indian political theorist can make original contributions only if he masters both the Western and Indian traditions of political theory, whereas most Indian scholars find such a double burden too heavy to bear. He writes:

The West can help him [i.e., the Indian political theorist] understand *what it is to do political theory*; his own society can help
him decide *what kind of political theory to do*. To master one
tradition is difficult enough; to acquire an adequate command
of two is beyond the reach of most. The Indian political theorist
needs to go West *in order to* get back to the East. This is a long
way back home, but it is the only way. Not surprisingly some
never leave home either physically or theoretically; some others
stay West both physically and theoretically; a few do return
home but only physically and continue to think West. (p. 558)

While Parekh correctly highlights a genuine difficulty experienced
by the Indian political theorists, his analysis, I feel, needs to be
extended to indicate that several important problems which the
Indian *and* Western political theorists have to address are or have
been *jointly* made by India and the West (during the colonial and
neo-colonial eras) so that the sort of division of labour between
Western and Indian political theory, which is indicated by Parekh,
may not address the problem of the *shared* poverty of Indian *and*
Western political theories.

In some of the literature surveyed above (e.g., Parekh's *Colonialism, Tradition and Reform* or Ashis Nandy's *The Intimate Enemy*
or the *Subaltern Studies*), there is a clear recognition that some of
the socio-historical or social-psychological problems which need to
be addressed by present-day moral-political theory have been
jointly made by India and the West during the eras of colonialism
and neo-colonialism. Hence the dominant political theory of neither
the Indian tradition nor Western modernity can *singly* guide us in
facing and resolving those problems. In other words, neither
Western ethnocentrism nor Indian relativism/historicism can help
us address the political problems (e.g., the problem of the grossly
unfair distribution of the resources of the earth between the presently rich and the presently poor countries) in the making of
which they have both been complicit as colonizer and colonized.

While the weaknesses, rigidities, failures, etc., of Indian tradition
have been well recognized in both the liberal and Marxist theories
of modernization and development, the complicity of modern
Western political theory in the political economy of colonialism/
neo-colonialism is beginning to be recognized only now. This,
however, does not seem to me to be as worrying as the fact that the

moral-political ideas of decolonization or post-coloniality (e.g., *satya/ahimsa, swaraj, sarvodaya and satyagraha*) that have been initiated and experimented with in India's world-historic freedom movement are not being incorporated into the moral-political discourses of the world today. The exploration of those ideas as terms of a non-ethnocentric moral-political discourse for a post-colonial world or cosmopolis is of the calling of Indian political theory—a calling, which, as the previous pages show, has hitherto received only a very, very feeble response.

It is also of the calling of Indian political theorists today to give priority attention to the task of reconstructing democratic political institutions at both the domestic and transnational levels of the Indian polity. Concerning the domestic sphere, it can be said, *with* Atul Kohli, that '[n]o problem in contemporary India is likely to prove more serious than the disintegration of its major problem-solving institution: the democratic state' (Kohli, 1991, as cited in chapter 2 *supra*). As I have tried to indicate in chapters 2 and 6, we need to take steps to halt the current trend of political deinstitu-tionalization and to reconstruct our democratic political institutions.

I have also tried to indicate that the present trend of economic liberalization and globalization should not be interpreted as signi-fying the so-called end of the history of political ideations about the state but rather as calling for a *redefinition* of the role of the state—and other political institutions—in a truly democratic direc-tion. So redefined, the tasks of the state, to quote Sridharan, would include 'skimming some of the gain from industry's growth and putting it into long-neglected, productivity-raising (and equal-izing and empowering) investment in education, health, rural infrastructure, and minimum needs' (Sridharan, 1991). It is a democratically constituted state, and not a deinstitutionalized, arbitrary, authoritarian rule, that can be expected to play this role. Concerning the former, political theorists are expected to make important contributions through their critical and reconstructive thinking and writing. In India, as the present survey of the literature has shown, such contributions have not been forthcoming in suffi-cient measure.

The urgently needed democratic reconstruction of political insti-tutions has to be attempted not only at the national or local levels of the polity but also at the international or transnational levels (cf. Rana, 1983 and Kothari, 1988 & 1988a & b). In the present phase of global capitalism, business corporations, financial institutions, communications networks, etc., which are multinational, transnational or global in character, have brought about a marked decrease in the sovereignty or autonomy of the nation-state. The former, i.e., the transnational or global corporations or networks, whose management or dispensations of the economic, cultural, informational or security affairs affect our lives—and deaths—deeply, are not the ideal or adequate embodiments of the values or principles of democracy. Even the United Nations Organization is not sufficiently democratic. In this situation, a nation-state-centric conception of the project of reconstructing democratic political institutions will not suffice. Attention has also to be given to a multi-faceted project of transnational, regional or global democratization.

The modern system of nation-states, which began with the Peace of Westphalia of 1648, has been characterized, to use David Held's apt words, by such features as: 'democracy *in* nation-states and non-democratic relations *among* states; the entrenchment of accountability and democratic legitimacy *inside* state boundaries and the pursuit of power politics *outside* such boundaries; democracy and citizenship rights for *insiders* and their frequent negation for *outsiders* (Held, 1993: 266). This Westphalian system, which did not have a conception of democracy *beyond* the boundaries of the nation-state, has only been partially or weakly modified by the U.N. system. While in some respects, the U.N. does recognize such democratic principles as the equality of all states (e.g., in the General Assembly), the Declaration of Universal Human Rights and the principle of national self-determination, in other respects (e.g., the membership and voting system of the Security Council), it accommodates itself to the vast inequalities of political, economic, military and technological power among the member-states (cf. Held, 1993).

What all this means for our present concerns is that the conjunction of the emergence of an insufficiently democratic 'new world order' of international/transnational economic, political, communications and security organizations and networks on the one hand and on the other the decrease in the autonomy of the nation-state as well as the weakening of democratic political organizations at the national level has resulted in a massive denial of *swaraj* or democratic rights *with* ethico-political responsibilities to the people.

In this emerging 'new world order,' the *swarajist* or decolonizing/
postcolonizing affirmation of the basic liberal-democratic ideal of
the *freedom and equality of all* will have no competitive chance
against the might-is-right non-principle. It is in this situation that
we need critical and reconstructive thought about the institutional
expressions (or dis-expressions?) of the basic ideals of *swaraj* and
sarvodaya at not only the local and national levels but also the
international and global levels of our material existence.

Bibliography

Chapter 1: Political Theories and Social Reconstruction: An Introduction

Anderson, B. 1983. *Imagined Communities: Reflections on the Origin and Spread of Nationalism*. London: Verso.

Austin, Granville. 1966. *The Indian Constitution: Cornerstone of a Nation*. Oxford: Clarendon Press.

Bakshi, O.P. 1987. *The Crisis of Political Theory*. Delhi: Oxford University Press.

Benhabib, Seyla. 1986. *Critique, Norm, and Utopia*. New York: Columbia University Press.

Berlin, Isaiah. 1962. 'Does Political Theory Still Exist?,' in P. Laslett and W.G. Runciman, eds., *Philosophy, Politics and Society*, Second Series. Oxford: Basil Blackwell.

Bernstein, Richard. 1976. *The Restructuring of Social and Political Theory*. Oxford: Basil Blackwell.

——————. 1991. *The New Constellation*. Cambridge: Polity Press, and Oxford: Basil Blackwell.

Bondurant, Joan V. 1959. *Conquest of Violence: The Gandhian Philosophy of Conflict*. Bombay: Oxford University Press.

Bottomore, Tom, ed., 1983. *A Dictionary of Marxist Thought*. Delhi: Oxford University Press.

Callinicos, A., ed., 1989. *Marxist Theory*. Oxford: Oxford University Press.

Chatterjee, Partha. 1977. 'Stability and Change in the Indian Political System,' *Political Science Review*, XVI (1), January–March.

Connolly, William. 1974. *The Terms of Political Discourse*. Lexington, Mass.: D.C. Heath.

Dallmayr, Fred. 1991. *Life-World, Modernity and Critique*. Cambridge: Polity/ Oxford: Basil Blackwell.

Deutsch, Karl. 1963. *The Nerves of Government*. New York: Free Press of Glencoe.

Dunn, John. 1985. *Rethinking Modern Political Theory*. Cambridge: Cambridge University Press.

——————. 1990. *Interpreting Political Responsibility*. Cambridge: Polity/Oxford: Basil Blackwell.

——————, ed., 1992. *Democracy: The Unfinished Journey*. Oxford: Oxford University Press.

Dutta, Ratna. 1971. *Values in Models of Modernization*. Delhi: Vikas.

Dworkin, Ronald. 1977. *Taking Rights Seriously*. London: Duckworth.

Fay, Brian. 1975. *Social Theory and Political Practice*. London: George Allen and Unwin.

Gray, J. 1986. *Liberalism*. Milton Keynes: Open University Press.

Habermas, Jurgen. 1990. *Moral Consciousness and Communicative Action*. Cambridge: Polity/Oxford: Basil Blackwell.

Harre, R. 1976. 'The Constructive Role of Models,' in L. Collins, ed., *The Use of Models in the Social Sciences*. London: Tavistock.

Held, David. 1987. *Models of Democracy*. Cambridge: Polity.

—————. 1989. *Political Theory and the Modern State*. Cambridge: Polity.

Horton, John. 1990. 'Weight or Lightness? Political Philosophy and Its Prospects,' in A. Leftwich, ed., *New Developments in Political Science*. Aldershot: Edward Elgar.

Jessop, B. 1982. *The Capitalist State: Marxist Theories and Methods*. Oxford: Martin Robertson.

Kaviraj, Sudipta. 1979. 'Concept of Man in Political Theory,' Parts I & II, *Social Scientist*, Nos. 87 and 88, October and November.

—————. 1986. 'Marxian Theory and Analysis of Indian Politics,' in *A Survey of Research in Political Science, Vol. IV: Political Thought*. New Delhi: Indian Council of Social Science Research; and Allied Publishers.

Keohane, N.O. 1976. 'Philosophy, Theory, Ideology: An Attempt at Clarification,' *Political Theory*, IV (1), February.

Kohli, Atul. 1991. *Democracy and Discontent: India's Growing Crisis of Governability*. Cambridge: Cambridge University Press. Indian edition, 1992, New Delhi: Foundation Books.

Kothari, Rajni. 1976. *Democratic Polity and Social Change*. Bombay: Allied.

—————. 1986. 'Contributions to Theory,' in *A Survey of Research in Political Science, Vol. IV: Political Thought*. New Delhi: Indian Council of Social Science Research; and Allied Publishers.

Kuhn, Thomas. (1962)/1970. *The Structure of Scientific Revolutions*. Chicago: University of Chicago Press.

Kumar, Ravinder. 1983. *Essays in the Social History of Modern India*. Delhi: Oxford University Press.

Kymlicka, Will. 1990. *Contemporary Political Philosophy*. Oxford: Clarendon Press.

Lloyd, C. 1989. 'Realism, Structuralism, and History: Foundations for a Transformative Science of Society,' *Theory and Society*, Vol. 18.

MacIntyre, A. 1983. 'The Indispensability of Political Theory,' in D. Miller and L. Siedentop (1983).

Macpherson, C.B. 1973. *Democratic Theory*. Oxford: Clarendon Press.

—————. 1977. *Life and Times of Liberal Democracy*. Oxford University Press.

McCarthy, Thomas. 1991. *Ideals and Illusions: On Reconstruction and Deconstruction in Contemporary Critical Theory*. Cambridge, Mass.: MIT Press.

Miller, D. 1987. 'Political Theory,' in *Blackwell Encyclopedia of Political Thought*. Oxford: Blackwell.

Miller, D. and **L. Siedentop**, eds., 1983. *The Nature of Political Theory*. Oxford: Clarendon Press.

Mohanty, Manoranjan. 1979. 'Value Movement and Development Models in Contemporary India,' *Teaching Politics*, V (1 & 2).

—————. 1989. 'Changing Terms of Discourse: A Poser,' *Economic and Political Weekly*, 16 September.

Nehru, Jawaharlal. (1938)/1948. *The Unity of India*. London: Lindsay Drummond.

Ostergaard, G. and **M. Currell.** 1971. *The Gentle Anarchists*. Oxford: Clarendon Press.

Rao, K. Raghavendra. 1966. 'Political Process and Social Change in Modern India,' in G.S. Halappa, ed., *Dilemmas of Democratic Political Behaviour in India*. Bombay.

Roy, Ramashray. 1982. *Against the Current: Essays in Alternative Development*. New Delhi: Satvahan.

Ryan, Alan. 1972. '"Normal" Science or Political Ideology?,' in P. Laslett, W.G. Runciman and Q. Skinner, eds., *Philosophy, Politics and Society*. Fourth Series, Oxford: Basil Blackwell.

Skinner, Quentin. 1978. *Foundations of Modern Political Thought*, Vols. I and II. Cambridge: Cambridge University Press.

Taylor, Charles. 1983. 'Political Theory and Practice,' in C. Lloyd, ed., *Social Theory and Political Practice*. Oxford: Clarendon.

——————. 1985. *Philosophical Papers, Vol. 2: Philosophy and the Human Sciences*. Cambridge: Cambridge University Press.

Wolin, Sheldon. 1968. 'Paradigms and Political Theories,' in Preston King and Bhikhu C. Parekh, eds., *Politics and Experience*. Cambridge: Cambridge University Press.

Chapter 2: Models of Liberal Democracy and Modernization

Almond, Gabriel. 1960. 'Introduction,' in Almond and J.S. Coleman, eds., *The Politics of the Developing Areas*. Princeton: Princeton University Press.

——————. 1970. *Political Development*. Boston: Little Brown.

Almond, Gabriel et al., eds., 1973. *Crisis, Choice, and Change*. Boston: Little Brown.

Almond, Gabriel and **S. Verba.** 1963. *The Civic Culture*. Princeton: Princeton University Press.

Amin, Samir. 1977. 'Self-reliance and the New International Economic Order,' *Monthly Review*, 29 (3), July–August.

Apter, D. 1965. *The Politics of Modernization*. Chicago: University of Chicago Press.

Arora, S.K. 1968. 'Pre-empted Future? Notes on Theories of Political Development,' *Behavioural Sciences and Community Development*, II (2), September.

Austin, G. 1966. *The Indian Constitution: Cornerstone of a Nation*. Oxford: Clarendon Press.

Bagchi, A.K. 1980. Review of Frankel (1978). *Indian Book Chronicle*, 1 September.

Barker, Ernest. 1951. *Principles of Social and Political Theory*. London: Oxford University Press.

Baxi, Upendra. 1990. 'The Recovery of Fire: Nehru and Legitimation of Power in India,' *Economic and Political Weekly*, XXV (2), 13 January, pp. 107–12.

Bhambhri, C.P. 1976. 'Theoretical Perspectives on Political Science,' *Indian Journal of Political Science*, 37 (4), October–December.

Bharadwaj, Krishna. 1989. 'The Resurgence of Political Economy,' in Bharadwaj and Kaviraj, 1989.

Bharadwaj, Krishna, and **Sudipta Kaviraj,** eds., 1989. *Perspectives on Capitalism: Marx, Keynes, Schumpeter and Weber*. New Delhi: Sage.

Brandt Report of the Independent Commission on International Development Issues. 1980. *North-South: A Programme for Survival*. London: Pan Books.

Brass, Paul. 1990. *The Politics of India Since Independence*. New Delhi: Orient Longman.

Brown, J.. 1985. *Modern India: The Origin of an Asian Democracy*. Delhi: Oxford University Press.

Byres, T.J. 1988. 'A Chicago View of the Indian State: An Oriental Grin Without an Oriental Cat and Political Economy without Classes,' *Journal of Commonwealth and Comparative Politics*, November.

Chakravarty, Sukhamoy. 1987. *Development Planning: The Indian Experience*. Oxford: Clarendon Press.

——————. 1989. 'Keynes as a Theorist of Capitalism,' in K. Bharadwaj and S. Kaviraj, 1989.

Chandra, Bipan et al., (1984). 'The Communists, the Congress and the Anti-Colonial Movement,' *Economic and Political Weekly*, XIX (17), 28 April.

Chatterjee, Partha. 1974. 'Modern American Political Theory with Reference to Underdeveloped Nations,' *Social Scientist*, September. Also reproduced in S. Kaviraj, P. Chatterjee et al., *The State of Political Theory*. Calcutta: Research India Publications, 1978.

——————. 1986. *Nationalist Thought and the Colonial World: A Derivative Discourse?* New Delhi: Oxford University Press.

Coleman, James. 1960. In G. Almond and J.S. Coleman, eds., *The Politics of the Developing Areas*. Princeton: Princeton University Press.

——————. 1973. 'The Resurrection of Political Economy,' in N. Uphoff and W.F. Ilchman, eds., *The Political Economy of Development*. Berkeley: University of California Press.

Cox, Robert W. 1979. 'Ideologies and the New International Economic Order,' *International Organization*, 33 (2), Spring.

Crozier, M.J. et al., 1975. *The Crisis of Democracy: Report on the Governability of Democracies to the Trilateral Commission*. New York: New York University Press.

Dahl, Robert. 1956. *A Preface to Democratic Theory*. Chicago: University of Chicago Press.

Dasgupta, J. 1989. 'India: Democratic Becoming and Combined Development,' in L. Diamond et al., eds., *Democracy in Developing Countries*. Boulder, Colo.: Lynne Rienner.

Desai, A.R. 1984. *India's Path of Development, A Marxist Approach*. Bombay: Popular Prakashan.

Dube, S.C. 1989. 'Development Theory: From Present Impasse to a Fresh Orientation,' in I. Narain, 1989.

Evans, Peter, and **J.D. Stephens.** 1988. 'Studying Development since the Sixties: The Emergence of a New Comparative Political Economy,' *Theory and Society*, XVII, pp. 713–748.

Evans, P. et al., 1985. *Bringing the State Back In*. Cambridge: Cambridge University Press.

Franda, Marcus. 1980. *India's Rural Development: An Assessment of Alternatives*. Bloomington, Indiana: Indiana University Press.

Frankel, Francine. 1978. *India's Political Economy, 1947–1977: The Gradual Revolution*. Bombay: Oxford University Press.

——————. 1989. 'Modernization and Dependency Theories: Is a Social Science of Development Possible?' in I. Narain 1989.

Frankel, Francin and **M.S.A. Rao**, eds., 1989–90. *Dominance and State Power in India*, 2 vols. Delhi: Oxford University Press.

Galtung, John, Peter O'Brien and **Roy Preiswerk**, eds., 1980. *Self-Reliance: A Strategy for Development*. London: Bogle L'Ouverture Publications Ltd. (The Annexure on pp. 401–411 contains the COCOYOC Declaration of 1974.)

Gopal, S. 1980. 'The Formative Ideology of Jawaharlal Nehru,' in K.N. Panikkar, ed., *National and Left Movements in India*. New Delhi: Vikas.

——————. 1984. *Jawaharlal Nehru: A Biography. Vol. III*. New Delhi: Oxford University Press.

Gupta, S.D. 1978. 'The Concept of Political development and its Meaning as an Ideology,' in S. Kaviraj, S.D. Gupta et al., eds., *The State of Political Theory*. Calcutta: Research India Publications.

Hardgrave, Robert. 1984. *India Under Pressure: Prospects for Political Stability*. Boulder, Colo.: Westview Press.

Held, David. 1987. *Models of Democracy*. Cambridge: Polity Press.

Herrera, A.O. et al., 1976. *Catastrophe or New Society? A Latin American World Model*. Ottawa: International Development Research Centre.

Higgott, R.A. 1983. *Political Development Theory*. London: Croom Helm.

Hoogvelt, A.M.M. 1978. *The Sociology of Developing Societies*. Second edition. London: Macmillan.

——————. 1982. *The Third World in Global Development*. London: Macmillan.

Huntington, S.P. 1968. *Political Order in Changing Societies*. New Haven: Yale University Press.

——————. 1975. 'The United States,' in M.J. Crozier, S.P. Huntington and J. Watanuki, eds., *The Crisis of Democracy*. New York: New York University Press.

Joshi, P.C. 1979. 'Gandhi and Nehru: The Challenge of a New Society,' in B.R. Nanda et al., 1979.

Kaviraj, Sudipta. 1980. 'Apparent Paradoxes of Jawaharlal Nehru,' *Mainstream*. 15, 22 and 29 November and 6 and 13 December.

——————. 1984. 'On the Crisis of Political Institutions in India,' *Contributions to Indian Sociology*. 18 (2).

——————. 1988. 'A Critique of the Passive Revolution,' *Economic and Political Weekly*, Special Number, November.

Kegley, C.W. and **E.R.W. Wittkopf.** 1981. *World Politics: Trend and Transformation*. New York: St. Martin's Press.

Khaliq, Zoya. 1977. 'A Critical Note on the Tradition-Modernity Framework,' *Teaching Politics*, III (1 & 2).

Kochanek, S.A. 1986. 'Regulation and Liberalization Theology in India,' *Asian Survey*, 26: 12.

Kohli, Atul. 1980. 'Democracy, Economic Growth, and Inequality in India's Development,' *World Politics*, 32 (4), July.

——————. 1987. *The State and Poverty in India*. Bombay: Orient Longman.

——————. 1991. *Democracy and Discontent: India's Growing Crisis of Governability*. Cambridge: Cambridge University Press. Indian edition, 1992 from New Delhi: Foundation Books.

Kothari, Rajni. 1988. 'Political Economy of the Indian State: The Rudolph Thesis,' *Contributions to Indian Sociology*, 22 (2), pp. 273–78.

Krishna, Daya. 1979. *Political Development: A Critical Perspective*. Bombay: Oxford University Press.

Krishna, Raj. 1978. 'The Next Phase in Rural Development,' *Voluntary Action*, 20 (7), July.

Kumar, Sushil. 1978. 'The Concept of Political Development,' *Political Studies*, XXVI (4), December.

Lerner, D. 1965. *The Passing of Traditional Society*. New York: Free Press.

Lipset, S.M. 1960. *Political Man*. New York: Doubleday.

Macpherson, C.B. 1972. *The Real World of Democracy*. Oxford: Oxford University Press.

——————. 1973. *Democratic Theory*. Oxford: Clarendon Press.

——————. 1977a. *The Life and Times of Liberal Democracy*. Oxford: Oxford University Press.

——————. 1977b. 'Do We Need a Theory of the State?,' *Arch. Europ. Sociol.*, 18 (2), pp. 223–44.

——————. 1978. 'The False Roots of Western Democracy,' in Fred Dallmayr, ed., *From Contract to Community*. New York: Marcel Dekker.

Manor, J. 1983. 'Anonie in Indian Politics,' *Economic and Political Weekly*, 18: 19.

——————. 1990. 'How and Why Liberal Representative Politics Emerged in India,' *Political Studies*, 38(1).

Mathur, Gautam. 1989. 'Economic Order in a Firm State,' in I. Narain, 1989.

Mehta, V.R. 1983. *Ideology, Modernization and Politics in India*. New Delhi: Manohar.

Mesarovic, M. and E. Pestel. 1976. *Mankind at the Turning Point*. New York: New American Library.

Mitra, Subrata, ed., 1990. *The Postcolonial State in Asia*. Herrel Hemstead: Harvester Wheatsheat.

——————. 1991. 'Crisis and Resilience in Indian Democracy,' *International Social Science Journal*, August.

Mohanty, Manoranjan. 1979. 'Value Movement and Development Models in Contemporary India,' *Teaching Politics*, V (1 & 2), pp. 40–66.

Morris-Jones, W.H. 1971. *The Government and Politics of India*. Third revised edition. London: Hutchinson University Library.

——————. 1980. 'The West and the Third World: Whose Democracy, Whose Development?' in B.K. Nehru and Morris-Jones 1980.

——————. 1984. 'India—More Questions than Answers,' *Asian Survey*, 24: 8, August.

Mukherjee, A., and M. Mukherjee. 1988. 'Imperialism and Growth of Indian Capitalism in Twentieth Century,' *Economic and Political Weekly*, 12 March.

Muni, S.D. 1989. 'Dependency Theories and Development Dilemmas of the Third World,' in I. Narain, 1989.

Nanda, B.R., P.C. Joshi and Raj Krishna. 1979. *Gandhi and Nehru*. Delhi: Oxford University Press.

Nandy, Ashis. 1983. *The Intimate Enemy: Loss and Recovery of Self Under Colonialism*. New Delhi: Oxford University Press.

Narain, Iqbal, ed., 1989. *Development, Politics and Social Theory:. Essays in Honour of Professor S.P. Varma*. New Delhi: Sterling.

Nayar, Baldev Raj. 1972. *The Modernization Imperative and Indian Planning*. New Delhi: Vikas.

Nayar, Baldev Raj. 1989. *India's Mixed Economy: The Role of Ideology and Interests in its Development*. Bombay: Popular Prakashan.

——————. 1992. 'The Politics of Economic Restructuring in India: The Paradox of State Strength and Policy Weakness,' *Journal of Commonwealth and Comparative Politics*, 30: 2.

Nehru, B.K. 1980. 'Western Democracy and the Third World,' in Nehru and Morris-Jones, *Western Democracy and the Third World*. London: Third World Foundation.

Nehru, B.K. and **W.H. Morris-Jones**. 1980. *Western Democracy and the Third World*. London: Third World Foundation. This first appeared in *Third World Quarterly*, I (2 and 3), 1979.

Nerfin, M. 1977. *Another Development: Approaches and Strategies*. Uppsala: Dag Hammarskjold Foundation.

O'Brien, Donald Cruise. 1972. 'Modernization, Order, and the Erosion of a Democratic Ideal: American Political Science 1960–70,' *Journal of Development Studies*, VIII (6), July.

Offe, Claus. 1984. *Contractions of the Welfare State*. London: Hutchinson.

Panikkar, K.M. 1955. *Hindu Society at the Crossroads*. Bombay: Asia Publishing House.

Palmer, N. 1977. 'Development: The Need for an Effective Dialogue,' in S.K. Sharma, ed., *Dynamics of Development*. Delhi: Concept Publishing.

Pantham, Thomas. 1976–77. 'On the Theory of Democracy: A Critique of the Schumpeter-Dahl Axis,' *Journal of the Maharaja Sayajirao University of Baroda*, XXV–XXVI (2), pp. 65–86.

——————. 1980. 'Elites, Classes and the Distortions of Economic Transition in India,' in Sachchidananda and A.K. Lal, eds., *Elite and Development*. New Delhi: Concept Publishing House. (This article also appears in N.R. Inamdar, ed., *Contemporary India: Socio-Economic and Political Processes*. Poona: Continental Prakashan, 1982.)

——————. 1985. 'Some Trends in American Theorizing on Political Development,' in R.M. Crunden, ed., *Traffic of Ideas Between India and America*. Delhi: Chanakya.

——————. 1985a. 'The Crisis of Liberal Democracy: Three Theories,' *Teaching Politics*, XI (1), pp. 1–15.

——————. 1991. 'Understanding Nehru's Political Ideology,' in Amal Ray et al., eds., *The Nehru Legacy: An Appraisal*. New Delhi: Oxford and IBH Publishing Co.

Parekh, Bhikhu. 1991. 'Nehru and the National Philosophy of India,' *Economic and Political Weekly*, XXVI (1 & 2), 5–12 January, pp. 35–48.

——————. 1992. 'The Cultural Particularity of Liberal Democracy,' *Political Studies*, XL, Special Issue.

Patel, I.G. 1987. 'On Taking India into the Twenty-first Century,' *Modern Asian Studies*, 21: 2.

Pateman, C. 1970. *Participation and Democratic Theory*. Cambridge: Cambridge University Press.

Pool, Ithiel de Sola. 1967. 'The Public and the Polity,' in Pool, ed., *Contemporary Political Science*. New York (26).

Prasad, Bimal. 1985. *Gandhi, Nehru and JP*. Delhi: Chanakya Publications.

Pye, L. 1966. *Aspects of Political Development*. Boston: Little Brown.

Raj, K.N. 1973. 'The Politics and Economics of Intermediate Regimes,' *Economic and Political Weekly*, B (27), pp. 1189–98.

Rana, A.P. 1976. *The Imperatives of Non-Alignment*. New Delhi: Macmillan.

——————. 1983. 'Non-Alignment and International Change: Strategic and Socio-economic Dimensions,' *The Non-Aligned World*, I (3), July–September.

——————. 1987. 'The Legitimacy Crisis of Contemporary Non-Alignment: A Paradigmatic Enquiry and Research Proposal,' *Paradigms: The Kent Journal of International Relations*, I (2), December.

——————. 1989. 'The Non-aligned Regulation of India's National Security Problematic, and the Universalization of International Society: A Conceptual Study of Nehru's International Legacy,' paper presented at the Seminar on Nehru Legacy, held at the Institute for Social and Economic Change, Bangalore, February 1989.

Rao, V.K.R.V. and **P.C. Joshi.** 1982. 'Some Fundamental Aspects of Socialist Transformation in India,' *Man and Development*. IV (2), June.

Reshaping the International Order. A Report to the Club of Rome. New York: E.P. Duttin and Co. 1976.

Riggs, F. 1964. *Administration in Developing Countries*. Boston: Houghton Mifflin.

Rudolph, Lloyd I. and **Susanne H. Rudolph.** 1967. *The Modernity of Tradition: Political Development in India*. New Delhi: Orient Longman.

——————. 1987. *In Pursuit of Lakshmi: The Political Economy of the Indian State*. New Delhi: Orient Longman.

Sandbrook, Richard. 1976. 'The "Crisis" in Political Development Theory,' *Journal of Development Studies*, 12 (2), January.

Sen, Amartya. 1981. 'Public Action and the Quality of Life in Developing Countries,' *Oxford Bulletin of Economics and Statistics*, no. 43.

——————. 1982. 'How is India Doing?' *New York Review of Books*, 16 December.

——————. 1983. 'India: The Doing and the Undoing,' *Economic and Political Weekly*, 12 February.

Sharma, S.K., ed., 1977. *Dynamics of Development: An International Perspective*, Vol. I and II. Delhi: Concept Publishing Co.

Sheth, D.L. 1989. 'State, Nation and Ethnicity: Experience of Third World Countries,' *Economic and Political Weekly*, 25 March.

Shils, E. 1963. 'On the Comparative Study of the New States,' in C. Geertz, ed., *Old Societies and New States*. Princeton: Princeton University Press.

——————. 1972. *The Intellectuals and the Powers*. Chicago: University of Chicago Press.

Shourie, Arun. 1978. *Symptoms of Fascism*. New Delhi: Vikas Publishing House.

Singh, H.K.M. 1975. 'Jawaharlal Nehru and Economic Change,' *Economic and Political Weekly*, Special Number, August.

Singh, Yogendra. 1974. 'Concepts and Theories of Social Change: A Trend Report,' in *A Survey of Research in Sociology and Social Anthropology*, Vol. I. New Delhi: ICSSR, and Bombay: Popular Prakashan.

——————. 1989a. 'Relevance of Max Weber for the Understanding of Indian Reality,' in Bharadwaj and Kaviraj, 1989.

——————. 1989b. 'Facing upto Modernity: The Web of Mystifications and Contradictions,' in I. Narain, 1989.

Smith, A.D. 1973. *The Concept of Social Change: A Critique of the Functionalist Theory of Social Change*. London: Routledge and Kegan Paul.

Smith, T. 1979. 'The Underdevelopment of Development Literature,' *World Politics*, 31 (2), January.

Somjee, A.H. 1978. 'Ethnocentricity and Value Ambiguity in Political Development Studies,' *Political Studies*, June.

——————. 1982. *Political Capacity in Developing Societies*. London: Macmillan.

——————. 1989. 'Core Issues in Political Development,' in I. Narain, 1989.

Sridharan, E. 1991. 'Leadership Time Horizons in India: The Impact of Economic Restructuring,' *Asian Survey*, 31: 12.

——————. 1993. 'Economic Liberalisation and India's Political Economy: Towards a Paradigm Synthesis,' *Journal of Commonwealth and Comparative Politics*, 31: 3.

Thapar, Romesh. 1968. Review of G. Myrdal's *Asian Drama. Yojana*, 13 May.

Toye, J. 1987. Dilemmas of Development. Oxford: Basil Blackwell.

Varma, S.P. 1989. 'Models of Development: Search for Alternatives,' in Iqbal Narain, 1989.

Ward, R. 1963. 'Political Modernization and Political Culture in Japan,' *World Politics*, 15 (4), July.

Weiner, M. 1983. 'The Wounded Tiger: Maintaining India's Democratic Institutions,' in P. Lyon and J. Manor, eds., *Transfer and Transformation*. Leicester University Press.

Yadav, Yogendra. 1990. 'Theories of the Indian State,' *Mainstream*, March.

Chapter 3: Marxist and Neo-Marxist Theories of Social Transformation

Alam, Javeed. 1983. 'Peasantry, Politics and Historiography: Critique of New Trends in Relation to Marxism,' *Social Scientist* 11 (May): 5 (No. 117), pp. 43–54.

——————. 1983a. 'Dialectics of Capitalist Transformation and National Crystallisation: The Past and Present of the National Question in India,' *Economic and Political Weekly*, 29 January.

Alavi, Hamza. (1972) 1973. 'The State in Postcolonial Societies,' in Gough and Sharma, 1973.

——————. 1975. 'India and the Colonial Mode of Production,' *Economic and Political Weekly*, Special Number, August.

——————. 1980. 'India: Transition from Feudalism to Colonial Capitalism,' *Journal of Contemporary Asia*, X (4), pp. 359–99.

——————. 1982. 'State and Class under Peripheral Capitalism,' in Alavi and T. Shanin, eds., *Introduction to the Sociology of Developing Societies*. London: Macmillan.

Amin, Samir. 1974. *Accumulation on a World Scale. Vol. I & II*. New York: Monthly Review Press.

——————. 1976. *Unequal Development*. Sussex: Harvester Press.

——————. 1977. *Imperialism and Unequal Development*. Sussex: Harvester Press.

——————. 1980. *Class and Nation, Historically and in the Current Crisis*. London: Heineman.

Avineri, S., ed., 1968. *Karl Marx on Colonialism and Underdevelopment*. New York.

Bagchi, A.K. 1982. *The Political Economy of Underdevelopment*. Cambridge: Cambridge University Press.

————. 1986. 'Towards a Correct Reading of Lenin's Theory of Imperialism,' in P. Patnaik, ed., 1986.

————. 1988. 'Colonialism and the Nature of the "Capitalist" Enterprise in India,' *Economic and Political Weekly*, 30 July.

Bains, J.S. and **R.B. Jain**, eds., 1981. *Political Science in Transition*. New Delhi: Gitanjali Prakashan.

Banaji, J. 1972. 'For a Theory of Colonial Modes of Production', *Economic and Political Weekly*, VII (52), December.

————. 1975. 'Comment on India and the Colonial Mode of Production,' *Economic and Political Weekly*, 10.

————. 1977. 'Modes of Production in a Materialist Conception of History,' *Capital and Class*, 3, Autumn.

Banerjee, Diptendra, ed., 1985. *Marxian Theory and the Third World*. New Delhi: Sage.

————. 1987. 'The Historical Problematic of Third World Development,' *Social Scientist*, August–September.

Banerjee, D., ed., 1976. *Essays in Honour of Prof. S.C. Sarkar*, New Delhi.

Banerjee, Sumanta. 1982. 'The Island of Dr. Marx,' *Economic and Political Weekly*, 23 January.

Bardhan, Pranab. 1984. *Political Economy of Development in India*. Delhi: Oxford University Press.

————. 1993. 'The "Intermediate Regime": Any Sign of Graduation?' in Bardhan et al., eds., *Development and Change*. Bombay: Oxford University Press.

Bayly, C.A. 1988. 'Rallying Round the Subaltern,' *Journal of Peasant Studies*, 16: 1, October, pp. 110–20.

Berberoglu, Berch. 1978. 'The Meaning of Underdevelopment: A Critique of Mainstream Theories of Development and Underdevelopment,' *International Studies*, XVII (1), January–March.

Bhadra, Bula. 1989. *Materialist Orientalism: Marx, Asiatic Mode of Production and India*. Calcutta: Punthi Pustak.

Bhambhri, C.P. 1981. 'Contemporary Frameworks of Comparative Politics: A Critique,' in Bains and Jain 1981.

————. 1984. 'The State in Contemporary India,' *Mainstream*, Republic Day (January 26): 44–48.

————. 1986. 'Indian Capitalism: Competition and Collaboration with World Monopoly Capitalism,' in P. Patnaik, 1986.

————. 1988. *Politics in India*. New Delhi: Vikas.

————. 1989. 'The Indian State: Conflicts and Contradictions,' in Hasan et al., 1989.

————. 1989a. 'Marxist Concept of Political Economy and its Application to India,' in I. Narain, 1989 (cf. bibliography of chapter 2).

Bharadwaj, Krishna. 1986. 'A Note on Emmanuel's "Unequal Exchange",' in P. Patnaik, 1986.

————. 1989. 'The Resurgence of Political Economy,' in Bharadwaj and Kaviraj, eds., 1989.

Bharadwaj, Krishna and **Sudipta Kaviraj**, eds., 1989. *Perspectives on Capitalism: Marx, Keynes, Schumpeter and Weber*. New Delhi: Sage.

Bhatnagar, Rashmi. 1986. 'Uses and Limits of Foucault: Study of the Theme of Origins in Edward Said's "Orientalism",' *Social Scientist*, No. 158, July.

Booth, D. 1975: 'Andre Gunder Frank: An Introduction and Appreciation,' in I. Oxaal et al., eds., 1975.

Bose, Arun. 1986. 'G. Adikari,' 'J. Basu,' 'P. Das Gupta,' 'A. Ghosh,' and 'B.T. Ranadive,' in Gorman, 1986.

——————. 1989. *India's Social Crisis: An Essay on Capitalism, Socialism, Individualism and Indian Civilization*. Delhi: Oxford University Press.

Brewer, Anthony. 1980. *Marxist Theories of Imperialism: A Critical Survey*. London: Routledge & Kegan Paul.

Carver, T. 1985. 'Marx and Non-European Development,' in Diptendra Banerjee, ed., *Marxian Theory and the Third World*. New Delhi: Sage.

Chakrabarty, Dipesh. 1985. 'Discussion: Invitation to a Dialogue,' in R. Guha, ed., *Subaltern Studies, IV*. New Delhi: Oxford University Press.

——————. 1991. 'History as Critique and Critiques of History,' *Economic and Political Weekly*, 14 September.

Chandra, Bipan. 1979. *Nationalism and Colonialism in India*. New Delhi: Orient Longman.

——————. 1981. 'Karl Marx, His Theories of Asian Societies, and Colonial Rule,' *Review*, V (1), Summer.

——————. 1983. *The Indian Left: Critical Appraisals*. New Delhi: Vikas.

——————. 1988. *The Indian National Movement: The Long-term Dynamics*. New Delhi: Vikas.

Chandra, N.K. 1979. 'Political Economy of India,' *Economic and Political Weekly*, XIV (42 & 43), 27 October.

Chatterjee, Partha. 1974. 'Modern American Political Theory with Reference to Underdeveloped Nations,' *Social Scientist*, September.

——————. 1977. 'Stability and Change in the Indian Political System,' *Political Science Review*, XVI (1), January–March.

——————. 1978. 'Political Development and the Question of Political Stability,' in Kaviraj et al., 1978.

——————. 1978a. 'Violence, Revolution and Political Theory,' *Teaching Politics*, IV (3 & 4).

——————. 1983. 'Peasants, Politics and Historiography: A Response,' *Social Scientist*, May.

——————. 1983a. 'More on Modes of Power and the Peasantry,' in R. Guha, ed., 1983.

——————. 1985. 'Modes of Power: Some Clarifications,' *Social Scientist*, February.

——————. 1986. *Nationalist Thought and the Colonial World: A Derivative Discourse*. Delhi: Oxford University Press.

——————. 1986a. 'The Colonial State and Peasant Resistance in Bengal 1920–1947,' *Past and Present*, Number 110, February, pp. 169–204.

——————. 1987. 'The Constitution of Indian Nationalist Discourse,' in B. Parekh and T. Pantham, eds., *Political Discourse: Explorations in Indian and Western Political Thought*. New Delhi: Sage.

Chattopadhyay, P. 1972. 'On the Question of the Mode of Production in Indian Agriculture: A Preliminary Note,' *Economic and Political Weekly*, VII (13), March.

Chattopadhyay, P. 1972a. 'The Mode of Production in Indian Agriculture: An Anti-kritik,' *Economic and Political Weekly*, VII (53), December.

Chaube, S.K. 1973. *Constituent Assembly of India: Springboard of Revolution.* New Delhi: People's Publishing House.

————. 1978. 'Studies on the Constitution of India: A Methodological Survey,' *Teaching Politics*, IV (1 & 2).

————. 1978. 'Politics among the Social Sciences,' in Kaviraj et al., 1978.

Chopra, Suneet. 1982. 'Missing Correct Perspective,' *Social Scientist*, X (8), August.

Dandekar, V.M 1978. 'Nature of Class Conflict in Indian Society,' *Mainstream*, Republic Day.

Das, Arvind. 1974. 'Three Misconceptions about the State,' *Social Scientist*, November.

————. 1986. 'D.D. Kosambi,' in Gorman, 1986.

Das, Veena. 1989. 'Subaltern as Perspective,' in Ranajit Guha ed., *Subaltern Studies VI*.

Dasgupta, Biplab. 1974. *The Naxalite Movement*. Bombay: Allied Publishers.

Dasgupta, Jyotirindra. 1982. 'Development and Poverty Reduction in South Asia – A Review Article,' *Journal of Asian Studies*, XLII (1), November.

Desai, A.R. 1984. *India's Path of Development: A Marxist Approach*. Bombay: Popular Prakashan.

Dhanagare, D.N. 1983. *Peasant Movements in India*. New Delhi: Oxford.

Dube, Saurabh. 1985. 'Peasant Insurgency and Peasant Consciousness,' *Economic and Political Weekly* 20 (16 March): 11, pp. 445–48.

Emmanuel, A. 1972. *Unequal Exchange: A Study of the Imperialism of Trade.* London: New Left Books, and New York: Monthly Review Press.

————. 1974. 'Myths of Development versus Myths of Underdevelopment,' *New Left Review*, 85, May/June.

Foster-Carter, Aidan. 1976. 'From Rostow to Gunder Frank: Conflicting Paradigms in the Analysis of Underdevelopment,' *World Development*, IV (3), March.

————. 1978. 'The Modes of Production Controversy,' *New Left Review*, 107, January/February.

Frank, Andre Gunder. 1967. *Capitalism and Underdevelopment in Latin America.* New York: Monthly Review Press.

————. 1972. *Lumpenbourgeoisie: Lumpendevelopment*. London: Monthly Review Press.

————. 1973. 'On Feudal Modes, Models and Methods of Escaping Capitalist Reality,' *Economic and Political Weekly*, VIII (1), 6 January.

————. 1977. 'Emergence of Permanent Emergency in India,' *Economic and Political Weekly*, XII (11), 12 March.

Ghosh, Sankar. 1974. *The Naxalite Movement: A Maoist Experiment*. Calcutta: Firma K.L. Mukhopadhyaya.

Gorman, R.A., ed., 1985. *Biographical Dictionary of Neo-Marxism*. Westport, Connecticut: Greenwood Press.

————. 1986. *A Biographical Dictionary of Marxism*. Westport, Connecticut: Greenwood Press.

Gough, K. 1980. 'Modes of Production in South India,' *Economic and Political Weekly*, February.

Gough, K. and **H. Sharma**, eds., 1973. *Imperialism and Revolution in South Asia*. New York: Monthly Review Press.

Guha, Amalendu. 1985. 'Marxist Approach to Indian History—A Framework,' in Kurian, 1985.

Guha, Ranajit. 1981. *A Rule of Property for Bengal: An Essay on the Idea of Permanent Settlement.* Delhi: Orient Longman.

——————, ed., 1982–89. *Subaltern Studies: Writings on South Asian History and Society*, Volumes I to VI. New Delhi: Oxford University Press (referred to in the text as S.S. I to VI).

——————. 1982. 'On Some Aspects of the Historiography of Colonial India,' in Guha, ed., S.S. I.

——————. 1983. *Elementary Aspects of Peasant Insurgency in Colonial India*, Delhi: Oxford University Press.

——————. 1989. 'Dominance without Hegemony and Its Historiography,' in Guha, ed., S.S. VI.

—————— and Gayatri Chakravorty Spivak, eds., 1988. *Selected Subaltern Studies*. New York: Oxford University Press.

Gulap, Haldun. 1981. 'Frank and Wallerstein Revisited: A Contribution to Brenner's Critique,' *Journal of Contemporary Asia*, pp. 169–88.

Gupta, Bhabani Sen. 1973. 'Communism in South Asia,' *Problems of Communism*, XXII, January–February.

——————. 1978. *Communism in Indian Politics*. New Delhi: Young Asia.

Gupta, Dipankar. 1985. 'On Altering the Ego in Peasant History: Paradoxes of the Ethnic Option,' *Peasant Studies*, XIII (1), Fall.

Gupta, Sobhanlal Datta. 1978. 'The Concept of Political Development and Its Meaning as an Ideology,' in Kaviraj et al., 1978.

——————. 1980. *Comintern, India and the Colonial Question.* Calcutta: K.P. Bagchi.

Habib, Irfan. 1975. 'Problems of Marxist Historical Analysis,' in Kurian, 1985.

——————. 1983. 'The Peasant in Indian History,' *Social Scientist*, 118, 2(3), March.

——————. 1983a. 'Marx's Perception of India,' *The Marxist*, 1(1), July–September.

Hardiman, David. 1986. ' "Subaltern Studies" at Crossroads,' *Economic and Political Weekly*, XXI (7), 15 February.

——————. 1987. 'The Nationalist Trap' (Review of Partha Chatterjee 1986), *Economic and Political Weekly*, XXII (3), 17 January.

Hasan, Zoya, S.N. Jha and **Rasheeduddin Khan**, eds., 1989. *The State, Political Process and Identity: Reflections on Modern India.* New Delhi: Sage.

Higgott, R.A. 1983. *Political Development Theory.* London: Croom Helm.

Hobsbawm, E.J., ed., 1964. *Karl Marx: Pre-capitalist Economic Formations.* London: Lawrence and Wishart.

Hoogvelt, Ankie M.M. 1982. *The Third World in Global Development.* London: Macmillan.

Inden, Ronald. 1990. *Imagining India.* Oxford: Basil Blackwell.

Jaksic, M. 1985. 'Marx's Theory of Modes of Production Problems of Colonialism and Underdevelopment,' in D. Banerjee 1985.

Jha, Prem Shankar. 1980. *India—A Political Economy of Stagnation.* New Delhi: Oxford University Press.

Johari, J.C. 1971. 'Naxalite Politics in Andhra Pradesh,' *Indian Journal of Politics*, V (1).

Josh, Bhagwan. 1992. *Struggle for Hegemony in India, 1920–1947, Vol. II: 1934–41.* New Delhi: Sage.

Joshi, P.C., ed., 1969. *Homage to Karl Marx*. New Delhi: People's Publishing House.

——————. 1980. 'Reflections on Marxism and Social Revolution in India,' in K.N. Panikkar, ed., 1980. *National and Left Movements in India*. New Delhi: Vikas.

——————, ed., 1986. *Marxism and Social Revolution in India and Other Essays*. New Delhi: Patriot Publishers.

Kaviraj, Sudipta. 1977. 'The Subtler Side of Domination,' *Teaching Politics*, Vol. III (1 & 2).

——————. 1981. 'Political Culture in Independent India,' *Teaching Politics*, VII (3 & 4), pp. 1–22.

——————. 1983. 'On the Status of Marx's Writings on India,' *Social Scientist*, No. 124, September.

——————. 1984. 'On the Crisis of Political Institutions in India,' *Contributions to Indian Sociology*. 18 (2), pp. 223–43.

——————. 1986. 'Marxian Theory and Analysis of Indian Politics,' in *A Survey of Research in Political Science, Vol. IV: Political Thought*. New Delhi: ICSSR.

——————. 1988. 'A Critique of the Passive Revolution,' *Economic and Political Weekly*, Special Number, November.

——————. 1989. 'On Political Explanation in Marxism,' in Bharadwaj and Kaviraj, eds., 1989.

——————. 1990. Review of Arun Bose 1989. *Contributions to Indian Sociology*, 24 (1): 105–15.

Kaviraj, Sudipta et al., 1978. *The State of Political Theory: Some Marxist Essays*. Calcutta: Research India Publications.

Kohli, Atul. 1989. 'The Politics of Economic Liberalisation in India,' *World Development*, 17: 3.

Kurian, K. Mathew, ed., 1975. *India—State and Society, A Marxian Approach*. Bombay: Orient Longman.

Laclau, E. 1971. 'Feudalism and Capitalism in Latin America,' *New Left Review*, 67, May/June, reprinted with postscript, in Laclau, 1977.

——————. 1977. *Politics and Ideology in Marxist Theory*. London: New Left Books.

Lin, Sharat G. 1980. 'Theory of a Dual Mode of Production in Post-Colonial India,' *Economic and Political Weekly*, 8 March.

Marx, K. 1969. *On Colonialism and Modernization*. ed. with introduction by S. Avineri. New York: Doubleday Anchor.

——————. 1970. *A Contribution to the Critique of Political Economy*. Moscow: Progress Publishers.

Meillassoux, Claude. 1972/1980. 'From Reproduction to Production,' in H. Wolpe, ed., *Articulation of Modes of Production*. London.

——————. 1973. 'Are there Castes in India?,' *Economy and Society*, 2 (1), February.

Mohanty, Manoranjan. 1977. *Revolutionary Violence: A Study of the Maoist Movement in India*. New Delhi: Sterling.

——————. 1979. 'Value Movement and Development Models in Contemporary India,' *Teaching Politics*, V (1 & 2).

——————. 1986. 'Ideology and Strategy of the Communist Movement in India,' in Thomas Pantham and K.L. Deutsch, eds., *Political Thought in Modern India*. New Delhi: Sage, 1986.

Mohanty, Manoranjan. 1991. 'Socialism Tomorrow,' *Janata*, Annual Number.

Mukherjee, Mridula. 1988. 'Peasant Resistance and Peasant Consciousness in Colonial India: "Subalterns" and Beyond,' Parts I & II. *Economic and Political Weekly*, 8 and 15 October.

Mukhia, Harbans. 1985. 'Marx on Pre-Colonial India: An Evaluation,' in D. Banerjee, 1985.

Naqvi, S. 1985. 'Marx on India's Pre-Asiatic Society,' in Kurian, 1985.

Nayar, Baldev Raj. 1989. *India's Mixed Economy: The Role of Ideology and Interests in its Development*. Bombay: Popular Prakashan.

———————. 1992. 'The Politics of Economic Restructuring in India: The Paradox of State Strength and Policy Weakness,' *Journal of Commonwealth and Comparative Politics*, 30: 1.

O'Brien, P.J. 1975. 'A Critique of Latin American Theories of Dependency,' in I. Oxaal et al., eds., 1975.

O'Hanlon, Rosalind. 1988. 'Recovering the Subject: *Subaltern Studies* and Histories of Resistance in Colonial South Asia,' *Modern Asian Studies*, XXII (1), February.

O'Hanlon, Rosalind and **David Washbrook**. 1992. 'After Orientalism: Culture, Criticism and Politics in the Third World,' *Comparative Studies in Soicety and History*, 34 (1), January.

Oxaal, I. et al., eds., 1975: *Beyond the Sociology of Development: Economy and Society in Latin America and Africa*, London: Routledge and Kegan Paul.

Pai, Sudha. 1989. 'Dependency Theory: What Directions has it Taken in Explaining Third World Reality?' *Teaching Politics*, XV (2).

Palat, R. et al., 1987. 'The Incorporation and Peripheralisation of South Asia,' 1600–1950, *Review*, X (1), Summer.

Palma, Gabriel. 1979. 'Marxist Debate on Capitalist Development,' *Mainstream*, 20 January.

Pandey, Gyanendra. 1990. *The Construction of Communalism in Colonial North India*. New Delhi: Oxford University Press.

Pantham, Thomas. 1980. 'Elites, Classes and the Distortions of Economic Transition in India,' in Sachchidananda and A.K. Lal, eds., *Elites and Development*. New Delhi: Concept Publishing House. Also in N.R. Inamdar et al., eds., _Contemporary India: Socio-Economic and Political Processes_. Poona: Continental Prakashan, 1982.

———————. 1986. 'Manabendra Nath Ray,' in Gorman, 1986.

Parekh, Bhikhu. 1982. *Marx's Theory of Ideology*. New Delhi: Ajanta.

———————. 1991. 'The Marxist Discourse on Gandhi,' in D. Tripathi, ed., *Business and Politics in India*. Delhi: Manohar.

———————. 1992. 'Marxism and the Problem of Violence,' *Development and Change*, 23 (3): 103–20.

Patankar, B. and **G. Omvedt**. 1977. 'The Bourgeois State in Postcolonial Social Formations,' *Economic and Political Weekly*, 31 December.

Patnaik, Prabhat. 1973. 'On the Political Economy of Underdevelopment,' *Economic and Political Weekly*, Annual Number, February.

———————. 1973a. 'Imperialism and the Growth of Indian Capitalism,' in Owen and Sutcliffe, 1973.

———————. 1975. 'Imperialism and the Growth of Indian Capitalism,' in Kurian, 1975.

———————. 1986. *Lenin and Imperialism*. New Delhi: Orient Longman.

Patnaik, U. 1971. 'Capitalist Development in Agriculture: A Note,' *Economic and Political Weekly*, VI (39), September.

——————. 1972. 'On the Mode of Production in Indian Agriculture: A Reply,' *Economic and Political Weekly*, VII (40), September.

——————. 1986. 'Neo-Marxian Theories of Capitalism and Underdevelopment: Towards a Critique,' in P. Patnaik, 1986.

——————, ed., 1990. *Agrarian Relations and Accumulation: The Mode of Production Debate in India*. New Delhi: Oxford University Press.

Pilling, Geoffrey. 1973. 'Imperialism, Trade and Unequal Exchange: The Work of Aghiri Emmanuel,' *Economy and Society*, II (2), May.

Prakash, Gyan. 1990. 'Writing Post-Orientalist Histories of the Third World: Perspectives from Indian Historiography,' *Comparative Studies in Society and History*, 32 (2), April.

——————. 1992. 'Can the "Subaltern" Ride? A Reply to O'Hanlon and Washbrook,' *Comparative Studies in Society and History*, 34 (2).

Rai Haridwar and **K.M. Prasad.** 1972. 'Naxalism: The Challenge to the Proposition of Peaceful Transition to Socialism,' *Indian Journal of Political Science*, 30 (4), October–December.

Raj, K.N. 1973. 'The Politics and Economics of Intermediate Regimes,' *Economic and Political Weekly*, 8 (27), pp. 1189–98.

Ray, A.K. 1989. 'Towards the Concept of a Post-Colonial Democracy: A Schematic View,' in Hasan, et al., 1989.

Roemer, J.E. 1985. 'Rational Choice Marxism,' *Economic and Political Weekly*, 20: 34.

Sarkar, Sumit. 1969. 'Marx on Indian History,' in P.C. Joshi, 1969.

Sarkar, S.C. 1976. *Essays in Honour of Prof. S.C. Sarkar*. New Delhi: People's Publishing House.

Sathyamurthy, T.V. 1990. 'Indian Peasant Historiography: A Critical Perspective on Ranajit Guha's Work,' *Journal of Peasant Studies*, pp. 92–144.

Sau, R. 1973. 'On the Essence and Manifestation of Capitalism in Indian Agriculture,' *Economic and Political Weekly*, VIII (13), March.

——————. 1978. *Unequal Exchange: Imperialism and Underdevelopment*. Calcutta: Oxford University Press.

Sen, Asok. 1969. 'Marxism and the Pettybourgeois Default,' in P.C. Joshi, ed., *Homage to Karl Marx*, New Delhi: People's Publishing House.

——————. 1976. 'Bureaucracy and Social Hegemony,' in Sarkar, 1976.

——————. 1985. 'Weber, Gramsci and Capitalism,' *Social Scientist*, 13: 1, January.

——————. 1987. 'Subaltern Studies: Capital, Class and Community,' in R. Guha, ed., S.S. V.

——————. 1989. 'Weber, Gramsci and Capitalism,' in K. Bharadwaj and S. Kaviraj, eds., 1989.

Sen, M. 1976. 'Class Methodology and India,' in Sarkar, 1976.

Seshadri, K. 1986. 'K. Damodaran,' 'T.N. Reddy,' and 'Mohit Sen,' in Gorman, 1986.

Shah, Ghanshyam. 1986. 'A.K.R. Desai,' in Gorman, 1986.

——————. 1990. *Social Movements in India: A Review of the Literature*. New Delhi: Sage.

Shah, S.A., ed., 1982. *India: Degradation and Development*, Parts I & II. Secunderabad: M. Venkatarangaiya Foundation; Bombay: India Book House.

——————. 1990. *Relevance of Marxism in the Contemporary World*. Delhi: Patriot Publishers.

Sharma, T.R. 1990. *Relevance of Marxism in the Contemporary World*. Delhi: Patriot Publishers.

Singh, Randhir. 1989. 'Politics: The Dialectics of Science and Revolution in Karl Marx,' in Bharadwaj and Kaviraj, eds., 1989.

————. 1990. *Of Marxism and Indian Politics*. New Delhi: Ajanta.

————. 1991. 'Communalism and the Struggle against Communalism: A Marxist View,' in Panikkar 1991 (cf. bibliography of chapter 5 *infra*.).

Smith, T. 1979. 'The Underdevelopment of Development Literature,' *World Politics*, 31 (2), January, pp. 247–88.

Spivak, Gayatri Chakravorty. 1985. 'Subaltern Studies: Deconstructing Historiography,' in R. Guha, ed., S.S. IV.

————. 1988. 'Can the Subaltern Speak?' in Cary Nelson and Lawrence Grossberg, eds., *Marxism and the Interpretation of Culture*. Urbana: University of Illinois Press.

Sridharan, E. 1993. 'Economic Liberalisation and India's Political Economy: Towards a Paradigm Synthesis,' *Journal of Commonwealth and Comparative Politics*, 31: 3, November.

Taylor, J.G. 1979. *From Modernisation to Modes of Production: A Critique of the Sociologies of Development and Underdevelopment*, London: Macmillan.

Telang, G.M. 1989. 'The State of the State' (review of Zoya Hasan et al., 1989), *Indian Express*, 30 April.

Thorner, Alice. 1982. 'Semi-Feudalism or Capitalism? Contemporary Debates on Classes and Modes of Production in India,' *Economic and Political Weekly*, XVII (49–50), 4, 11 and 18 December.

Thorner, Daniel. 1966. 'Marx on India and the Asiatic Mode of Production,' *Contributions to Indian Sociology*, Vol. 9.

Toye, J. 1987. *Dilemmas of Development*, Oxford: Basil Blackwell.

Tripathy, Laxman Kumar. 1990. 'Marxism and Social Change: Some Theoretical Reflections,' *Journal of Indian Council of Philosophical Research*, 8 (3), May–August.

Upadhyaya, Prakash Chandra. 1988. Review of *Subaltern Studies* III and IV. *Social Scientist*, 16 (3), March.

Varshney, Ashutosh. 1984. 'Political Economy of Slow Industrial Growth in India,' *Economic and Political Weekly*, 1 September.

Wallerstein, Immanuel. 1974a. 'Dependence in an Interdependent World: The Limited Possibilities of Transformation within the Capitalist World Economy,' *African Studies Review*, XVII (1), April.

————. 1974b. *The Modern World System*, Vol. 1, New York: Academic Press (Vol. II, 1980).

————. 1979. *The Capitalist World Economy*. Cambridge: Cambridge University Press.

————. 1984. *The Politics of the World Economy*. Cambridge: Cambridge University Press.

————. 1986. 'Incorporation of Indian Subcontinent into Capitalist World Economy,' *Economic and Political Weekly*, XXI (4), 25 January.

Washbrook, David. 1990. 'South Asia, the World System, and World Capitalism,' *Journal of Asian Studies*, 49 (3), August.

Weisskopf, Thomas E. (1977) 1978. 'The Persistence of Poverty in India—A Political Economic Analysis,' *Teaching Politics*, Vol. IV (1 & 2).

Yadav, Yogendra. 1989. 'Wither Subaltern Studies?' *New Quest*, July–August.

————. 1990. 'Theories of the Indian State,' *Seminar*, March.

Chapter 4: Gandhi: *Swaraj, Sarvodaya* and *Satyagraha*

Brahmananda, P.R. 1978. Review of Charan Singh 1977. *Indian Book Chronicle*, Vol. III, No. 5, March 1.

Brown, Judith. 1990. *Gandhi: Prisoner of Hope*, Delhi: Oxford University Press.

Chandra, Bipan. 1988. *Indian National Movement: The Long-term Dynamics*. New Delhi: Vikas.

Chatterjee, Partha. 1986. *Nationalist Thought and the Colonial World*. New Delhi: Oxford University Press.

——————. 1987. 'The Constitution of Indian Nationalist Discourse,' in B. Parekh and T. Pantham, 1987.

Conrad, Dieter. 1982. 'Gandhi's Egalitarianism and the Indian Tradition,' in G.D. Sontheimer and P.K. Aithal, eds., *Indology and Law*, Wiesbaden.

——————. 1987. 'The Influence of Western Liberal Ideas on Gandhi's Constitutional Philosophy,' in Mahendra P. Singh, ed., *Comparative Constitutional Law*. Lucknow: Eastern Book Co.

Dallmayr, Fred. 1989. 'Gandhi as Mediator between East and West,' in Dallmayr, *Margins of Political Discourse*. Albany: State University of New York Press.

Dalton, Dennis. 1986. 'The Ideology of Sarvodaya,' in T. Pantham and K.L. Deutsch, eds., *Political Thought in Modern India*. New Delhi: Sage.

Dandekar, V.M. 1978. 'Gandhian Economic System: A Path to Non-economic Goals,' *Mainstream*, XVI, (29 and 30), 18 and 25 March.

Das, A. 1979. *Foundations of Gandhian Economics*. New Delhi: Allied.

——————. 1985. 'Implicit Socio-economic Analysis in Gandhian Thought,' in Diwan and Lutz 1985.

Datta, Babatosh. 1978. Review of Charan Singh 1977. *Indian Book Chronicle*, III (5), 1 March.

Dhanagare, D.N. 1975. *Agrarian Movements and Gandhian Politics*, Agra: Agra University.

Diwan, Romesh and **Mark Lutz**, eds., 1985. *Essays in Gandhian Economics*. New Delhi: Gandhi Peace Foundation.

Fox, R.G. 1987. 'Gandhian Socialism and Hindu Nationalism: Cultural Domination in the World System,' *Journal of Commonwealth and Comparative Politics*, XXV (3), November.

——————. 1989. *Gandhian Utopia*. Boston: Beacon Press.

Ganguli, B.N. 1977. 'Political Economy in the World of Gandhi and Nehru,' in Ganguli, *Indian Economic Thought*. New Delhi: Tata McGraw-Hill.

Grover, D.C. 1980. 'New Left in India: Theory of Social and Political Change,' in J.S. Bains and R.B. Jain, eds., *Perspectives in Political Theory*, New Delhi: Radiant Publishers.

Guha, Ranajit. 1989. 'Dominance without Hegemony and its Historiography,' in Guha, ed., *Subaltern Studies, VI*. Delhi: Oxford University Press.

Haksar, Vinit. 1988. *Civil Disobedience, Threats and Offers: Rawls and Gandhi*. Delhi: Oxford University Press.

Handa, Madan. 1980. 'The Existing World Order: A Gandhian Interpretation,' *Gandhi Marg*, November.

——————. 1985. 'The Elements of a Gandhian Social Theory,' in Selbourne, 1985.

Iyer, Raghavan. 1973. *The Moral and Political Thought of Mahatma Gandhi*. Delhi: Oxford University Press.

Iyer, Raghavan. 1979. *Parapolitics.* New York: Oxford University Press.
————. 1985. 'Gandhi on Socialism and Communism,' *Gandhi Marg*, October.
Josh, Bhagwan. 1992. *Struggle for Hegemony in India, 1920–1947, Vol. II: 1934–41.* New Delhi: Sage.
Joshi, P.C. 1979. 'Gandhi and Nehru: The Challenge of a New Society,' in Nanda et al., 1979.
Kantowsky, D. 1980. *Sarvodaya: The Other Development.* New Delhi: Vikas.
Karlekar, Malavika. 1991. 'Hinduism Revisited: The Relevance of Gandhi Today,' Occasional Paper No. 18. Centre for Women's Development Studies, New Delhi.
Kumar, Ravinder. 1983. 'Class, Community or Nation? Gandhi's Quest for a Popular Consensus in India,' in his *Essays in the Social History of Modern India.* Delhi: Oxford University Press.
Lutz, Mark. 1983. 'Human Nature in Gandhian Economics,' *Gandhi Marg*, March. Reprinted in Diwan and Lutz 1985.
Mohanty, M. 1979. 'Value Movement and Development Models in Contemporary India,' *Teaching Politics*, V (1 & 2).
Mukherjee, Partha N. 1986. 'Sarvodaya after Gandhi: Contradiction and Change,' in Roy, 1986.
Nanda, B.R. et al., 1979. *Gandhi and Nehru.* Delhi: Oxford University Press.
Nandy, Ashis. 1980. 'Final Encounter: The Politics of the Assassination of Gandhi,' in his *At the Edge of Psychology.* New Delhi: Oxford University Press.
————. 1983. *The Intimate Enemy.* New Delhi: Oxford University Press.
————. 1986. 'Oppression and Human Liberation: Towards a Post-Gandhian Utopia,' in Pantham and Deutsch, 1986.
————. 1987a. 'Cultural Frames for Transformative Politics: A Credo,' in Parekh and Pantham 1987.
————. 1987b. *Traditions, Tyranny and Utopias.* Delhi: Oxford University Press.
Oommen, T.K. 1972. *Charisma, Stability and Change.* New Delhi: Thompson Press.
————. 1979. 'Rethinking Gandhian Approach,' *Gandhi Marg*, October, 416–423.
Ostergaard, Geoffrey. 1977. 'Marxism and Gandhism as Strategies for Social Change,' in K. Arunachalam and C. Sadler, eds., *On the Frontiers.* Madurai: Koodal Publishers.
————. 1985a. 'The Ambiguous Strategy of JP's Last Phase,' in Selbourne 1985.
————. 1985b. *Nonviolent Revolution in India.* Sevagram: J.P. Amrit Kosh and New Delhi: Gandhi Peace Foundation.
Pantham, Thomas. 1983. 'Thinking with Mahatma Gandhi: Beyond Liberal Democracy,' *Political Theory*, 11 (2) May. Reproduced in Pantham and Deutsch 1986.
————. 1986. 'Proletarian Pedagogy, Satyagraha and Charisma: Notes On Gramsci and Gandhi,' in Roy 1986.
————. 1986a. 'Habermas's Practical Discourse and Gandhi's Satyagraha,' *Praxis International*, VI (2), July. Reprinted in Parekh and Pantham 1987.

Pantham, Thomas. 1988. 'On Modernity, Rationality and Morality: Habermas and Gandhi,' *Indian Journal of Social Science*, I (2), April–June.

——————. 1989. 'Gandhi, Nehru, and Modernity.' (Paper presented at the India-China Seminar on Interactions between Tradition and Modernity, Chinese Academy of Social Sciences, Beijing, 30 October–2 November 1989. In U. Baxi and B. Parekh, eds., *Crisis and Change in Contemporary India*. New Delhi: Sage, 1995.

——————. 1991. 'Understanding Nehru's Political Ideology,' in Amal Ray et al., eds., *The Nehru Legacy: An Appraisal*. New Delhi: Oxford and IBH.

——————. 1991a. 'Postrelativism in Emancipatory Thought: The Significance of Gandhi's Swaraj and Satyagraha.' Paper presented at the Workshop on Rethinking Emancipation, Institute of Social Studies, The Hague, Netherlands, 30 January–1 February 1991. Forthcoming in D.L. Sheth and Ashis Nandy, eds., *The Multiverse of Democracy* (New Delhi: Oxford University Press, forthcoming).

Pantham, Thomas and **K.L. Deutsch**, eds., 1986. *Political Thought in Modern India*. New Delhi: Sage.

Parekh, Bhikhu. 1989a. *Gandhi's Political Philosophy*. London: Macmillan.

——————. 1989b. *Colonialism, Tradition and Reform*. New Delhi: Sage.

——————. 1991a. 'Gandhi's Quest for a Non-Violent Political Philosophy,' in L. Rouner, ed., *Celebrating Peace*. Notre Dame, Indiana: University of Notre Dame Press.

——————. 1991b. 'The Marxist Discourse on Gandhi,' in D. Tripathi, ed., *Business and Politics in India: A Historical Perspective*. Delhi: Manohar.

Parekh, Bhikhu and **Thomas Pantham**, eds., 1987. *Political Discourse: Explorations in Indian and Western Political Thought*. New Delhi: Sage.

Pillai, Vijay. 1982. 'Approaches to Development: A Critique,' *Alternatives*, 8 (3), September.

Prasad, Bimal, ed., 1980. *A Revolutionary's Quest: Selected Writings of Jayaprakash Narayan*. Delhi: Oxford University Press.

——————. 1985. *Gandhi, Nehru and JP: Studies in Leadership*. Delhi: Chanakya Publications.

Prasad, Kamta. 1986. 'Contemporary Relevance of Gandhian Economic Thought'. Paper presented at the Seminar on Gandhism and the Social Sciences, Gandhian Institute of Studies, Varanasi.

Prasad, Nageshwar, ed., 1985. *Hind Swaraj: A Fresh Look*. New Delhi: Gandhi Peace Foundation.

Pyarelal. 1956. *Mahatma Gandhi: The Last Phase, Vol. II*. Ahmedabad: Navajivan.

Raj, Sebasti L. 1986. *Total Revolution: The Final Phase of Jaya Prakash Narayan's Political Philosophy*. Madras: Satya Nilayam.

Rajasekharaiah, A.M. et al., 1977. *Reform of the Indian Political System: The Gandhian Alternative*. Dharwar: Lincoln Institute of Social Research and Public Opinion.

Ramamurthy, Acharya. 1986. 'Gandhian Perspective on the Reconstruction of the Indian Polity,' in Roy, 1986.

Rao, K. Raghavendra. 1985. 'State and Society: A Swarajist Framework,' in N. Prasad, 1985.

Rao, K. Raghavendra. 1986. 'Political Philosophy and the Transformation of Indian Politics,' in Roy, 1986.

——————. 1987. 'Communication against Communication: The Gandhian Critique of Modern Civilization in *Hind Swaraj*,' in Parekh and Pantham, 1987.

Rao, V.K.R.V. 1970. 'The Gandhian Alternative to Western Socialism,' *India Quarterly*, XXVI (4), October–December.

——————. 1979. 'Social Change and Relevance of Gandhi,' *Mainstream*, 10 November.

Rothermund, Dietmar. 1991. *Mahatma Gandhi: An Essay in Political Biography*. New Delhi: Manohar.

Rothermund, Indira. 1963. *The Philosophy of Restraint: Mahatma Gandhi's Strategy and Indian Politics*. Bombay: Popular Prakashan.

Roy, Ramashray. 1982. *Against the Current: Essays in Alternative Development*. New Delhi: Satvahan.

——————. 1985. *Self and Society*. New Delhi: Sage.

——————. 1987. 'One True World or Many? A Gandhian Perspective,' *Alternatives*, XII, July.

——————, ed., 1986. *Contemporary Crisis and Gandhi*. Delhi: Discovery Publishing House.

Rudolph, L.I. and **Susanne H. Rudolph.** 1967. *The Modernity of Tradition: Political Development in India*. Chicago: University of Chicago Press.

Rudolph, S.H. 1979. 'Beyond Modernity and Tradition: Theoretical and Ideological Aspects of Comparative Social Sciences,' in R.J. Moore, ed., *Tradition and Politics in South Asia*. New Delhi: Vikas.

Saran, A.K. 1969. 'Gandhi's Theory of Society and Our Times,' *Studies in Comparative Religion*, III (4).

——————. 1980. 'Gandhi and the Concept of Politics: Towards a Normal Civilization,' *Gandhi Marg*, February.

Sarangi, Prakash. 1989. 'Gandhi and Rawls on Civil Disobedience,' *Indian Journal of American Studies*, 19 (1–2).

Sarkar, Sumit. 1976. 'The Logic of Gandhian Nationalism,' *Indian Historical Review*, III (1), July.

Selbourne, David, ed., 1985. *In Theory and In Practice*. Delhi: Oxford University Press.

Sethi, J.D. 'Jayaprakash Narayan and His Revolution,' *Gandhi Marg*, 19.

——————. 1978. *Gandhi Today*. New Delhi: Vikas.

——————. 1985. 'Poverty, Alienation and the Way Out,' in Diwan and Lutz, 1985.

——————, ed., 1986a. *Trusteeship: The Gandhian Alternative*. New Delhi: Gandhi Peace Foundation.

——————. 1986b. 'Centralization, Decentralization, or Parallel Polities,' in Roy, 1986.

Shah, Ghanshyam. 1977. *Protest Movements in Two Indian States*. Delhi: Ajanta.

——————. 1979. 'Jayaprakash Narain's Ideology,' *Economic and Political Weekly*, 3 March.

Sharp, Gene. 1970. 'Non-Violence: Moral Principle or Political technique?' *Indian Political Science Review*, IV (1).

Singh, Charan. 1977. *India's Economic Policy: The Gandhian Blue-print.* New Delhi: Vikas.

Upadhyaya, Prakash Chandra. 1989. 'A Celebration of the Gandhian Alternative,' *Economic and Political Weekly,* 2 December.

————. 1992. 'The Politics of Indian Secularism,' *Modern Asian Studies,* 26, 4.

Yadav, Yogendra. 1992. 'JP's Changing Ideas on Social Change,' in N. Prasad, ed., *JP and Social Change.* New Delhi: Radiant.

Chapter 5: The Ideology of Hindu Nationalism

Aalst, Frank D. Van. 1969. 'The Secular State, Secularization, and Secularism,' *Quest,* No. 62, July.

Andersen, Walter K. 1978. 'The Political Philosophy of Deendayal Upadhyaya,' in Raje Sudhakar, ed., *Destination.* Delhi: Deendayal Research Institute, pp. 43–48.

Andersen, Walter K. and **Shridhar D. Damle.** 1987. *The Brotherhood in Saffron: The Rashtriya Swayamsevak Sangh and Hindu Revivalism.* New Delhi: Vistaar Publications.

Badrinath, Chaturvedi. 1989. 'The Quest for India's Secular Identity,' *Times of India* (Ahmedabad), 1 March.

————. 1990. 'Resolution of Conflicts: Potential of Dharmic Methods,' *Times of India* (Ahmedabad), 17 March.

————. 1991. 'Indian Nationalism: Borrowed Ideas, Ironies, Violence,' *Times of India,* 30 July.

Banerjee, Sumanta. 1991. 'Hindutva—Ideology and Social Psychology,' *Economic and Political Weekly,* 19 January.

Basu, Tapan. et al., 1993. *Khaki Shorts and Saffron Flags: A Critique of the Hindu Right.* New Delhi: Orient Longman.

Bhambhri, C.P. 1991. 'State and Communalism in India,' in Panikkar, 1991.

Bhargava, Rajeev. 1991. 'The Right to Culture,' in Panikkar, 1991.

Bidwai, Praful. 1991. 'Countering Majoritarianism: Another Approach to Ayodhya Dispute,' *Times of India,* 4 January.

Bjorkman, J.W., ed., 1988. *Fundamentalism, Revivalists and Violence in South Asia.* New Delhi: Manohar.

Chandra, Bipan. 1984. *Communalism in Modern India.* New Delhi: Vikas.

————. 1991. 'Communalism and the State: Some Issues in India,' in Panikkar, 1991.

Chakrabarty, Bidyut, ed., 1990. *Secularism and Indian Polity.* New Delhi: Segment Book distributors.

Chandramohan, P. 1987. 'Popular Culture and Socio-Religious Reform: Narayana Guru and the Ezhavas of Travancore,' *Studies in History,* III (1).

Dasgupta, Swapan. 1990. 'Journey to Ayodhya: Hindu Nationalism Comes of Age,' *Times of India.* 20 October.

————. 1991. 'Truncated India: Revisionist View of Partition,' *Times of India,* 12 August.

Devdutt. 1981. 'The BJP and Gandhian Socialism: A Case of Ideology-transplant,' *Gandhi Marg,* July.

Dixit, Prabha. 1986. 'The Ideology of Hindu Nationalism,' in Thomas Pantham and K.L.Deutsch, 1986.

Doctor, Adi H. 1991. 'Low Caste Protest Movements in 19th and 20th Century Maharashtra: A Study of Jyotirao Phule and B.R. Ambedkar,' *Indian Journal of Social Science*, IV (2), April–June.

Dube, S.C. and **V.N. Basilov**, eds., 1983. *Secularisation in Multi-Ethnic Societies*. New Delhi: Concept.

Embree, Ainslee T. 1991. *Utopias in Conflict: Religion and Nationalism in Modern India*. Delhi: Oxford University Press.

Engineer, Asghar Ali. 1989. *Communalism and Communal Violence in India: An Analytical Approach to Hindu-Muslim Conflict*. Delhi: Ajanta.

Engineer, Asghar Ali and **Moin Shakir**. 1985. *Communalism in India*. Delhi: Ajanta.

Fox, Richard. 1987. 'Gandhian Socialism and Hindu Nationalism: Cultural Domination in the World System,' *Journal of Commonwealth and Comparative Politics*, XXV (3), November.

—————. 1989. *Gandhian Utopia*. Boston: Beacon Press.

Golwalkar, M.S. 1939. *We, or Our Nation Defined*. Nagpur: Bharat Prakashan, 4th edition 1947.

—————. 1966. *Bunch of Thoughts*. Bangalore: Vikram Prakashan.

Gopal, S., ed., 1991. *Anatomy of a Confrontation: The Babri Masjid-Ramjanmabhumi Issue*. New Delhi: Penguin.

Graham, Bruce. 1990. *Hindu Nationalism and Indian Politics: The Origins and Development of the Bharatiya Jana Sangh*. Cambridge: Cambridge University Press.

Gupta, D. 1991. 'Communalism and Fundamentalism: Some Notes on the Nature of Ethnic Politics in India,' *Economic and Political Weekly*, March.

Gregorios, Paulos. 1989. *Enlightenment: East and West*. Delhi: B.R. Publishing Corporation.

—————. 1990. 'A Western Concept of Secularism Will Not Do for Us,' *Times of India*, 19 March.

Grewal, O.P. and **K.L. Tuteja.** 1990. 'Communalism and Fundamentalism: A Dangerous Form of Anti-Democratic Politics,' *Economic and Political Weekly*, 25 (47), 24 November.

Hasan, Mushirul. 1988. 'Indian Muslims Since Independence: In Search of Integration and Identity,' *Third World Quarterly*, X (2), April.

Hasan, Zoya. 1989. 'Minority Identity, Muslim Women Bill Campaign and the Political Process,' *Economic and Political Weekly*, 7 January.

—————. 1991. 'Changing Orientations of the State and the Emergence of Majoritarianism in the 1980s,' in Panikkar, 1991.

Jaffrelot, Christophe. 1993. 'Hindu Nationalism: Strategic Syncretism in Ideology Building,' *Economic and Political Weekly*, 20–27 March.

Jain, Girilal. 1992. 'Idiom of Public Debate: Combining Bhakti with Power,' *Times of India*, 30 December.

—————. 1993. 'Rise of the Kshatriya: Khalsa Influence on Hindutva,' *Times of India*, 9 April.

Joseph, Sarah. 1993. 'Identity, Culture and Community,' *Economic and Political Weekly*, 24 April.

Kapur, Ratna and **Brenda Cossman.** 1993. 'Communalising Gender/Engendering Community: Women, Legal Discourse and Saffron Agenda,' *Economic and Political Weekly*, 24 April.

Kavalekar, K.K. and **A.S. Chausalkar,** eds., 1989. *Political Ideas and Leadership of B.R. Ambedkar.* Pune: Vishwanil Publications.

Krishna, Gopal. 1991. 'Hinduism should be Semitised,' *Times of India*, 13 May.

Kumar, Krishna. 1991. 'BJP: Practising the Art of Delusion,' *Times of India*, 31 May.

—————. 1991. 'Hindu Revivalism and Education in North-Central India,' in Panikkar, 1991.

Kumar, Pramod, ed., 1992. *Towards Understanding Communalism.* New Delhi: Ajanta.

Kumar, Ravinder. 1983. *Essays in the Social History of Modern India.* Delhi: Oxford University Press.

—————. 1991. 'Contemporary Hinduism: Existential or Instrumental Religion,' *Times of India*, 24 April.

Madan, T.N. 1987. 'Secularism in its Place,' *Journal of Asian Studies*, 46 (4), November.

—————. 1991. 'Ram Bhakti or Power Play: Politics of Hindu Fundamentalism,' *Times of India*, 15 May.

Malik, S.C., ed., 1977. *Dissent, Protest and Reform in Indian Civilization.* Simla: Indian Institute of Advanced Study.

Mohanty, Manoranjan. 1989. 'Secularism: Hegemonic and Democratic,' *Economic and Political Weekly*, 3 June.

Nambissan, Geeta B. et al., 1990. 'Advertising Hate: BJP's Campaign,' *Times of India*, 19 December.

Nandy, Ashis. 1988. 'The Politics of Secularism and the Recovery of Religious Tolerence,' *Alternatives*, vol. XIII: 177–94.

—————. 1991. 'Hinduism Versus Hindutva: The Inevitability of a Confrontation,' *Times of India*, 18 February.

O'Hanlon, Rosalind. 1985. *Caste, Conflict and Ideology: Mahatma Jyotirao Phule and Low Caste Protest in Nineteenth Century Western India.* Bombay: Orient Longman.

Omvedt, Gail. 1971. 'Jyotirao Phule and the Ideology of Social Revolution in India,' *Economic and Political Weekly*, 6 (37), 11 September.

—————. 1990. 'Hinduism and Politics,' *Economic and Political Weekly*, 7 April, 723–29.

Organizer. 1981. 'Gandhi and BJP: Two Emanations of the same spirit,' 25 October.

Padgaonkar, Dileep. 1990. 'India in 1990: Advent of the Advani Age,' *Times of India*, 31 December.

Pandey, Gyanendra. 1990. *The Construction of Communalism in Colonial North India.* Delhi: Oxford University Press.

—————. 1991. 'Hindus and Others: The Militant Hindu Construction,' *Economic and Political Weekly*, 28 December.

Panikkar, K.N., ed., 1991. *Communalism in India: History, Politics and Culture.* New Delhi: Manohar.

Pantham, Thomas and **K.L Deutsch,** eds., 1986. *Political Thought in Modern India.* New Delhi: Sage.

Punalekar, S.P. 1988. 'Identities and Consciousness: An Overview of Dalit Literature in Maharashtra,' *Man and Development*, 10 (4), December.

Raghavan, T.C.A. 1983. 'Origins and Development of Hindu Mahasabha Ideology: The Call of V.D. Savarkar and Bhai Paramanand,' *Economic and Political Weekly*, 9 April, pp. 595–600.

Rothermund, Indira. 1990. 'Fundamentalism has no Legitimacy in Hindu *dharma*,' *Times of India*, 28 August.

Rudolph. L.I. and S.H. Rudolph. 1984. 'Rethinking Secularism: The Genesis and Implications of the Textbook Controversy,' in Rudolph, ed., *Cultural Policy in India*. Delhi.

Savarkar, V.D. 1909/1947. *The Indian War of Independence, 1857*. Bombay: Phoenix Publications, 1947.

—————. 1923. *Hindutva or Who is a Hindu?* Bombay: Veer Savarkay Prakashan.

Shah, Ghanshyam. 1990. *Social Movements in India: A Review of the Literature*. New Delhi: Sage.

Shakir, Moin. 1986. 'Dynamics of Muslim Political Thought,' in Pantham and Deutsch, 1986.

Sharma, G.S., ed., 1966. *Secularism: Its Implications for Law and Life in India.*

Sheth, D.L. 1992. 'Movements, Intellectuals and the State: State Policy in Nation-Building,' *Economic and Political Weekly*, 22 February.

Singh, Randhir. 1988. 'Theorizing Communalism: A Fragmentary Note in the Marxist Mode,' *Economic and Political Weekly*, Vol. 23 (No. 30), 23 July: 1541–48.

—————. 1991. 'Communalism and the Struggle Against Communalism: A Marxist View,' in Panikkar, 1991.

Smith, D.E. 1963. *India as a Secular State*. Bombay: Oxford University Press.

Thapar, Romila. 1989. 'Imagined Religious Communities? Ancient History and the Modern Search for a Hindu Identity,' *Modern Asian Studies*, 23 (2), pp. 209–31.

—————. 1991. 'Communalism and the Historical Legacy: Some Facets,' in Panikkar, 1991.

Upadhyaya, Deendayal, Sri Guruji and D.B. Thengdi. 1979. *The Integral Approach*. New Delhi: Deendayal Research Institute.

Upadhyaya, Prakash Chandra. 1992. 'The Politics of Indian Secularism,' *Modern Asian Studies*, 26 (4).

Varma, V.P. 1979. *Philosophical Humanism and Contemporary India*. Delhi: Motilal Banarsidass.

Vempeny, Ishanand. 1990. 'An Idealist's View of Ayodhya', *Times of India*, 26 October.

—————. 1990a. 'Indian Secularism and Ayodhya,' *Times of India*, 2 November.

Vora, Rajendra. 1986. 'Two Strands of Indian Liberalism: The Ideas of Ranade and Phule,' in Pantham and Deutsch, 1986.

Zelliot, Eleanor. 1986. 'The Social and Political Thought of B.R. Ambedkar,' in Pantham and Deutsch, 1986.

Chapter 6: Theories of 'Integral Pluralism' and 'Alternative Democracy'

Bhambhri, C.P. 1973. 'Functionalism in Politics,' *Indian Journal of Political Science*, 34 (4).

Bhambhri, C.P. 1974. 'Functionalism in Politics: A Rejoinder,' *Indian Journal of Political Science*, April–June.

Chittick, W.O. and **M. Steiner.** 1982. 'Unity in Diversity: Cultural autonomy or panculture?' *Alternatives*, 8.

Chopra, Nina. 1972. Review of R. Kothari, 1970. *Social Scientist*, October.

Cox, Robert W. 1981. 'Social Forces, States and World Orders: Beyond International Relations Theory,' *Millennium: Journal of International Studies*, 10 (2).

Frobel, F. et. al., 1980. *The New International Division of Labour*. Cambridge University Press.

Gupta, Sobhanlal Datta. 1976. 'Rajni Kothari and the "Centre-Periphery" Model: A Critique,' *Socialist Perspective*, III, Special Number, May.

Hoogvelt, A.M.M. 1982. *The Third World in Global Development*. London: Macmillan.

Karat, Prakash. 1984. 'Action Groups/Voluntary Organizations: A Factor in Imperialist Strategy,' *The Marxist*, II (2).

————. 1985. 'Justification for Imperialist-Financed Activities, *Economic and Political Weekly*, 20 (18).

Kaviraj, Sudipta. 1981. 'Political Culture in Independent India: An Antiromantic View,' *Teaching Politics*, 7 (3–4).

Khaliq, Zoya. 1978. Reivew of R. Kothari, 1976a. *Social Scientist*, 7 (7).

Kothari, Rajni. 1970. *Politics in India*. New Delhi: Orient Longman.

————. 1974a. *Footsteps into the Future*. New Delhi: Orient Longman.

————. 1974b. Communication to the editor. *Indian Journal of Political Science*, January–March.

————. 1974c. 'A Reply,' *Indian Journal of Political Science*. April–June.

————. 1976a. *Democratic Polity and Social Change*. Bombay: Allied.

————. 1976b. *State and Nation-building*. Bombay: Allied.

————. 1977. 'India: An Alternative Framework for Rural Development,' in M. Nerfin, ed., *Another Development: Approaches and Strategies*. Uppsala: Dag Hammarskjold Foundation.

————. 1980. 'Towards a Just World,' *Alternatives*, V (4).

————. 1983. 'The Crisis of the Moderate State and the Decline of Democracy,' in P. Lyon and J. Manor, eds., *Transfer and Transformation: Political Institutions in the New Commonwealth*. Leicester University Press.

————. 1984. 'The Non-Party Political Process,' *Economic and Political Weekly*, 19 (5), February.

————. 1986. 'Masses, Classes and the State,' *Alternatives*, 11 (2), April.

————. 1988. *Transformation and Survival: In Search of a Humane World Order*. Delhi: Ajanta.

————. 1988a. *State Against Democracy: In Search of Humane Governance*. Delhi: Ajanta.

————. 1988b. *Rethinking Development: In Search of Humane Alternatives*. Delhi: Ajanta.

————. 1988c. 'Political Economy of the Indian State: The Rudolph Thesis,' *Contributions to Indian Sociology*, 22 (2), pp. 273–78.

————. 1989a. *Politics and the People: In Search of a Humane India*. Vol. I. Delhi: Ajanta.

————. 1989b. *Politics and the People: In Search of a Humane India*, Vol. II. Delhi: Ajanta.

Kothari, Rajni. 1992. 'Pluralism and Secularism: Lessons of Ayodhya,' *Economic and Political Weekly*, 19–26 December.

Krishna, Daya. 1976. 'Global Vision in a Gandhian Perspective,' *Indian Book Chronicle*, 1 March.

Mazrui, Ali. 1975. 'Eclecticism as an Ideological Alternative: An African Perspective,' *Alternatives*, 1 (December).

Mehta, Pratap Bhanu. 1991–92. 'India's Disordered Democracy,' *Pacific Affairs*, 64 (4), pp. 536–48.

Mehta, V.R. 1978. *Beyond Marxism*. New Delhi: Manohar.

—————. 1983. *Ideology, Modernization and Politics in India*. New Delhi: Manohar.

—————. 1989. 'The Concepts of Modernization: A Critique From the Third World Perspective,' in I. Narain, 1989.

Mendlovitz. Saul. 1981. 'On the Creation of a Just World Order: An Agenda for a Program of Inquiry and Praxis,' *Alternatives*, 7 (3).

Mitra, Ashok. 1977. 'Nostalgia for the Nehru Era,' *Times of India*, 13 March.

Mohanty, Manoranjan. 1991. 'On Democratic Humanism: A Review of Rajni Kothari's Recent Works,' *Contributions to Indian Sociology*, 25 (1), pp. 151–60.

Nandy, Ashis. 1983. *The Intimate Enemy: Loss and Recovery of Self Under Colonialism*. New Delhi: Oxford University Press.

Narain, Iqbal. 1970. 'Ideology of Consensus,' *Economic and Political Weekly*, 26 September.

Nayar, Baldev Raj. 1989. *India's Mixed Economy*. Bombay: Popular Prakashan.

Pantham, Thomas. 1980. 'Elites, Classes and the Distortions of Economic Transition in India,' in Sachchidananda and A.K. Lal, eds., *Elite and Development*. New Delhi: Concept.

—————. 1988. 'Interpreting Indian Politics: Rajni Kothari and his Critics,' *Contributions to Indian Sociology*, XXII (2).

—————. 1991. 'Postrelativism in Emancipatory Thought: The Significance of Gandhi's Swaraj and Satyagraha.' Paper presented in the Workshop on Rethinking Emancipation, Institute of Social Studies, The Hague, Netherlands, 30 January–1 February 1991. Forthcoming in D.L. Sheth and Ashis Nandy, eds., *The Multiverse of Democracy* (New Delhi: Oxford University Press).

Sathyamurthy, T.V. 1991. 'A Unique Academic Understanding of Politics,' *Economic and Political Weekly*, 26 (36), 7 September.

Sheth, D.L. 1983. 'Grass-Roots Stirrings and the Future of Politics,' *Alternatives*, IX.

Sethi, Harsh. 1985. 'The Immoral "Other": Debate between Party and Non-Party Groups,' *Economic and Political Weekly*, 20 (8).

Singh, Randhir. 1991. 'Communalism and the Struggle against Communalism: A Marxist View,' in Panikkar 1991 (cf. bibliography of chapter 5 *supra*.).

Swarup, Shanti. 1977. Review of Kothari 1974a. *Political Science Review*, 16 (1).

Thakurdas, Frank. 1975. Review of Kothari 1974a. *Indian Journal of Political Science*, 36.

Chapter 7: Political Theorizations of Indian Society

Ahmad, Aijaz. 1993. *In Theory: Classes, Nations, Literatures.* Bombay: Oxford University Press. Originally published by Verso, London, 1992.

Bose, Arun. 1989. *India's Social Crisis: An Essay on Capitalism, Socialism, Individualism and Indian Civilization.* Delhi: Oxford University Press.

Chatterjee, Partha. 1986. *Nationalist Thought and the Colonial World: A Derivative Discourse.* Delhi: Oxford University Press.

Conrad, D. 1987. 'The Influence of Western Liberal Ideals on Gandhi's Constitutional Philosophy,' in Mahendra Singh, ed., *Comparative Constitutional Law.* Lucknow: Eastern Book Co.

Cox, Robert. 1981. 'Social Forces, States and World Orders: Beyond International Relations Theory,' *Millennium: Journal of International Studies*, 10 (2).

Dallmayr, Fred. 1992. 'Modernization and Postmodernization: Whither India?,' *Alternatives*, 17.

Das, Veena. 1989. 'Subaltern as Perspective,' in Guha, *Subaltern Studies*, VI.

de Souza, Peter Ronald. 1992. 'For and Against Participatory Democracy,' in N. Prasad, ed., *JP and Social Change.* New Delhi: Radiant.

Frobel, F. et al., 1980. *The New International Division of Labour.* Cambridge University Press.

Guha, Ranajit. 1989. 'Dominance without Hegemony and its Historiography,' in *Subaltern Studies: Writings on South Asian History and Society*, Vol. VI. New Delhi: Oxford University Press.

Habermas, Jurgen. 1990. *Moral Consciousness and Communicative Action.* Translated by C. Lenhardt and S.W. Nicholsen. Introduction by T. MacCarthy. Cambridge, Mass.: MIT Press.

Held, David. 1993. 'Democracy: Past, Present, and Possible Futures,' *Alternatives*, Vol. 18, No. 3, Summer.

Joseph, Sarah. 1987. 'Third World Critiques of Mainstream Social Science,' *Teaching Politics*, XIII (3 & 4).

Josh, B. 1992. *Struggle for Hegemony in India, 1920–1947, Vol. II: 1934–41.* New Delhi: Sage.

Kaviraj, Sudipta. 1990. Review of Arun Bose, 1989. *Contributions to Indian Sociology*, 24 (1), pp. 105–15.

Kohli, A. 1991. See Bibliography of chapter 1 above.

Kothari, Rajni. 1988. *Transformation and Survival: In Search of a Humane World Order.* Delhi: Ajanta.

————. 1988a. *State Against Democracy: In Search of Humane Governance.* Delhi: Ajanta.

————. 1988b. *Rethinking Development: In Search of Humane Alternatives.* Delhi: Ajanta.

Krishna, Daya. 1979. *Political Development: A Critical Perspective.* Bombay: Oxford University Press.

MacIntyre, Alasdair. 1983. Review of V.R. Mehta's *Beyond Marxism*, in *Political Theory*, II (4), November.

Marglin, S.A. 1990. 'Towards the Decolonization of the Mind,' in F.A. Marglin and S.A. Marglin, eds., *Dominating Knowledge: Development, Culture and Resistance.* Oxford: Clarendon Press.

Mehta, V.R. 1983. *Ideology, Modernization and Politics in India.* New Delhi: Manohar.

Mehta, V.R. 1987. 'Political Science in India: In Search of an Identity,' *Government and Opposition*, 22 (3).

Mohanty, Manoranjan. 1989. 'Changing Terms of Discourse: A Poser.' *Economic and Political Weekly*, 16 September.

—————. 1991. '*Swaraj* and *Jiefang*: Freedom Discourse in India and China,' *Social Scientist*, 19 (9–10), October–November.

Nandy, Ashis 1983. *The Intimate Enemy*. New Delhi: Oxford University Press.

—————. 1987. *Traditions, Tyranny and Utopias*. Delhi: Oxford University Press.

Offe, Claus. 1985. *Disorganized Capitalism*. Ed., John Keane. Cambridge, Mass.: MIT Press.

Pantham, Thomas. 1986. 'Habermas's Practical Discourse and Gandhi's Satyagraha' (cf. bibliography of chapter 4 *supra*).

—————. 1988. 'On Modernity, Rationality and Morality: Habermas and Gandhi,' *Indian Journal of Social Science*, I (2).

—————. 1991. 'Postrelativism in Emancipatory Thought: The Significance of Gandhi's Swaraj and Satyagraha' (cf. bibliography of chapter 4 *supra*).

—————. 1994. 'Gandhi's Intervention in Modern Moral-Political Discourse.' Revised version of a paper presented in an IIAS-sponsored seminar on 'Gandhi and the Present Global Crisis,' held at Nehru Memorial Museum and Library, New Delhi, March 1994.

Parekh, Bhikhu. 1991. 'Nehru and the National Philosophy of India,' *Economic and Political Weekly*, XXVI (1 & 2), 5–12 January, pp. 35–48.

—————. 1992. 'The Cultural Particularity of Liberal Democracy,' *Political Studies*, XL, Special Issue.

—————. 1992a. 'Marxism and the Problem of Violence,' Development and Change, 23 (3), pp. 103–20.

—————. 1992b. 'The Poverty of Indian Political Theory,' *History of Political Thought*, XIII (3), Autumn.

Rana, A.P. 1983. 'Non-alignment and International Change: Strategic and Socio-economic Dimensions,' *The Non-Aligned World*, I (3), July–September.

Rao, K. Raghavendra. 1985. *Religion, Society and State: A Theoretical Survey of an Epistemological Non-Encounter of India*. New Delhi: Indian Council of Social Science Research.

—————. 1986. Political Philosophy and the Transformation of Indian Politics,' in Roy, 1986.

Rawls, John. 1971. *A Theory of Justice*. Cambridge, Mass.: Harvard University Press.

—————. 1985. 'Justice as Fairness: Political Not Metaphysical,' *Philosophy and Public Affairs*, XIV.

Ray, Aswini K. 1986. 'Civil Rights Movement and Social Struggle in India,' *Economic and Political Weekly*, 12 July.

Sarkar, Sumit. 1984. 'The Conditions and Nature of Subaltern Militancy,' in R. Guha, ed., *Subaltern Studies*, Vol. III. Delhi: Oxford University Press.

Sathyamurthy, T.V. 1990. 'Terms of Political Discourse in India,' *Economic and Political Weekly*, 7 July.

Smith, D.E. 1963. *India as a Secular State*. Bombay: Oxford University Press.

Spivak, Gayatri Chakravorty. 1985. 'Subaltern Studies: Deconstructing Historiography,' in Guha, *Subaltern Studies*, IV.

Sridharan, E. 1991. 'Leadership Time Horizons in India: The Impact of Economic Restructuring,' *Asian Survey*, 31: 12.

——————. 1993. 'Economic Liberalisation and India's Political Economy: Towards a Paradigm Synthesis,' *Journal of Commonwealth and Comparative Politics*, 31: 3.

West, Cornell. 1991. 'The New Cultural Politics of Difference,' in Russell Fergusson et al., eds., *Out There: Marginalization and Contemporary Cultures*. Cambridge, Mass.: MIT Press.

Index